hand stitch
PERSPECTIVES

hand stitch
PERSPECTIVES

ALICE KETTLE & JANE McKEATING

BLOOMSBURY
LONDON · NEW DELHI · NEW YORK · SYDNEY

Front cover
Anne Jones
Buttonhole insertion stitch, 2011. Space dyed machine thread on a layer of sheer fabric over white cotton organdie. 18 x 18 cm (7 x 7 in.). MMU–Coats hand-stitch project. Photo: Mary Stark.

Frontispiece
Anne Jones
Buttonhole insertion stitch, 2011. Glacé thread, organdie, leather and knitted wire, layered. 8 x 8 cm (3¼ x 3¼ in.). MMU–Coats hand-stitch project. Photo: Mary Stark.

First published in Great Britain in 2012
Bloomsbury Publishing Plc
50 Bedford Square
London WC1B 3DP
www.bloomsbury.com

ISBN 9781408123416

Copyright © Alice Kettle and Jane McKeating 2012

CIP Catalogue records for this book are available from the British Library and the US Library of Congress.

All rights reserved. No part of this publication may be reproduced in any form or by any means – graphic, electronic or mechanical, including photocopying, recording, taping or information storage and retrieval systems – without the prior permission in writing of the publishers.

Alice Kettle and Jane McKeating have asserted their right under the Copyright, Design and Patents Act 1988 to be identified as the authors of this work.

Typeset in 11 on 14pt Photina
Book design: Susan McIntyre
Cover design: Sutchinda Rangsi Thompson
Publisher: Susan James
Project manager: Davida Forbes

Printed and bound in China

This book is produced using paper that is made from wood grown in managed, sustainable forests. It is natural, renewable and recyclable. The logging and manufacturing processes conform to the environmental regulations of the country of origin.

Manchester Metropolitan University

MANCHESTER SCHOOL OF ART

Contents

AUTHORS' NOTE	7
ACKNOWLEDGEMENTS	8
FOREWORD	10
Joanne Hall	
INTRODUCTION	12
Embroidery, Memory and Narrative	12
Professor Lesley Millar	
The Mindful Hand	16
Professor David Owen	
THE PERSONAL JOURNEY INTO HAND STITCH	18
The Lines in my Hands	18
Professor Tom Lundberg	
REAL OR IMAGINED: CONVERSATIONS ABOUT STITCHING	28
ON TO AND INTO:	
Ground in Cloth and Thread	28
Jane McKeating	
Sound, Light and Air	38
Professor Alice Kettle	
Air: off the Ground	48
Kate Egan	
PLACES AND PEOPLES, INDIVIDUALS AND COMMUNITIES	56
Stitching a Social Fabric	56
Heather Belcher	
From Hand to Hand: encounters with embroiderers from Kutch	64
Jane McKeating	
Outside, Inside and In Between	78
Professor Alice Kettle	
CAPTURING TIME, MOMENTS AND NARRATIVES	90
From Madras to Manchester: a narrative on the desire to hand-stitch	90
Professor Anne Morrell	
The Length of a Needle	104
June Hill	
Embroidery and the F-word	116
Dr Melanie Miller	
The Professional Embroiderer?	132
James Hunting	

MAKING: THE VOICES, MEMORIES AND ECHOES	138
The Enduring Trinity of Fingers, Thread and Needle	138
Ian Wilson	
Speaking up for Silence	146
Dr Nigel Hurlstone	
'Out of the Ordinary'	154
Lesley Mitchison	
THE PAST TO THE PRESENT	164
But what can the Museum do to Encourage Embroidery? Museums, collectors and embroidery	164
Ann French	
Research and the Imprint of Stitch	176
Tracy Gill	
The Staircase Stitchers: re-stitching the past	186
Sue Prestbury	
Contemporary Practices: where are we now?	196
Professor Alice Kettle and Jane McKeating	
GLOSSARY OF STITCHES	208
Jane McKeating	
ARTISTS' PROFILES	216
FURTHER READING	220
INDEX	223

Authors' Note

BEFORE COMPLETION OF *MACHINE STITCH: PERSPECTIVES* in 2010, the idea of a companion volume had emerged. It is testament to the spirit of that last collaborative publication that many of the authors were happy to work with us again. The model of having contributors give voice to their own particular perspectives on stitch, in its many forms, needed the addition of hand stitch to complete an overview of embroidery for the many professional and amateur scholars and practitioners that this book is aimed at.

This book has expanded the list of contributing authors and includes a very broad vision of hand stitch, and the way that its impact is felt in contemporary society: the emphasis is not only on stitching, but on the people and the communities, systems and organisations that support hand stitch. The volume has the richness and experience of embroiderers' voices alongside the expert knowledge and vision of historians, curators and educators. It is this rich mix that has made it such a rewarding publication to work on.

In putting together the text, we have been supported by a huge number of organisations and individuals who have contributed their experience of hand stitch, and especially those at Manchester Metropolitan University, where it has been an area of research education and professional practice over the last 60 years. Hundreds of students and staff have contributed in many ways to the wealth of knowledge on the subject and it is to them that we would like to give particular thanks.

Jane McKeating and Alice Kettle

Acknowledgements

With support from MIRIAD, Manchester School of Art, Manchester Metropolitan University

The staff and students at Manchester School of Art, Manchester Metropolitan University

Alastair McMinn, Coats Threads UK

White Cube Gallery, London

Dr Jennifer Harris and Frances Pritchard, Whitworth Art Gallery, Manchester

The National Maritime Museum, London

Marc Steene, Pallant House Museum and Gallery, Chichester

Valerie Elmore

Jean-Charles Durand, Côté Salons, Paris

The Indianapolis Museum of Art

Andrew Salmon and Jan King, Creative Exhibitions

Dick Christensen

Clare Browne, Victoria and Albert Museum, London

Dr Johann Feilacher

Tom di Maria, Director of the Creative Growth Center, California, USA

Heritage and Archives Team, London Borough of Newham

Prinzhorn Collection Centre for Psychosocial Medicine, Universitätsklinikum Heidelberg, Austria

The Bourgeois Trust

Antonia Harrison, Compton Verney, UK

James Brett, The Museum of Everything

Dr Amanda Ravetz, Senior Research Fellow MIRIAD, Manchester School of Art, Manchester Metropolitan University

Museo Bispo Rosário Arte Contemporanea, Prefeitura da Cidade do Rio de Janeiro

John Davis, Visual Resources, Manchester School of Art, Manchester Metropolitan University

Stephanie Boydell, Special Collections, Manchester School of Art, Manchester Metropolitan University

Villoo Mizra, STFC, Ahmedabad, India

Pankaj Shah, Qasab, India

Judy Frater, Kala Raksha Trust, India

Gail Marsh, Mike Millward, Jennifer Hacking and Tracy Gill, Rachel B. Kay-Shuttleworth Collection, Gawthorpe Hall, Burnley

ACKNOWLEDGEMENTS

Mixed hand techniques in the style of Rebecca Crompton, date unknown. 74 x 54 cm (29 x 21¼ in.). Special Collections at Manchester Metropolitan University. Photo: Mary Stark.

Staircase House, Stockport MBC

Thelma Nye

Diana Phillips and Robert Phillips

Elizabeth Elvin

Lisa Rostron

Diana Springall

The Dean and Chapter of Canterbury Cathedral

The Dean and Chapter of Chelmsford Cathedral

The Beryl Dean Archive

The Embroiderers' Guild

The PCC of the Priory Church of St Margaret, King's Lynn

Pauline Rushton, Liverpool Museums

Amalia Kakissis and Penny Wilson, British School at Athens

Amanda Odlin

Most photography courtesy of Mary Stark

Photo credits for profiles of artists: Dick Christensen (Tom Lundberg), Tom Hopkins Gibson (James Hunting), Claire Barber (June Hill), Joe Low (Alice Kettle, David Owen), David Bullock (Ian Wilson), Michael Pollard (Anne Morrell)

All other portraits by Mary Stark

JOANNE HALL

Foreword

IN THE DECADE THAT I HAVE BEEN EDITOR OF *EMBROIDERY* MAGAZINE, I've had the good fortune to interview a host of talented people from all walks of the textile world – from artists, students and curators to collectors, tutors and designers – and I have learnt a great deal from each of them. Embroiderers tend to be universally passionate about their practice. Some I would describe as innovators, their devotion resulting in the expansion of new techniques, applications or approaches to embroidery as a creative medium.

One such person is Alice Kettle. I studied embroidery at Goldsmiths College in the 1980s, at the same time that Kettle was completing her postgraduate diploma. When the end-of-year shows arrived, I recall the buzz around the college about one of the studio exhibitions. It turned out to be that of Alice Kettle. I recall my amazement (and what seemed to be the amazement of the entire art department) at the ambitious scale of the work and sensitive interpretation of the subject matter. I gained a new perspective on machine stitch that day.

Alice Kettle is now a Senior Research Fellow at Manchester School of Art, Manchester Metropolitan University (MMU), in which the genesis of this book is firmly rooted. Many influential embroiderers have passed through the school, whether as students, technicians, research fellows or tutors. Jane McKeating, now Director of Studies there, is one such person. Over the years, she has continued the work begun by Professor Anne Morrell in shaping a highly successful programme area that is dedicated to developing embroidery within every imaginable arena. It is thanks to Jane's tenacity that the embroidery discipline continues to thrive within new programming. This she manages while continuing to develop her own artistic practice, which focuses on hand embroidery. Jane exhibits widely, and her work continues to earn awards and the admiration of her peers within the textile world.

Over the years, those who have passed through MMU have consistently contributed to the canon of traditional and contemporary embroidery practice. Perhaps less well known outside the University is the unique teaching collection made up of samples of embroidery that have been collected from students and tutors since the 1960s. This rich resource prompted the publication of *Machine Stitch: Perspectives* in 2010, very much a sister compendium to this new volume dedicated to hand stitch.

Nearly all those who work with hand stitch talk of the importance, in their creative journey, of the handing down of hand stitch by a mother, aunt or teacher. Many revel in the pleasure of working with their hands in an age of overarching

FOREWORD

technology. They delight in the simple act of working a piece of stitch in the hand. The intimacy and immediacy of working this way conjures a kind of magic – there are no interventions and no interruptive processes, no preparation or machinery required. Many mention the almost meditative effect of stitching. Others speak of the pull on their senses: the sound of a needle as it plucks or stabs the canvas; the distinctive smell of a particular cloth; the feel of starched linen or the roughness of sacking; those fibres that stick at the back of the throat. There are layers of meaning within each recollection and each connection: so many stories and so many perspectives.

In *Hand Stitch: Perspectives*, all the contributors, most of whom have links to the embroidery area in Manchester School of Art, bring years of accumulated knowledge and insight to bear in their interpretations of the reach and potential of hand stitch. In short, each offers a unique perspective.

If the last decade has taught me anything, it is that the exploration of new perspectives of all forms of embroidery, traditional and contemporary, past and present, is a vital part of keeping the humble hand stitch alive.

Joanne Hall
Editor, *Embroidery* magazine

Farzana Ullah
Interlaced Running Stitch, 2011. A slice of tree trunk drilled and stitched with raffia. 23 x 23 cm (9 x 9 in.). MMU–Coats hand stitch project. Photo: Mary Stark

Introduction

LESLEY MILLAR

Embroidery, Memory and Narrative

I HAVE BEEN TOLD THAT THE MOST BEAUTIFUL SOUND in the world is that of a linen thread being pulled through a taut piece of cloth stretched on an embroidery frame.[1]

> *The phrase 'hand stitch' carries with it an intense visual and haptic resonance – as captured by Reiko Mochinago Brandon: under a dim light, during a freezing winter night in Tsugaru, northern Japan, a woman's hand steadily sews exact stitches to reinforce and decorate her handwoven cloth. Counting each warp and weft thread, she brings the stark white cotton strand to the surface at exactly calculated intervals. Gradually she builds a mosaic of precise, pure white diamonds and squares over the deep indigo-blue ground.*[2]

As this example shows, the embroidered thread is an additive mark, which could be a dynamic edge, a punctuation point, or an accumulation of lines, all of which have the potential to create a narrative plane. However, hand embroidery has potency far deeper than its decorative surface: it is a form of handwriting delineating the domestic, the social and the political. It also contains the physical traces of the stitcher. According to textile artist Maxine Bristow, 'The laborious working of row upon row of stitching, the hand turning of buttonholes and cracking of gesso-encrusted cloth [–] every centimetre of the surface within my work bears the trace of my own DNA trapped within the fibres of the cloth.'[3] Such trace elements were embedded in the embroidered belt that a Japanese soldier wore underneath his uniform. On the belt were stitches made by each of the people in his village, so that he carried with him, in the cloth and next to his skin, an embodiment of their good wishes, warmth and confidence. As such, hand embroidery becomes the witness of both the soldier and the embroiderer.

Hand embroidery is also witness to culture, society and the time. In China long ago, the Hmong people were forcibly divided by the Han Chinese and their language outlawed, its use punishable by death. To preserve their language, Hmong women hid their alphabet in the intricate designs of *pa ndau*, the flower-cloth embroidered textiles used for clothes and burial shrouds. Their original alphabet

EMBROIDERY, MEMORY AND NARRATIVE

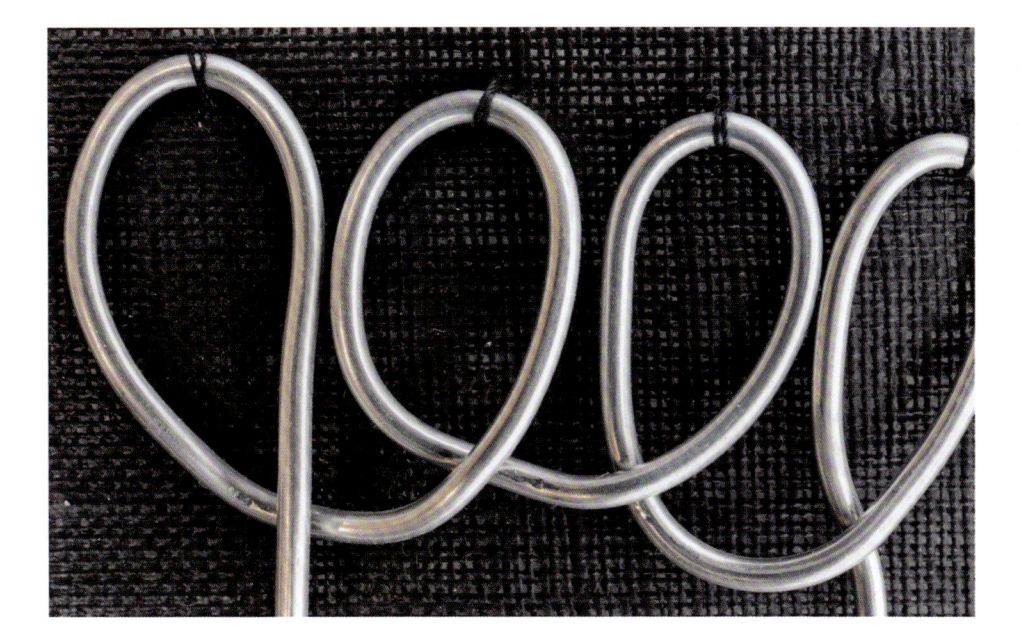

Anne Jones
Couched Chain, 2011. Aluminium wire and cotton thread on Holland linen, a simple chain couched to the surface. 10 x 12 cm (4 x 4¾ in.). MMU–Coats hand stitch project. Photo: Mary Stark.

has now long been forgotten: the sounds were written only in pictorial form, handed down as design motifs from one generation to the next. The flower-cloth patterns reinforced their ethnic identity for centuries. Indeed, one of the names Hmong tribes called themselves was 'embroidery people'.[4]

Far away in space and time, in Juarez, a city on the border of the USA and Mexico, the Norwegian textile artist Lise Bjørne Linnert is using hand-embroidered name tags to bear witness to the desperate situation in this city.[5] Here, more than 600 women have been found tortured, abused and murdered and hundreds more have disappeared: it is suspected that they have been kidnapped for trafficking. Linnert invites people globally to embroider the name of a murdered woman from Juarez on to 2 x 8 cm (¾ x 3¼ in.) name tags, which are then affixed to a wall. So far, almost 2,000 people in 22 countries have participated creating 5,700 name tags. This work embodies memory at all levels, most particularly the memory of the women who have died, but also that of the people who have embroidered the names. Through the act of embroidery, as our fingers struggle with the tiny piece of cloth and the unfamiliar movements as we shape the letters, we become one with the name: we bear the mark.

And it is a powerful mark: one than has been used on many occasions for resistance, for covert communication, acknowledging those things which cannot be spoken so that others would know; moving from the hidden to the public.

For her collaborative piece *Women at Work: Under Construction*, the Serbian artist Maja Bajević worked with five displaced Muslim women from the region around Srebrenica. At that time they were living as refugees in Sarajevo, the capital of Bosnia and Herzegovina. All five had lost a husband, father or brother during the war in the 1990s, and the bodies had not been recovered. This meant, under Muslim law, that there could be no formal period of mourning, no acknowledgement of loss. Bajević, a non-Muslim, invited each of these women to create an embroidered

Alice Kettle
(*opposite*) *Saki* (detail), 2010. Digital stitch, hand stitch. Cotton rayon, threads and glass beads on cotton. 120 x 220 cm (47¼ x 86½ in.). Photo: Joe Low.

work in public as an act of catharsis and repair, which she would video. On scaffolding erected to enable the reconstruction of the Sarajevo Art Museum, the women stretched fabric and here they sat, day and night, embroidering traditional patterns and symbols. They worked in total silence, when normally they would sing, finally cutting the work from the scaffolding, rolling it up and leaving. Their rite of passage, one that could not take place in life, had been performed and communicated through the act of making, of hand embroidery.[6] The stitch and the story, the pattern and the performance, become intertwined and inter-resonant, holding the memory and bearing witness.

As this book eloquently demonstrates, hand-embroidered cloth is many things – it may be a work of art to view behind glass or a beautiful decoration on a humble household item; it may represent the role of the highest in the land, and it may be an intimate acknowledgement of love. The meticulously worked sampler is a measure of individual endeavour which may have been achieved alone or within a supportive community. It can be absolute luxury and it can be the last resort of those whose voice is denied. The hand-embroidered cloth may be any of these, and so much more, created from the simple combination of a piece of cloth, a needle, a thread and a skilled, knowing hand.

Professor Lesley Millar MBE
Professor of Textile Culture and Director of the Anglo-Japanese
Textile Research Centre, University for the Creative Art

Since 1987, Lesley Millar has worked as an exhibition organiser and curator specialising in textiles, and has been project director for seven major international touring exhibitions: 'Revelation' (1996–98), 'Textural Space' (2001), 'Through the Surface' (2003–05), '21:21 – The Textile Vision of Reiko Sudo and NUNO' (2005–10), 'Cloth & Culture NOW' (2008), 'Cultex: Textiles as a Cross-Cultural Language' (2009–11) and 'Lost in Lace' (2011–12). In 2008, she received the Japan Society Award for significant contribution to Anglo-Japanese relations and in 2011 was appointed MBE for her contribution to higher education.

NOTES

[1] Becker, Lutz and Millar, Lesley, *What Is Cloth to Me?* (video, London, 2005).

[2] Brandon, Reiko Mochinaga, 'Japan' in *The Extraordinary in the Ordinary*, ed. M. Kahlenberg (New York: Harry N. Abrams, 1998), p. 55.

[3] Bristow, Maxine, 'Continuity of Touch: Textiles as Silent Witness'. See http://www.cpara.co.uk/events/repeatrepeat/labour/Bristow.html (accessed 24 October 2009).

[4] Fournier, Merlinda, (1987) 'Hmong Stories and Story Cloth' (1987). See article 13437, www.worldandihomeschool.com/public_articles/1987/september/wis13437.asp (accessed 24 September 2008).

[5] See 'Stitching a Social Fabric', Belcher, Heather, pp. 56–63.

[6] For my understanding of the work of Maja Bajević, I am greatly indebted to Dr Bojana Pejić and her essay 'The Matrix of Memory' in *Maja Bajević: Women at Work*, Blažević (Sarajevo: National Gallery of Bosnia and Herzegovina, 2002), pp. 69–97

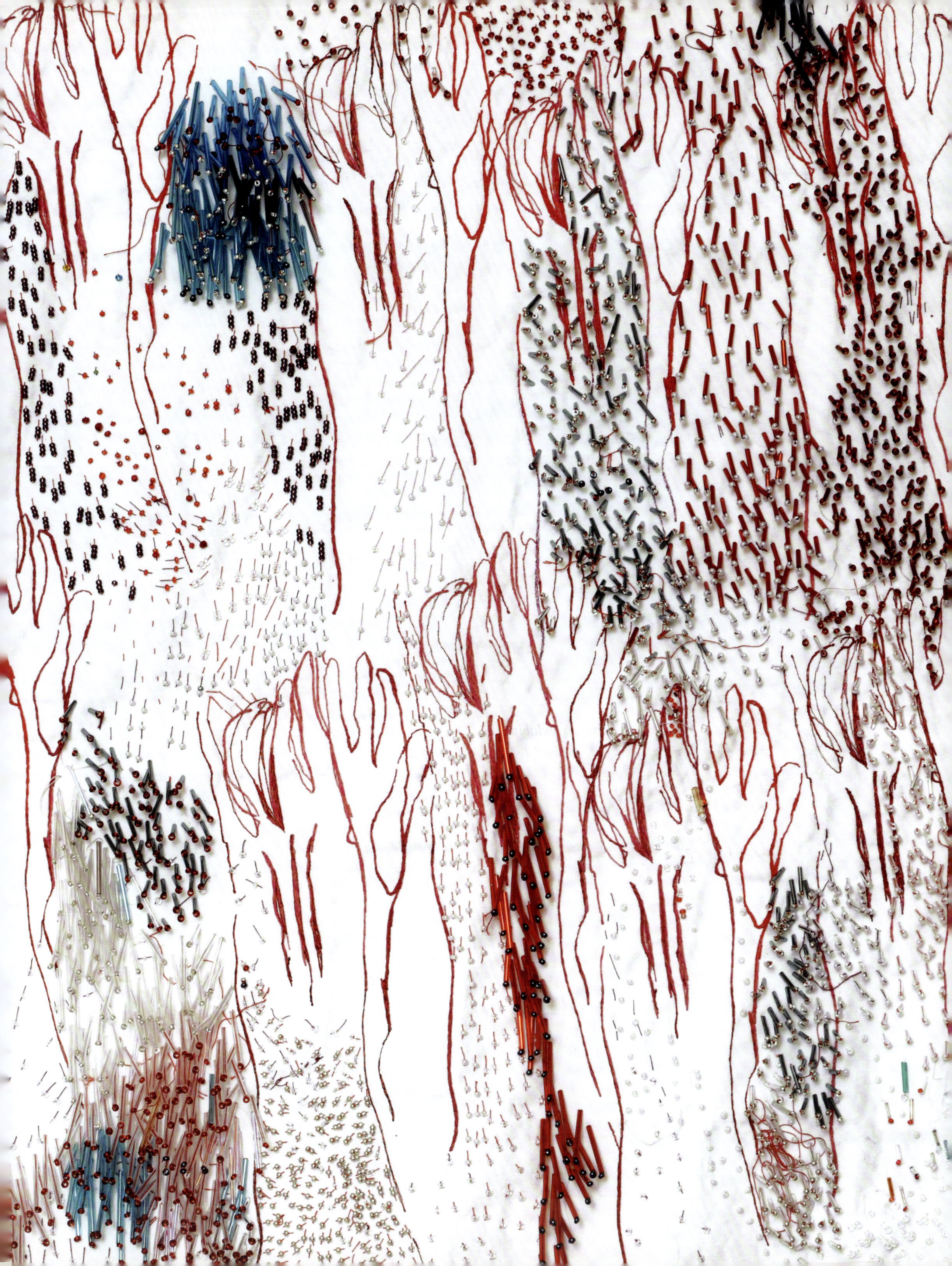

DAVID OWEN

The Mindful Hand

TRADITIONS ARE HANDED ON. Traditions in 'handicrafts' are handed on through a training of the hand; an education of the hand as, at once, a technical and expressive medium of mind. But what is the hand?

Considered in the everyday terms of classical surface anatomy, the hand starts at the wrist and extends to the fingertips. But underneath the skin, it is a highly complex structure of bones, tendons and nerves. From this perspective, that of biomechanical anatomy, the hand 'is an integral part of the entire arm, in effect a specialized termination of a crane-like structure suspended from the neck and the upper chest'.[1] We also now know that hand functions can be affected by a variety of brain injuries and, hence, from the standpoint of physiological or functional anatomy, the hand is directly related through the nervous system to several areas of the brain.[2] These biomechanical and functional perspectives raise fundamental issues concerning the evolution of the hand and its role in relation to the evolution of the brain, which have been compellingly explored in the neurologist Frank Wilson's 1998 book *The Hand: How Its Use Shapes the Brain, Language and Human Culture*, and which also offers a range of insights into the significance of working creatively with one's hands (Wilson's own interest was in part sparked by his experience of working with musicians). At the least, though, Wilson's reflections indicate that an education of the hand is much more than simply an education of the appendage extending from wrist to fingertips; it is also an education in the comportment of a minded body. Support for this thesis concerning the significance of the hand can be further drawn from recent work on drawing and cognition carried out by John Tchalenko (Camberwell College of Arts) who used an Eyemouse (an instrument through which the computer cursor is controlled with the eyes) to discover how much control artists and student artists have over their voluntary eye movements. He found that although most people have little control over the path that their eyes take in moving from one scene to another, 'There were some remarkable exceptions, namely amongst painters who drew regularly from life. They seemed to have strong control over their eyes and could move them very slowly and smoothly to write their names or draw a simple picture on a blank screen.'[3] Here, at least, the artist's eye is trained by practices of the artist's hand.

Such scientific studies on the hand and on the relationship of hand and eye are both intrinsically fascinating and help to develop a fuller understanding of the hand, most notably of why and how it can perform the complex technical feats of expression of which it is capable. But we also have another interest in the hand in which we address it less in terms of the causes (and causal consequences) of its dexterity than in relation to its phenomenology, an inquiry in which issues of orientation, meaning and value come to the fore.

Consider: the eye observes, focuses and gazes, while the hand touches, holds and wields. Through the eye, we encounter the appearance of the world as spectators and, within the context of the face, express reactions: the subtle glance, the wide-eyed stare, the cheeky wink, the frank or hooded gaze. Through the hand, we encounter the appearance, and engage the substance, of the world as agents: we run our fingers across the ply of fabric, stretch it between our hands, fold or tear it into shapes. (The importance of the difference becomes clear if we try to imagine a world in which it is the look that acts physically on the material of the world and the hand that spectates.) But even as we distinguish the orientations of eye and hand, we need to acknowledge that both can serve as media of mediation, although they do so in ways that reveal the contrast between them. In the first, the body is anchored stillness and the eye serves as the medium through which the ego loses itself in the wider visual field. In the second, it is the repetitive rhythmic movement of the hand in activity (say, stitching) that serves as the point of focus, the channel through which the mind is cleared and subject unites with object. The difference between hand and eye also points to a more complex phenomenological condition, that of the combination of hand and eye, of the to and fro cooperation of the two media in which observer and agent unite in giving expression to mind; this is the possibility of art.

We may notice, however, that there is a further difference of significance that is indicated in the contrast between the two modes of mediation, namely, that the hand enables us to extend and specialise the operations of the minded body further through tools that, once mastered, can be experienced as continuous with the body. It is a feature of the craftsman or woman that the pen or paintbrush or needle or chisel is not (for the most part) experienced as an alien object applied, but as an extension of the body itself (this is why, say, hand and needle can serve as a locus of meditation). This raises an interesting point with respect to the scope of the 'hand stitch' because it suggests that this notion need not be limited to a hand and needle combination, but could be extended to further modes of instrumentality in which the key issue is the continuity of hand and instrument, the responsiveness of instrument to hand. In this respect, one could reasonably argue that the use of a sewing machine is simply an extension of the 'hand stitch', just as the piano is an extension of the 'hand pluck' instanced in playing the guitar. Can this thought be extended further to encompass programmed stitching by computer-guided looms? In so far as we can still intervene, adjust, alter within the process itself, we can sustain this thought. But there is often a trade-off here: a machine may greatly expand the range and speed of stitching at the price of responsiveness, and pre-planned responses do not amount to expressive responsiveness. In this respect at least it is meaningful to retain the concept of the hand stitch.

NOTES

[1] Wilson, Frank, *The Hand: How Its Use Shapes the Brain, Language and Human Culture* (New York: Pantheon, 1998).
[2] Ibid.
[3] See www.arts.ac.uk/research/drawing_cognition/eyecontrol.htm (accessed 17 August 2011).

The personal journey into hand stitch

TOM LUNDBERG

The Lines in my Hands

'YOU'VE HAD GOOD TEACHERS', said the woman reading my palm. The first time she entered the studio I'd been startled by her resemblance to my grandmother. The white-haired person assessing my fingertips was a new student who was learning to weave. Her earlier life as a fashion model somehow seemed to be qualification enough: as she decoded the lines of my hand, this lady was right on target.

It would have been rude to mention the likeness to Babi. A teacher can't tell his student, a one-time beauty, that she reminds him of an immigrant in a babushka. In most ways, their lives could not have been more dissimilar. Not that

Tom Lundberg
Lucky Buttonhole, 2011. Embroidery on linen fabric woven by Barbara Eckhardt and cotton and rayon fabrics. 8 x 11.5 cm (3¼ x 4¾ in.). Photo: Tom Lundberg. Collection of the estate of Martha Hibberd.

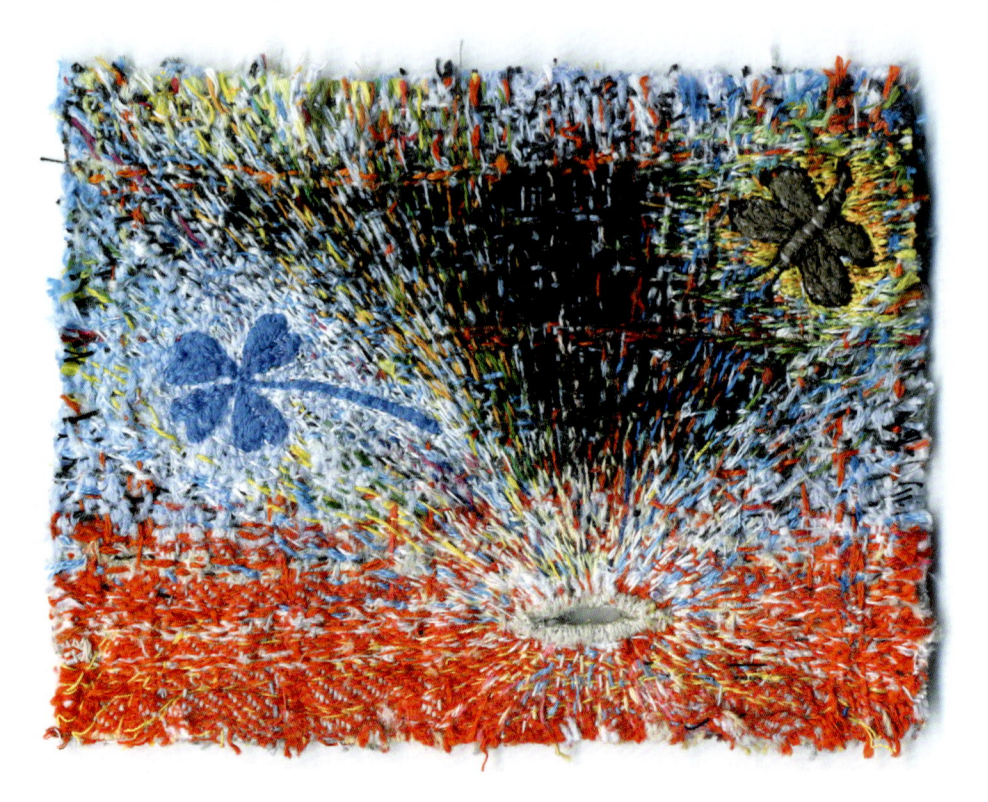

our Moravian grandmother didn't appreciate well-made clothes: to augment the income of their family, her father and a brother had become tailors. Like other village girls, she had picked up needles and crochet hooks at an early age – at about the same time that she was shown the ropes of herding geese and cattle. During her decades on an Iowa farm, Frances Straka sewed for the family and, like many of her neighbours during and after the Depression, became adept at patching things. Using scrap fabrics, she sewed repairs with the closest pattern matches at hand; an everyday apron or housedress could be given a second life with jarring new accents.

The oldest cloth we knew had been made into a bag; our grandfather had carried it to America. His name was pencilled inside wooden handles that were attached to scratchy fabric. Inside its dull stripes, someone had stitched a stained green lining into place. In our grandparents' back bedroom was a white fabric the size of a small flag. It was hemmed with red blanket stitches and embroidered with red lines to make a picture of soldiers. They were pointing bayonets and were surrounded by flames, clouds, and arching Czech words. This, we learned, was a splash cloth made by a neighbour in the old days, to be pinned behind a water pitcher and basin to protect the wallpaper.

Barely anything was thrown away on that farm. An old feed sack became a curtain to keep the wind out of the doghouse. The dog had another getaway spot inside the shed; over the low dog-door was tacked a braided rug that once had been in the kitchen. On a table inside the shed was a basket made of grasses; no one could remember when a mouse had chewed the big hole in the bottom. We also found heavy shuttles used for weaving rag rugs. The shuttles were hand-carved from oak, and had been used by our grandfather a long time ago.

Our father's parents saved things, too. In their South Dakota attic was a stack of military uniforms that belonged to our father and our uncle. In the middle of summer, our band of cousins wore the big wool coats and caps. We seemed to belong together in these uniforms, with their coordinated badges and brass buttons. At home, my brother and I spent hours with the World Book Encyclopedia, studying insignia of the United States Army and pages with flags of the world all lined up in rows.

In rural Benton County, our teachers had tried their best to equip us for the bigger world. Textiles were not central to their mission, yet some items couldn't be missed. We took a bus to the Herbert Hoover Presidential Library, with its collection of First World War flour sacks. These were important to the story of Hoover and Belgian food relief, and were stitched with messages in French. The empty bags were in frames and decorated with the colours of Belgium and the United States, and with lions, roosters and eagles. One year, for a class project on the Indians of North America, my father made a loom by notching a Masonite panel; on this we wove acrylic yarns back and forth with plastic Popsicle-stick shuttles. A teacher showed us how to use pinking shears and needles to construct gifts for Mother's Day: owl-shaped pouches designed to hold scissors, edged with red buttonhole stitches.

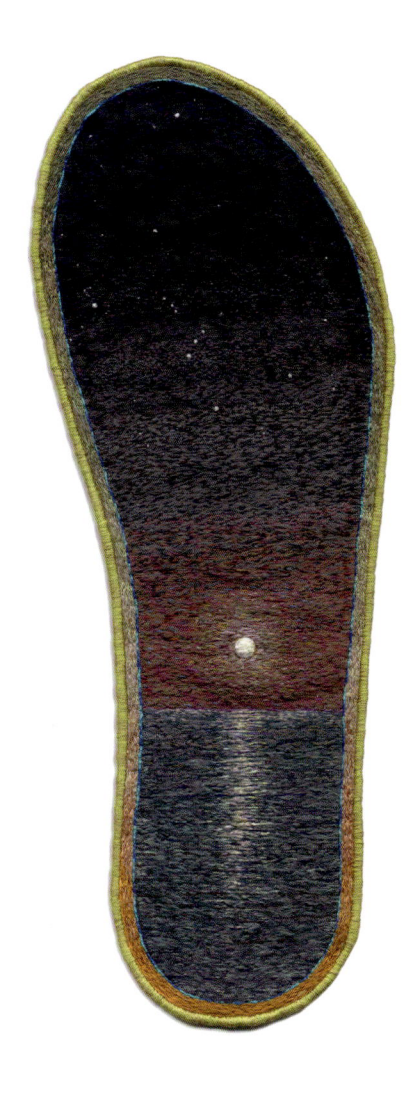

Tom Lundberg
Orion Diving, 1997. Cotton and silk threads on cotton fabric. 29.2 x 10.8 cm (11½ x 4¼ in.). Collection of Carol and Randy Shinn. Photo: Tom Lundberg.

Our mother joined a group of women from the Presbyterian Guild to make altar hangings for the simple wooden church. For a few weeks, as they planned the project, the ladies traded brochures that arrived in the mail from church supply companies. Sales catalogues showed men in robes, swatches of fancy fabric, and an assortment of machine-embroidered symbols. The women constructed four sets of altar cloths – in purple, white, red and green – to mark the seasons of the church calendar. Each item in a set was decorated with matching emblems. Crowns and crosses, triangles and trefoils, and overlapping Greek letters were stitched into place. Each piece then was finished with a band of gold fringe. Once completed, the big project was dedicated with a string of Sunday sermons that decoded the meaning of these new textiles. Each lesson featured the symbols of the day, which appeared to float within the fields of coloured cloth. At intervals throughout the year, the trappings were stored and rotated, kept at the base of the belfry in a box that our father helped to build.

As a new college student, it never once crossed my mind that my future would be wrapped up in textiles. In our freshman year at Iowa State University, my friend Corry and I analysed leaf scars in a botany class called Local Flora, a course that required hikes in the woods to inspect twigs and buds. Then, with the supervision of our calligraphy teacher, we drew serifs over and over with pen and ink, attempting to keep black blobs from forming on the nibs. Nearby, a fabric sculptor and a well-known weaver were introducing their students to textile arts, but my mind was elsewhere. I declared new majors three times in the first year.

Eventually, I did find my place. I met friends and mentors who knew what they were doing and who put a lot of thought into their work. Now I am a teacher, too. In the studios, I see beginners plugging along and advanced students who are on their way to mastering the language of textiles. Around me are individuals at crossroads and artists on the thresholds of careers. They are discovering what they love, coaxing materials to give form to something that comes from within. As they labour away, it sometimes feels like I'm in two places at once: at looms or dye pots with them, yet simultaneously time travelling, remembering people who helped me to see what was right before my eyes. I can't deny that there are moments when I blurt out 'When I was a student …', but these people in the classroom have no idea how much of that internal chatter I keep to myself.

When I was a student, I discovered that I like to work with simple tools and techniques. By the time I'd completed a graduate degree in textiles at Indiana University, the stitch was at the heart of my studio life. For the last several decades, I've embroidered pictures that combine a few easy techniques: long-and-short stitch, split stitch, and couching, in which threads laid on the surface of a ground material are anchored or couched into place by other stitches. These pictures often look like small bound badges. Sometimes their outer silhouettes are familiar shapes: pockets, cuffs or the soles of slippers. When I make slightly bigger panels, densely stitched details get surrounded by little seed stitches or by lines in patterns.

It would take me a few years to figure out how I might work this way. At the end of my sophomore year, I moved in with my parents for the summer and

THE LINES IN MY HANDS

Clary Illian
Porcelain soup bowls, 2000. Size: 18 cm (7 in.) in diameter and 10 cm (4 in.) high. Photo: Clary Illian.

worked as an apprentice to a potter, Clary Illian, who lived in a town a few miles away. A photograph taken outside her studio frames a large wooden reel, the kind used to package ropes and cables. One round end of the giant spool rests on the ground; the other end serves as a circular tabletop and holds an arrangement of my little vases and pitchers. Even the biggest pots look like miniatures on this chunky pedestal.

Clary had worked in the Bernard Leach Pottery in St Ives, Cornwall, producing standard ware for the showroom. When she returned to Iowa, Clary established her own pottery and began to turn out sturdy vessels – pots – that are pleasing to handle and easy on the eye. I came to regard the table and the kitchen sink as research stations: so much revolved around these mugs and plates. At certain points in the day, bowls and coffee cups could become the centre of the universe. I'd never heard this much talk about craft or about functional forms, nor ever been so fixated on earth and fire.

By the time I entered the University of Iowa that fall, my focus was on painting, drawing and ceramics – in that order. After three months of working with a master, I could see the writing on the wall when it came to my future in pottery. By the age of 20 I had seen famous paintings in museums, but still could not imagine the immensity of the field of art, nor the thousands of art students who, like me, were groping their way through school.

Near the end of the degree programme, after months of dropping in on friends in the textiles studio, I enrolled on a weaving course, and then a print and dye class. As a painting student, it was easy to create the impression of mud whenever I mixed pigments for too long on a canvas. But when warp and weft colours meshed together at the loom, they became livelier. Fabrics woven with a variety of hues, like pointillist paintings, could appear to change depending on where you stood. Up close, a

HAND STITCH: PERSPECTIVES

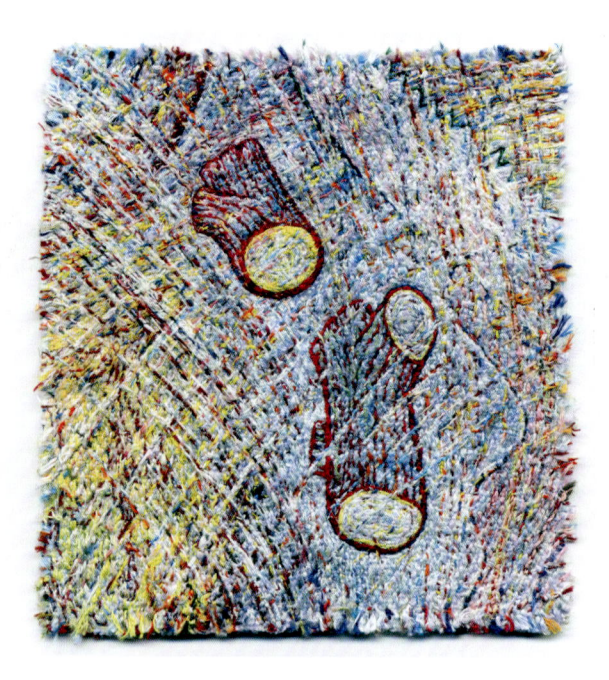

Tom Lundberg
(*left*) *Summer Vortex*, 1997. Cotton and silk threads on cotton fabric. 15.9 x 15.2 cm (6¼ x 6 in.). Photo: Colorado State University Department of Communications and Creative Services.

(*right*) *Crosscut*, 2011. Cotton and silk threads on linen woven by Barbara Eckhardt. 14.5 x 13.5 cm (5¾ x 5¼ in.). Photo: Tom Lundberg.

confetti of bright specks could hurt your eyes, but then suggest a dreamy sky from across the studio. For this type of fluctuating colour, common terms were inadequate; such tones required – and often defied – new names. It was curious how these optical surprises developed from threads laid methodically into place. Compared to mapping out a painting, the preliminary stages of a weaving required much more measuring and counting, and over time, this kind of preparation helped to focus my mind. Gradually, ideas could take shape on the loom as weavings scrolled through their beginnings, middles and endings.

Weaving and surface design courses at Iowa were taught by Naomi Kark Schedl. Naomi had begun art studies in her native Cape Town, South Africa, and completed degrees in painting at Yale. By the 1970s, she was making woven and coiled containers that looked like empty nests or shelters. Naomi's teaching message was direct: learn technical skills and think like an artist. Embroidery wasn't a formal part of her curriculum, but in an attempt to give my clothes a hippie look, I took needle and thread to work shirts and bellbottoms.

My friend Barbara Eckhardt had already immersed herself in more advanced courses and had fallen in love with historic textiles. She was charmed by the birds in Coptic weavings and adored the flattened spaces of medieval tapestries. For her, a Gothic niche was not that different from her own closet. Her weavings began to suggest ritual window shades, with views of interiors and veiled distances. Barbara's studies in reversible weave structures came shortly after reading Carl Jung's *Man and His Symbols* (first published in 1964). Jung's connections between art and the unconscious clicked with Barbara's knack for remembering dreams. If rooms in houses could be interpreted as dream symbols, then woven fabrics could represent levels of awareness. Overlapping shapes could create the sensation of separate moments existing together.

Barbara Eckhardt
At Night Looking In, 1986. Weaving with interlocking supplementary warps, weft inlay; cotton, linen, ramie. 79 x 72 cm (31¼ x 28½ in.). Collection of Dick Christensen and Tom Lundberg. Photo: David Caras.

For all her technical virtuosity, Barbara felt that it was essential for her weavings to connect with something basic. She understood that fabrics, like music, arise from nature. Her pictures began to fill with vines, meandering lines of linen and cotton that she couched into place along borders and between geometric shapes. Like flora in medieval art, her plants sometimes dwarfed the shapes of buildings. In museums, Barbara and I found medieval vestments stitched with grapevines in shades of brown, yellow and green.

At Indiana University, the textiles faculty paid serious attention to colour. With Budd Stalnaker, we dyed skeins and stocked a storeroom with a full spectrum of wool and cotton yarns. Joan Sterrenburg applied a similar strategy to fabric dyeing, teaching us to control tints and shades in measured steps. My friend Anne McKenzie Nickolson adapted these methods to her work with reverse appliqué, which she had seen in North American Indian ribbon work. She snipped into layers of dyed fabric, then added embroidery to give the effect of scattered shapes dancing across fields of colour. Anne continues to investigate how flat strips of cloth can evoke deep spaces,

HAND STITCH: PERSPECTIVES

Anne McKenzie Nickolson
(*above*) *Extinct, Unknown*, 1997.
Embroidery on French cutwork. 18 x 18
cm (7 x 7 in.). Collection of Nancy
Dasenbrock. Photo: Anne McKenzie
Nickolson.

Renie Breskin Adams
(*right*) *Lunar Drift*, 2000. Hand embroidery,
cotton. 16.5 x 22.5 cm (6½ x 8⅞ in.).
Photo: Renie Breskin Adams.

piecing together rich and surprising harmonies. In certain works, like those made with found fabrics, Anne also explores how things fade away.

My Indiana classmates and I could see how two recent alumni were translating colour skills into works that glowed. Renie Breskin Adams was drawing on her love of Bonnard and packing small worlds into needlework pictures. Renie offered windows into emotional states that were funny and anxious, full of weird creatures and people she knew. The objects themselves could look homey and calm, but they contained scenes of panic, silliness and giddy joy.

Diane Itter's career also was kicking into gear. Like Renie, Diane usually made small works, with colours that pulled you in from across the room. Both artists used threads that were loose and pliable, but you couldn't call their compositions relaxed: with stitches and knots appearing in dots and dashes, even neutral tones could tug your attention from one corner to the next. Even in the dullest grey patches, you could sense the tension involved in tightly bound ridges, casting row after row of fine shadows.

Diane's studio looked out over the front porch, in the house that she shared with her artist husband Bill. They were filling the place with stuff – with fantastic things from flea markets, auctions and traders. Their kente cloths, rugs and quilts filled Diane and Bill with ideas about pattern and abstraction. As Diane moved from embroidery and weaving to what would become her signature half-hitch-knot technique, she charted out where shapes could meet and mingle. On her work board, each knotted piece grew out from the middle. Her output was invariably compared to painting, but there was no denying that these dazzling concentrations of colour could only be achieved with yarn and basic hand movements.

THE LINES IN MY HANDS

As a professor of art, Bill introduced his students to the paradox and poetry of the two-dimensional universe. The rooms in his studio were stacked with drawings and paintings. In finely drawn still lifes, cones and cylinders balanced in elegant silence. In other drawings, you could see how he was improvising as he reinterpreted the rhythms of textiles. Big canvases teemed with hundreds of painted nooks and crannies, which seemed to flutter and lead in all directions, each square inch throbbing with light and shifting shadows. There was so much to absorb, so many details to take in that sometimes I had to look away for a while; certain tribal textiles could have this same dizzying effect.

Why should it surprise me that there are so many of us who try to connect the big rhythms of life to the smallest of marks? I look at the work of Ilze Aviks and identify with her trembling targets, and with the incessant tap of time that she stitches out in all directions. Yes, those floating marks, like quivering iron filings, merge with the clouds that drift through her fabric panels, yet I can't shake the image of a needle's sharp tip piercing the cloth over and over. The combined effect reminds me of Italian velvets from the Renaissance – luxurious, soft and appealing, but with big patterns full of thorns.

Could weavers and needleworkers of the Renaissance ever have imagined that their famous fabrics might come to rest in the middle of America? Maybe yes, since textile workers had to endure their own relocations and knew the value of their labours. As I tried to make something worthwhile, I could see my own slow progress as a weaving student and my floor littered with samples. In books from the library, I browsed pictures of old fabrics and their designs of artichokes and

Diane Itter
(*left*) *Triangles 2*, 1977. Silk threads on cotton fabric. 21 x 20.5 cm (8¼ x 8¹⁄₁₆ in.). Collection of Susan and Malcolm Knapp. Photo: Diane Itter.

William Itter
(*right*) *Modular Transformations*, 1971. Graphite pencil on rag paper. 33 x 33 cm (13 x 13 in.). Photo: William Itter.

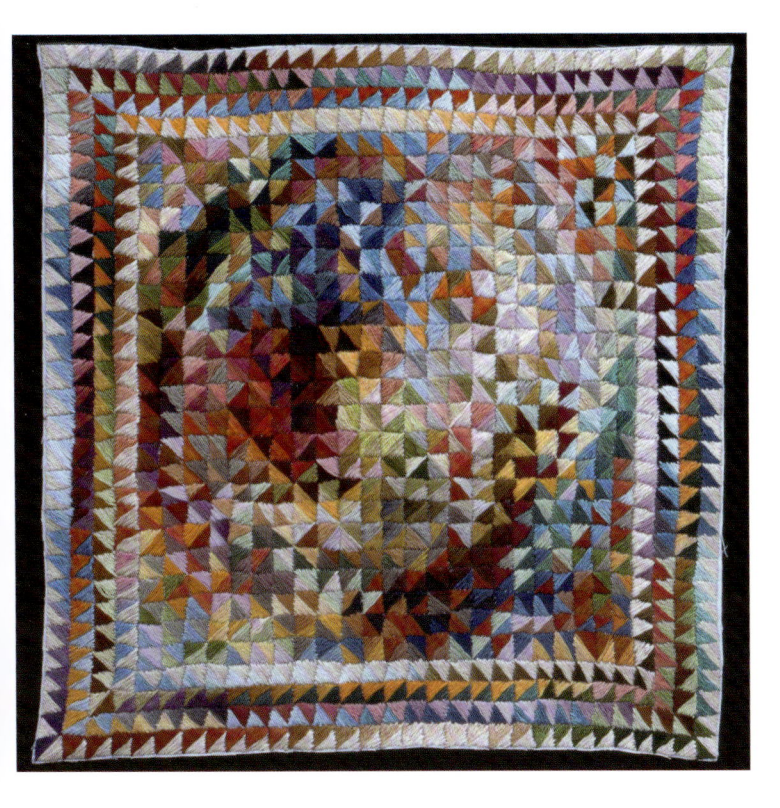

HAND STITCH: PERSPECTIVES

Ilze Aviks
(*left*) *Release* (detail), 2009. Pigment on linen, cotton thread. Painting, resist, hand embroidery. 198 x 102 cm (78 x 40 in.). Photo: Paul Pennington.

(*right*) Chasuble (Italian), (back), late 1700s. Collection of Indianapolis Museum of Art, the Orville A. and Elma D. Wilkinson Fund, ref no: 74.114. Velvet, about 1475; orphreys, 1500–1550. Silk velvet, silk and metallic threads. 69 x 117 cm (27 x 46 in.). Photo: courtesy of Indianapolis Museum of Art.

prickly pomegranates. In a few volumes, there were details of embroideries like those that Barbara and I had seen in glass cases: saints holding their special props and gesturing with their hands.

An hour away from campus, in study rooms at the Indianapolis Museum of Art, someone helped me to find a vestment that was in remarkable condition; it was Italian and hundreds of years old. Its velvet sides were deep red, framing long panels of embroidery. These held images of St Barbara, with her tower, and St Peter holding his keys. Above their heads were the grinning profiles of leafy Green Men. The backgrounds were worked with gold-wrapped threads in couched patterns. Silk threads in little split stitches softened the skin tones and the shadows of robes. Back at home I tested my own version of these techniques. I filled a patch of fabric with marks stitched in cotton thread, and then added new stitches on top of the first ones. The combination was thick and bulky compared to what I'd seen in the museum, but I could see colours begin to blend together as I poked away with the needle. Little pictures started to take shape. This had potential.

THE LINES IN MY HANDS

Tom Lundberg
Flare, 2011. Cotton, silk, rayon and metallic threads on rayon velvet. 10 x 25 cm (4 x 10 in.). Photo: Tom Lundberg.

Tom Lundberg
Breviary, 2010. Cotton, silk, rayon and metallic threads on rayon velvet. 18 x 13 cm (7 x 5 in.). Collection of Wendy and Jim Franzen. Photo: Tom Lundberg.

Real or imagined: conversations about stitching on to and into

JANE MCKEATING

Ground in Cloth and Thread

Asif Shaikh
Kutchchi Ari, 2009. Chain stitch with ari needle and twisted silken floss. Detail of Kutchchi ari border, embroidered with twill weave pure silk, embellished with badla (flat metal strip) and sequins. The collections are stitched in Ahmedabad for international clients. The designs are inspired by and adapted from traditional Kutchchi designs held in the V&A collection. 10 x 18 cm (4 x 7 in.). Collection revival of Kutchchi ari. Photo: Asif Shaikh.

THE CLOTH AND THE THREAD

AS I SEW, A CONVERSATION WITH EMBROIDERER ASIF SHAIKH earlier this year in Ahmedabad keeps playing in my mind. Initially, I thought it was due to his intense use of miniature stitching, the way he had reduced the scale of his designs by half, challenging himself to make work where the minute stitches are hardly visible. However, on reflection, I now feel certain that it was his obsession with the straight grain that stayed with me. He stressed repeatedly, 'For me, geometry is very important, the grain lines keeping it very straight when you remove it from the frame.'[1] Asif's designs and stitches are neither geometric nor rigid, but beautifully placed, intricate motifs adorning immaculate garments. His determination is to perfect, to produce something of absolute quality, which for him required complete precision, order and control.

Reflecting on the conversation, analysing in turn the role of order in my own and others' practice, I understand that I stitch against the grain, marks going a little askew, the weave of the cloth distorting the image. The cloth's structure inflicts a grid to accept or ignore, a rule asking to be obeyed or broken. Sometimes a stitched line is moving happily along the warp and then shoots off, finding its own pattern. Stitching layers of overlaid cloth creates an intriguing, jarring mix.

I have observed artists select, absorb, reject and experiment with threads and grounds and have become interested in embroiderers' choice of, and sensitivity to, their materials. That a stitch can and does exist independently from a ground and is made from materials other than fibre is discussed elsewhere. Here I present responses to the relationship between thread and cloth and illustrate that the ground, its surface, structure and handle, is central to encapsulating the spirit of the work. A selection of apparently random examples illustrates a commonality that transcends the professional and amateur, the historic and the contemporary, the novice and the experienced. The commonality here being the stitches' connection to a base, as Gavin Fry describes it, the 'in and out, not the on'.[2]

Whether artists paint or stitch, I have recently begun to understand that the attraction of stitch for me is the connection of thread to cloth. Cloth dictates a history; it has tactile qualities and its structure, usually constructed of thread, suggests somewhere to start. Nigel Cheney expresses this well:

> *I went through a few years of thinking I had to be a painter and tried oils (allergic), canvas (too bouncy) MDF (better), acrylic (just can't get enough layers before it becomes fugitive), watercolours (too disciplined and can't leave the white of the paper) ... paint just isn't enough. I look at them and they are flat and dead and without the bounce, edge and depth that stitch has.*[3]

He goes on to describe hand stitch as 'like a highlighter pen'. Applied to the cloth, the stitch punctures and punctuates, heightens and distorts, even has a right and a wrong. It eventually obliterates the cloth in various proportions, the embroiderer judging how much of the cloth needs to remain visible. Stitch is physical colour in a multiplicity of guises, a means to imbue the cloth with ideas,

HAND STITCH: PERSPECTIVES

Eliza Matilda Baynham
(*right*) *Sampler*, 1813. Fine wool cloth with cross-stitch, satin stitch and long and short stitch, using filoselle-type silk. 39 x 31 cm (15½ x 12¼ in.). Rachel Kay-Shuttleworth Collection, Gawthorpe Hall (RBKS 6830). Photo: Mary Stark.

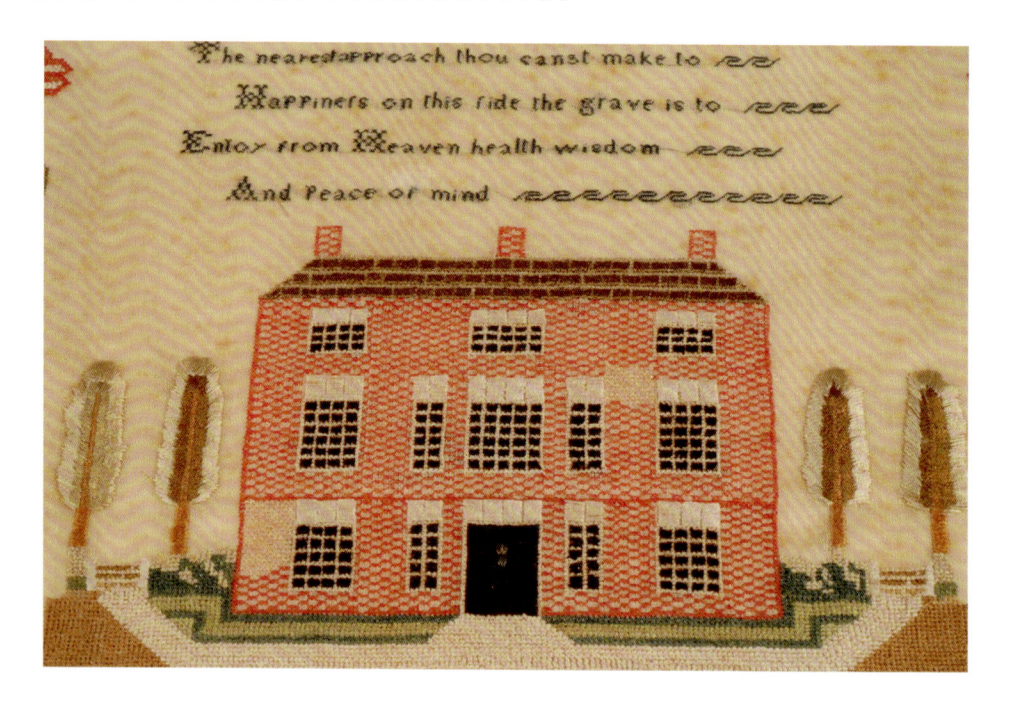

illustrate stories, and embellish artefacts; it serves as a record of filled time. The traditional sampler captures the practice at its most basic yet engaging level.

A COMMON THREAD

The embroidery on the bandana illustrated opposite densely covers the printed background in colours seemingly from nowhere, the original print only visible from the glimpse left at the edges. Why was this done? Possibly the embroiderer lacked the confidence or experience to create a design, and this was to hand. Embroidery has an advantage over drawing, which is perhaps why it's so popular with an unconfident amateur, because one can start with a structure or a print – lines to follow, threads to count, an image to embellish – there are rules and a formula. A child starts with a binca mat,[4] learning the stitches within the safe confines of the open-weave grid.

Embroidery, unlike other crafts, often responds to something that already exists. Does that explain the enduring popularity of the kit? The pattern, and the rules of the stitch vocabulary are clues. Could it explain the vast numbers of avid cross-stitch enthusiasts, who enjoy a mix of the mathematical with the manual?

Embroidery is a craft where professional and amateur frequently muddle along together in the same arenas. In the UK, at the popular 'Knitting and Stitching Show'[5] over 100,000 visitors encounter an eclectic mix, from stitch by numbers kits to feature exhibitions of the work of internationally renowned professional artists. This strange confluence is perhaps not echoed in any other creative sphere. Visitors buy volumes of pure colour, seduced by metallics, flosses and fluorescents, but the yarns and fabrics need to find form by application, and so emerge the popular crafts of quilt-making, patchwork, cross-stitch, counted thread and canvas

Embroiderer unknown. Bandana handkerchief, 1870–90. Long and short and satin stitch, basket stitch, French knots and raised satin stitch. Turkey red cotton twill embroidered with floss silk. 65 x 43 cm (25½ x 17 in.). Part of the collection used by Tracy Gill (see pp.176–85). Rachel Kay-Shuttleworth Collection, Gawthorpe Hall (RBKS 11984). Photo: Mary Stark.

work, each with a structure and set of rules in addition to their suitability for working with familiar and existing material.

In embroidery we utilise stitches, which we learn and adapt like a language. The method gives a therapeutic rhythm. Its repeat is like the beat of the heart, so simple that it seems to be at the very core of a natural instinct to make. It fulfils a human need that contributes to well-being.

It is the rhythmic and meditative quality of stitch that is, in part perhaps, what makes the work of Fine Cell so successful. Across 29 prisons, over 400 inmates stitch in their cells for, on average, 20 hours a week, some up to 40 hours. That the work earns money for the prisoners is clearly an incentive, but comments from many of the embroiderers demonstrate that the rewards from the stitching process itself can make a real difference to their mental health and outlook on life.[6]

> *You can't show any weakness inside. So it just gets more and more built up and then you get angry. Sewing made me stop and think about how things could have been different, and what I could have done differently. It helped me change the way I was, 'cos I used to be quite an angry fella when I went inside. I was quite moody and aggressive and people said I was defensive. I never knew I was, but when I was sewing I used to go back over my life and thought … perhaps I am. It gave me the space I needed.*

The stitching is purposeful, artefacts are completed and sold, there is satisfaction in the creative act of making something that gives pleasure, working with colour, feeling the tactile quality of the canvas in the hand and the concentration and skill required to carry out complex designs. There is a balance of the methodical and the visual – a multi-sensory activity. The result is a range of cushions or commissioned work that has a density and a solidity that give form to the hours spent.

Karl undertaking Fine Cell work in his cell. Photo: India Roper Evans.

HAND STITCH: PERSPECTIVES

GROUNDED ARTISTS

In talking to artists from many backgrounds, it becomes apparent that despite vastly different experiences, concepts, designs and outcomes, an equation is created within which the materials, the process and the pace are uniting factors.

Nigel Cheney's recent works reflect his interest in music, with the titles referring to fragments of lyrics. His multi-layered process is fundamental, his selection of fibre and structure in a cloth very specific: 'Cotton/linen mix with a coarse grain for the large crewelwork piece … then a vibrant cotton velvet that I want to etch into with stitch … then silk twill for the punch of a graphic image and some silk georgette – my favourite for layering and shadow.'[7]

Utilising digital media, he creates a base, which may eventually become obliterated with multiple processes. He comments:

> *The resulting textile itself is often then rescanned and so the process repeats, like a refrain lingering in the subconscious long after the sound has faded. Textiles are worked, dissected, assembled, overprinted, stitched and then cut up again … continually pulled apart and composed, until the compositions are in the discord and harmony associated with their original audible inspiration.*[8]

There has been a slow evolution towards the refinement of his current work. He discusses a time when as a student, any offcuts would do, but senses now that the choice of cloth is like a 'conversation between thread, technique and cloth … it's a language I think I could always hear, but used to scream in childish rants and now I try to tell stories'.[9] The pictorial outcome is a unified response to music, with its rich layers of sound. His pieces recount narratives, with his refined understanding of the relationships involved in the making process crucial to their success.

Similarly experienced, Gavin Fry describes his process as building rather than surface embellishment, placing increasing emphasis on the choice of ground: 'flattening, adding to and squashing down'.[10] Rather than use named stitches, he selects them as ranges of marks. He creates contrast between his highly raised hand stitch and flatter areas, which unembellished cloth helps to create, and uses found prints to give a versatility and greater depth.

Appreciating the pace of hand work, Gavin designs as he stitches, adjusting size and density instinctively. Working on a variety of different cloths, particularly woven wool, mohair (an influence of Eirian Short), and tea-towel linen, he enjoys a matt surface and prefers to add the gloss through needle-weaving with shiny threads. 'The fabric is like air and I can manipulate and layer it back on itself. Wool thread on woven wool is terrific to build stitches through and on. Looser cloths get bigger stitches first and then smaller ones, and finer cloths are the reverse.'[11]

The surface is allowed to pucker with stitches on open-weave cloths, creating an uneven surface against unstitched areas. Sometimes he works over a printed surface: Gavin describes this as doing 'embroidery by numbers'. The initial drawing is flat, almost diagrammatic. The three-dimensional nature of thread is ideal for creating an illusion; the work changes as he stitches, breaking away from the original drawing to give the embroidery a life of its own.

Nigel Cheney
Trinidad and Tobago (detail), 2011. Title is a reference to that Commonwealth currency, the full piece presenting a light-hearted response to the ludicrousness of money, subverting the image of Queen Elizabeth II with the TV presenter Trevor McDonald, who was born in Trinidad. The brightly-coloured chihuahuas were inspired by the dizziness of B-52s' 1980 album, 'Wild Planet'. Digital print on cotton panama with hand stitch in stranded cotton. 140 x 140 cm (55¼ x 55¼ in.). Photo: Nigel Cheney.

GROUND IN CLOTH AND THREAD

For Audrey Walker, the starting point for her pieces is something observed or remembered – a poem or myth, or perhaps a comment heard on the radio. Her interest in cloth goes beyond the physical – she is 'fascinated by this alternative history; stitching is in almost every culture and from thousands of years back'.[12] Describing the process using the terms 'manoeuvrable' and 'robust', Audrey goes on to comment:

[The cloth is] capable of a lot of punishment – layers of machine stitching to begin with – so it is usually plain, fine calico or a well-washed cotton sheet ... colour doesn't matter because it will be covered with layers of other fabric scraps, paint, dyes and finally a top layer of hand stitching.[13]

In the work, the strength of the ground allows the surface to be built up in layers, with the top layer adding tone. Through subtle changes in stitch direction, the form of the thread creates depth and provides a transparency that is perfect for the ethereal nature of the images, which contain mystery and secrecy. We glimpse through the forms to what lies beneath. In *Maud*, the figure of Maud works in harmony with the background. There is something about needle and thread that helps to integrate elements of an image, creating a sense in which forms emerge and retreat from their ground with seeming ease.

Gavin Fry
(*above*) Orlando on Her Return to England, 2010. From the 'Orlando' series, inspired by the book *Orlando*, a biography by Virginia Woolf. Needlepoint collage, found linen print, appliqué and hand embroidery in wool, cotton and silk. 20 x 16 cm (8 x 6¼ in.). From the collection of Michael Brennand Wood. Photo: Gavin Fry.

Audrey Walker
(*left*) Maud (detail), 2009. A section of *The Black Bat Night Has Flown*, made for an exhibition by the 62 Group in response to Tennyson's poem, 'Come into the Garden, Maud'. Hand and machine embroidery over collaged fabrics. 140 x 150 cm (56 x 59 in.). Collection of the artist.
Photo: Electric Egg.

33

HAND STITCH: PERSPECTIVES

Jane McKeating
Three pages from the *Transitions* rag book, part of the 'No Particular Value' series, 2010. Hand stitch on digital print. Whole book 15 pages; 40 x 40 cm (15¾ x 15¾ in.). Photo: Mary Stark

Anna Torma's 'Bagatelles' series is made up of six separate pieces in which Anna portrays imagined gardens. Named after the rose garden in the Bois de Boulogne in Paris, the composition is constructed from wildly imaginative imagery. She 'composed the gatekeeper monster depicting the uncertain territory of imagined plants, animals, high water and low lands'. She describes 'human-faced animals and animal-masked humans asking, "Who, may I ask, is the beast?"' Anna hand-paints a silk base and then uses stitch to distort the tension of the cloth, changing its two-dimensional quality to three dimensions, so it becomes a double-sided relief which wafts in the draught as a viewer passes by. Her work illustrates the capacity of cloth to change from the flat to a distorted surface by the pull of the thread, a further quality emerging from process, bringing the cloth to life.

The importance of the cloth is perhaps valued most through the experience of making – learnt but not taught, a gradual process of sensing. I discovered, after years of placing embroidery on a wall, that the remoteness of the visual response negated the tactile, which was so much a part of why I stitched. The handle and feel of the object and the surface of stitch as it relates to the hand is entirely missed: it avoids the point. So the cloth object as ground is one to be explored, for me currently as a rag book, which has to be handled to view. The use of fraying breaks down the cloth and subverts the image. Removing threads distorts or destroys the ground; just as stitches add a mark, I use fraying like a rubber.

For Antonia Riviere, the choice of cloth object is a familiar, worn-out skirt, which she has dyed, patched and continues to wear in reverse. She started stitching into it whilst working as a counsellor and artist-facilitator in 2008, and continues to do so:

I was feeling very drained, with all my energies going into other people's creativity and healing; my own creative practice wasn't getting a look-in, and I began to feel envious when I watched other people's absorption when stitching. The skirt became a place where I could attend to my own need to stitch/mend/heal, accompanied by the rhythm and slow pace of hand-stitching ... it's a piece about the process of hand-stitching, which explores the connectedness of psychological and material mending and the ongoing nature of both. I don't imagine it will ever be completed. The symbols are very obvious – clouds of small moths for falling apart, flowers/leaves for growth.[14]

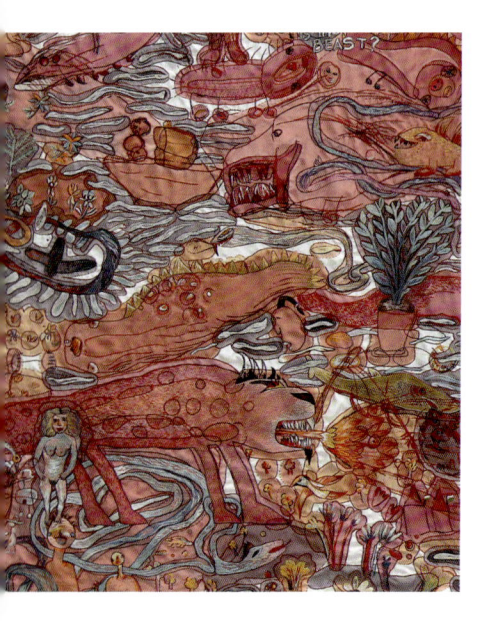

Anna Torma
Bagatelles 1, 2011.
Hand-painted and embroidered silk.
135 x 150 cm (53¼ x 59 in.). Collection of the artist. Photo: Istvan Zsako.

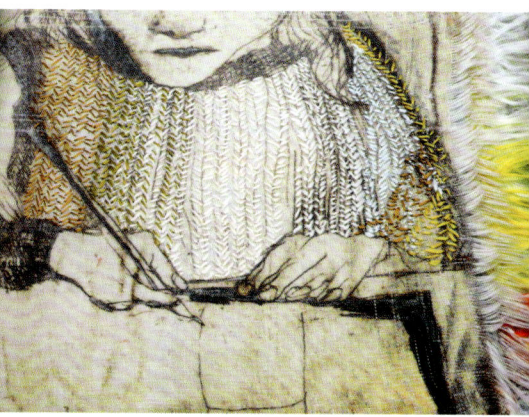

Jane McKeating
Three pages from *While I Was Gone, a Counting Book*, 2010. Hand stitch on digital print. Whole book 18 pages, 30 x 50 cm (12 x 20 in.). Collection of Alice Buckingham. Photo: Mary Stark.

Stitching takes time and marks time. It isn't meant to be quick. My current practice looks at stopping and starting; at interruptions, which may be short-term – a phone call, or longer term – personal demands of family or work. Do I pick up the same piece or do I move on? When is a piece really finished? Cloth allows me to constantly rework. My current *Indian Whispers* piece explores the way that time distorts memory, and how each time I recall an image it changes and is affected by the present and the past. By combining old and new imagery, through use of digital print, I can repeat images and marks constantly at different scales. Avoiding a linear approach to time, stitch has the perfect pace to represent the images in continually fresh ways. Old pieces become part of the new, just as the mind blends time and presents images affected by the past with possibilities for a future.

In *While I Was Gone, a Counting Book*, the form of a child's counting book is used to represent the growth of my daughter to adulthood, from 0 to 18. The reverse of each page records my parallel journey as we each become independent. The images are taken from drawings through the 18 years, but brought into the present through embellishment with stitch. The handle of the cloth and the stitched book construction are crucial parts of the object's resonance. The choice of thread is important, creating a balance between thick, shiny floss and fine matt glacé, a decision taken with each threading of the needle. The regularity of re-threading acts as a symbolic marker of interruption, so a change of thread type shows up on the surface as an interruption, a change to the rhythm. Pages are double-sided, so every mark is visible – a knot and a tangle like a blip in the smooth running of life.

The density of stitch in the *Self-Portrait* of Eirian Short demonstrates what happens when cloth is covered. On a ground of Welsh flannel, the image appears, drowned in the crewel wools that she has worked with for many years. The wool cloth, whilst not visible, is so important for its handle: 'I enjoy the sensual pleasure of hand-stitching so it is important for the threaded needle to pass through the fabric easily. I have used only straight stitches, treating them as "brushstrokes".'[15]

Portraying herself as others see her, this piece is part of a body of work exploring portraiture. Eirian's knowledge and understanding of the way thread works as it is laid densely into the surface of the cloth to create image and illusion, are powerful. Moving through ideas and themes over a lifetime of practice,

Antonia Riviere
Unfinished Mending, 2008 (ongoing). Altered linen skirt, overstitched patterned scrap cotton, hand-stitched with stranded embroidery thread. 68 cm (26¾ in.) long x 70 cm (27½ in.) wide at hem. Photo: Ruth Whitten.

influences and experiences, this image captures hand stitch in its most mesmerising form, making up the surface, yet presenting a much deeper construction.

Discussing all these works in terms of process and materials is not to negate meaning. Highly traditional techniques may be used for unexpected and powerful imagery. How could there be more meaning than exists in a church kneeler, lovingly made to commemorate a war, the canvas embroidered with a date of a death and imbued with the nature of the sacrifice? Without the grid of the canvas, the security and pleasure of the technique and the clarity of the function, would the community of stitchers be confident to contribute to the honouring of a soldier?

In recent years, many embroiderers have described their work by means other than process, reluctant to acknowledge the role played by methods and techniques in the production of work or the expression of an idea. But there is change towards a value being placed on the synthesis of technique and idea. Embroiderers' experience ensures that creativity is not subservient to materials, but enables a careful selection and balance between components. Sensitivity and knowledge help the work to make sense: to make it minimal, or drowned, to let the ground break through or to obliterate it, to work with the grain or against it.

NOTES

[1] Interview with Asif, February 2011, in Asif Shaikh's design studio, Ahmedabad, India.
[2] Correspondence with Gavin Fry, 2011.
[3] Conversation with Nigel Cheney, 2011. Nigel's website is: www.nigelcheney.com/.
[4] Binca is an open-weave cotton fabric used to teach young children basic stitches. It was particularly popular in the 1960s and 1970s.
[5] The 'Knitting and Stitching Show' is an annual exhibition and selling event that showcases both amateur and professional knit- and stitch-related artefacts and products over three venues in England and Ireland.
[6] Their website, www.finecellwork.co.uk, states: 'Fine Cell Work is a social enterprise that teaches needlework to prison inmates and sells their products. The prisoners do the work when they are locked in their cells, and the earnings give them hope, skills and independence.'
[7] Conversation with Nigel Cheney, 2011.
[8] Ibid.
[9] Ibid.
[10] Correspondence with Gavin Fry, 2011.
[11] Ibid.
[12] Audrey Walker, questionnaire responses, 2011.
[13] Ibid.
[14] Correspondence with Antonia Riviere, 2011.
[15] Eirian Short, questionnaire responses, 2011.

GROUND IN CLOTH AND THREAD

Eirian Short
Self-Portrait, 2006. Straight stitches in crewel wool on Welsh flannel. 47.3 x 37 cm (18⅝ x14½ in.). Collection of the National Library of Wales, Aberystwyth. Photo: National Library of Wales.

ALICE KETTLE

Sound, Light and Air

ARGUABLY, YOU CANNOT TOUCH OR SEE SOUND, LIGHT AND AIR, since they are insubstantial, ethereal and intangible. Yet these are the base materials for David Littler, Sally Morfill and Janet Echelman. All have moved far away from the tactile reassurance of stitching thread into cloth, transporting thread into realms that engage with other sensibilities such as sound, light, and the current of air, a move from the earthbound and local territory to a celestial space.

Their works remind me of the moment of recognition when Mary Magdelene saw Christ walking in the garden after his entombment. His words to her were 'Noli me tangere',[1] meaning 'Do not touch me'. Whilst, of course, these words refer to the important moment of the Christian Resurrection and a letting go of the physical and earthly to enter a spiritual place, in doing so they explore the notion of transformation. In the case of these artists they look up and away from the hand-held, tangible surface on which we concentrate our eye with stitch. In my own work, I look for transformation through the change from material touch to an emotional 'feeling' response, which is the metamorphosis of an inert thread into an animated, live line that can 'breathe' and 'talk'. My own line is bound into the cloth and I have wondered if I must have my feet on the ground to navigate my material landscape. I am the kite flyer holding on to the string whilst David Littler hears it whistle in the wind, Janet Echelman allows it to rise into the clouds, and Sally Morfill catches the moments of time. All their works let go of grounded surface and move the thread into the air, away from touch and into the surrounding atmosphere.

Hand stitching, with its proximity of cloth to a stitcher's hand, has a particular and magical intimacy between maker and made. The careful randomness of hand stitching traces the route of the maker's hand. There is a 'reciprocality of crafted and crafter'[2] as the cloth is closely studied to render each stitch in single marks, gathered groups or simple dotted lines.

Hand work has a contemplative and repetitive rhythm, producing an intimacy with, or closeness to touch in the thing made. These three artists expand our experience of the immediacy of close touch. As Paterson explains, 'A more explicit analysis of touch and space needs to depart from the body per se and the thingness of things, to see how the senses interact in our everyday, embodied experience of space.'[3]

The touch and feel of stitch provide the tangible affirmation of what we can see, verifying materiality. Yet, there are other sensations that are far less concrete and which David, Sally and Janet explore, playing with stitch at the very edge of its

SOUND, LIGHT AND AIR

Janet Echelman
1.26, 2010. Spectra© fibre, high-tenacity polyester fibre, lighting. Civic Center Park, suspended between the Denver Art Museum and Civic Center Park, Denver, Colorado. 7010 x 1920 x 914 cm (230 ft x 63 ft x 30 ft), suspended 2834 cm (93 ft) in the air. Photo: Sarah Rothwell.

form. They move us away from the embodied nature of thread and cloth to where the stitch has become formless and insubstantial, and yet nevertheless present and fundamental. The material, for them, is elemental and even non-existent. It is the wind, sound waves, flickering light and open space. Ingold describes it as an 'open world'[4] where the boundaries of sensation are permeable and 'not … stranded on a closed surface but … immersed in the fluxes of the medium, in the incessant movements of wind and weather. Life is borne on these fluxes which, felt rather than touched, permeate the inhabitant's entire being.'[5]

David Littler, sampler-cultureclash *Stills from an Oscilloscope Sound Drawing Experiment*, 2010. Drawing, paper, punched holes, piano player, sound recording, oscilloscope. Photo: David Littler.

So how do you hear the voice of thread? Or see it as an apparition of passing time? How do you stitch up air? The starting point for them all is the earthbound thread which loses its material ties. Their inspiring works seem to contain something of the spiritual, the cosmic and the infinite, which affect us through the sensations of air, light and movement and which conjure the imagination and echo with the currents of sound and breeze. They remind us of the abstract edges of the universe, the shifting, changing patterns of light and wave forms, the 'fluxes'[6] which are not separated by 'mutually exclusive hemispheres of sky and earth'.[7] Their lines and threads are animate and unconstrained, liberated from ground into a 'mingling'[8] of matter, sensation and thought.

David Littler and Sally Morfill have looked at the hidden voices and records of stitch in samplers.[9] The history of the sampler dates back some 400 years. Samplers were intended to be textile testimonials of the process of learning to sew. Made literally to be an 'example' (the word 'sampler' comes from the Latin *exemplum*[10]), they were the first experience of stitching for young girls. The samplers served as material sketchbooks to experiment in the mastery of stitch craft, 'for trialling, for experimenting, for making mistakes; to be rolled up, put away, referred back to and added to over time'.[11] Characteristically worked on linen, they contain repeated patterns, rows and text, 'extracts of moral and religious verse',[12] sometimes filled with motifs and florals. They are distinctive and acutely personal as the record of the individual maker and the moment of making; flat, measured cloth-works that document history and speak of private lives.

In *Palindromes*, a series started in 2005, Sally uses sampler text to establish this central moment of slow making which then stretches backwards and forwards in time.

> *Slowly on a dark screen stitches start to appear, moving outwards in two directions from a central axis. One image is taken from the top of the fabric, the other from the bottom, both are placed side by side, to form, over time, a word, a palindrome, which reads in bilateral symmetry … As I watch the letters slowly form, seeing the back and front develop together at once, I imagine the sewer planning her stitches to produce this evolving and intricate image.*[13]

In other works Sally cuts sampled words and lines in vinyl sheets. The words lose their location of ground as you look at their backs and fronts and as they are handed on for others to utilise. In *WAllAuTuMnMuTuAllAW*, Sally passes her line

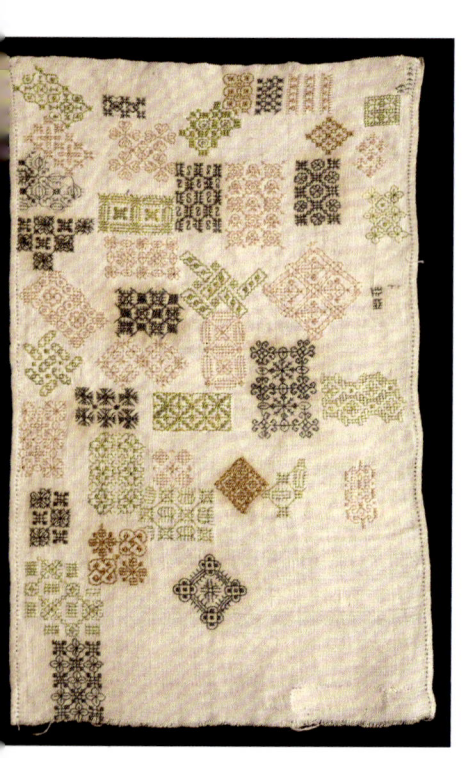

Sampler, English, 1625–50. Spot motif; linen embroidered with silk in running and double running stitch. 28.6 x 48.3 cm (11¼ x 19 in.). © Victoria and Albert Museum, London.

words on to performers and the composer Mark Lee Knowles to 'unpick' the piece in a vocal happening of exchanged words titled 'An Unforgivable Melancholy' (2009). 'I used a sentence from you, and made other sentences of similar shapes and alphabetic properties, and played around with palindromes and mirror images of the words, [mixing] these up in different ways around alliteration.'[14]

The voice within apparently mute cloth is fundamental to the work of David Littler and his colleagues Jason Singh (vocal percussionist and music producer), Yusra Warsama (actor and performance poet), Berit Greinke (textile designer and researcher), and several members of the New Embroidery Group and the Embroiderers' Guild in their group, 'sampler-cultureclash'. They use the marks, weave and stitch of cloth to play back and forth from stitch to sound, and sound to stitch, in a cyclical, repeated motif of textile and music 'sampling'. 'sampler-cultureclash' is a collective concerned with making and of orchestrating moments of stitch, time and sound. Their exploration is group led, a central aspect to their philosophy of shared making and creative growth. They mix the two worlds of sampling stitch and music, which share and exchange experiences, metaphorical resonances and the integrity of crafting. The works are fluid and constantly changing since they are put out freely for others to rework, remix and pass on.

David cites the 'random nature of the early sixteenth- and seventeenth-century spot samplers, which continue to inspire our approach' as his inspiration. 'Many of the samplers are the same, and take elements from each other. Motifs such as the boxer reappear over 300 years, as do pieces of text and designs that are also slightly changed by each maker – so a woman receiving the gifts from two male "boxers" has now become a flower. I like the fact that on one level they are intimate personal records, and at the same time part of a collective history of stitches, patterns, words and motifs.'[15]

The sampler-cultureclash group have used these stitched works as the impetus for 'sampling' into sound. The stitch becomes the notation for a musical note or chord, which when recorded and interpreted can become a pattern viewed on a screen or paper, and subsequently the basis for a new stitch. The musical 'sampling' is part of an idiom of collecting and generating spontaneous and fluid patterns of sound where musicians, like the early embroiderers who improvised with their stitches and patterns, bring disparate sounds together: a bass line from here, a drum break from there, a vocal from elsewhere, a field recording from somewhere else – all of which they combine into new musical experiences.

> *'Sampling', both in terms of music and embroidery, has been largely based on copying, adapting and passing on other people's works and knowledge, and as such is often referred to as stealing – especially if the original work which has been sampled is copyrighted. There is a very famous court case regarding [the] hip-hop artist Biz Markie, who sampled a section from one of Gilbert O'Sullivan's songs. In his final summing up (in which Biz Markie lost the case), the judge started by quoting from the Ten Commandments – 'Thou Shalt Not Steal' – [and] this has gone down in hip-hop history. This commandment often appears in embroidered samplers.*[16]

Derek Sheil performing *An Unforgivable Melancholy* in 2009, a performance by Matthew Lee Knowles in response to WAllAuTuMnMuTuAllAW. James Taylor Gallery, London, as part of 'Interrupted Correspondence/Vice Versa: Five Years Fragments', a project for JTP 09. Reproduced with permission of Derek Sheil. Photo: Sally Morfill.

HAND STITCH: PERSPECTIVES

From left to right:
David Littler, sampler-cultureclash 'Pairings 067'. Performance at 'Pairings: Conversations, Collaborations, Materials' conference, 2011, Manchester Metropolitan University. Photo: Kate Appleby.

sampler-cultureclash
Hacking a Stylophone, May 2010. Fabric, conductive thread, graphite powder, stylophone, live sampling, Bucharest, Romania. *Hacking a Stylophone®* with Berit Greinke, David Littler, Jason Singh, Catalin Matei, Carla Szabo, Pinar Basoglu and Gozde Ilkin. Part of the sampler-cultureclash workshop at MNAC, Bucharest supported by the British Council's Creative Collaboration programme. Photo: sampler-cultureclash.

sampler-cultureclash laboratory at Weißensee kunsthochschule, Berlin, November 2010. Photo: Linda Florence.

sampler-cultureclash
Work In Progess No. 3, live performance. Yusra Warsama performing as part of sampler-cultureclash's *Work in Progress No. 3* at the Craft Rally, London, 2010. Sampler-cultureclash was supported by a Crafts Council Spark Plug Award. Photo: Tas Kyprianou, © Crafts Council of Great Britain.

sampler-cultureclash are collectors of sounds, which they then orchestrate into live performances. They use a myriad of processes and approaches to gather and stitch together musical composition. Some are quietly intimate, where sound surfaces slowly from cloth or is spoken as memories from someone, whilst others are collective, spontaneous, noisy happenings.

They make recordings of people using embroidery machines or quietly hand-embroidering. Further recordings are made of readings of embroidered text, or the sound of the cloth as it is touched and stitched. Digital music software is utilised to pick up 'colour' and 'pattern' from cloth, which is reformed into musical concord. Sometimes a piano player plays strips of patterned paper based on 'samples' of embroidered designs and freestyle marks. Holes are punched in the patterned strips so the drawing becomes a musical score, much like the punch card used by jacquard looms and the first computers. Electronic musical instruments (such as stylophones) create textile buttons that play the machine – using conductive thread to connect the button to the instrument so that many individuals can participate to create a piece of music.

The library of marks from the fabric samples, which act as scores or notations for sound stitch music, are interpreted back into a voice or resonance in an experimental and cyclical sampling process. With all the sounds that are generated, sampler-cultureclash can record, copy, sample, cut, loop, repeat, reverse and distort in order to create a new sound which is re-sampled and repeated to build a continuous, but ever-evolving circle of sound.

This is a collective process, which links with community and live performance. It is a coming together and joining of hands. It is an acutely informed, insightful response from artists with a deep knowledge and understanding of textiles. The sympathy of this material response informs the music, which becomes loaded with the soul of textile and making.

Our approach to performing is inspired by those early spot samplers. The performances are laboratories of making. They are always improvised. Sometimes things don't always work, but at the same time it allows for serendipity: for beautiful moments when

SOUND, LIGHT AND AIR

unexpected elements connect. We start with a silence, the empty piece of linen; then add a single point akin to the first stitch, and end with a single point – the final stitch. In between we enter the unknown to create a playground of trials, experiments, conversations; an environment that becomes a collage of people, material, word, sound, image, pattern, movement and machine.[17]

Sally Morfill's recording is of her own stitching. Her projected images of stitch require our participation, our responses and interaction as the stitch reveals itself in a meditation on the order of things. Her focus is on the intimacy of quiet making, rather than the cacophony of sound within the cloth. The works are private, intense and conversely vast in their concentration on time and metaphysics. *Wipe* (1999) is a film of her hand-stitching and unstitching in a never-ending cycle, which she describes as 'a failed attempt to make the perfect loop'. She explains it as a durational piece lasting 17 hours, which shows her hand and the needle engaged in stitching half cross-stitch.[18] The image is vastly expanded and projected onto cloth canvas, and shifts from negative to positive, from black to white, day to night, light to dark, past to present. We are never sure if time moves backwards or forwards, or is recycled. The suggestion is that the samplers and the stitching are part of the universal pattern of life, which, whilst ordered and rhythmic, repeats in a changing form much like the wind – which blows but never has the same breath.

The thread, for Sally, is a continuum that connects one work to another. The sewn cloth of *Wipe* (1999) is part of the following work, *enough* (2001).[19] A small screen shows a line animated into a moving hand which stitches and unpicks a floating thread. 'The screen sits on a table and we can sit on a chair and peer at the screen in close observation as though it is our own hand doing the making.'

As with David and Janet, for Sally the old and new technologies are fluid tools in dialogue. They use the material fabric and thread as conduits for thoughts and heightened spatial experience. They ask us questions about the voice and feel of stitch, of temporal experience, of tacit knowledge, of material and of ambient sensation.

The work of sampler-cultureclash posits a new dimension of stitch, and David Littler emphasises the importance of ideas in his word manifesto: 'Sampling, Time, Silence, Soul, Community, Sound'. Sally Morfill's manifesto is in her titles and words, as in the palindrome: '**WAllAuTuMnMuTuAllAW**'.[20]

So it is that through starting with substance, David and Sally give us the reverberations of sound and light. In between, we listen and find the connections beyond the material to an all-encompassing experience that began with stitch. It is like 'the mystery of vision, the astonishment of the discovery that behind the sheer ordinariness of the sight of things lies the primal experience of being able to see'.[21]

Janet Echelman's work similarly implies expansive understanding as her giant works morph in the wind into billowing, volumetric forms without solid mass. She sculpts in response to a particular place, catching the air, the whispering movement of the wind, the shifts of sunlight and the changing seasons. The works

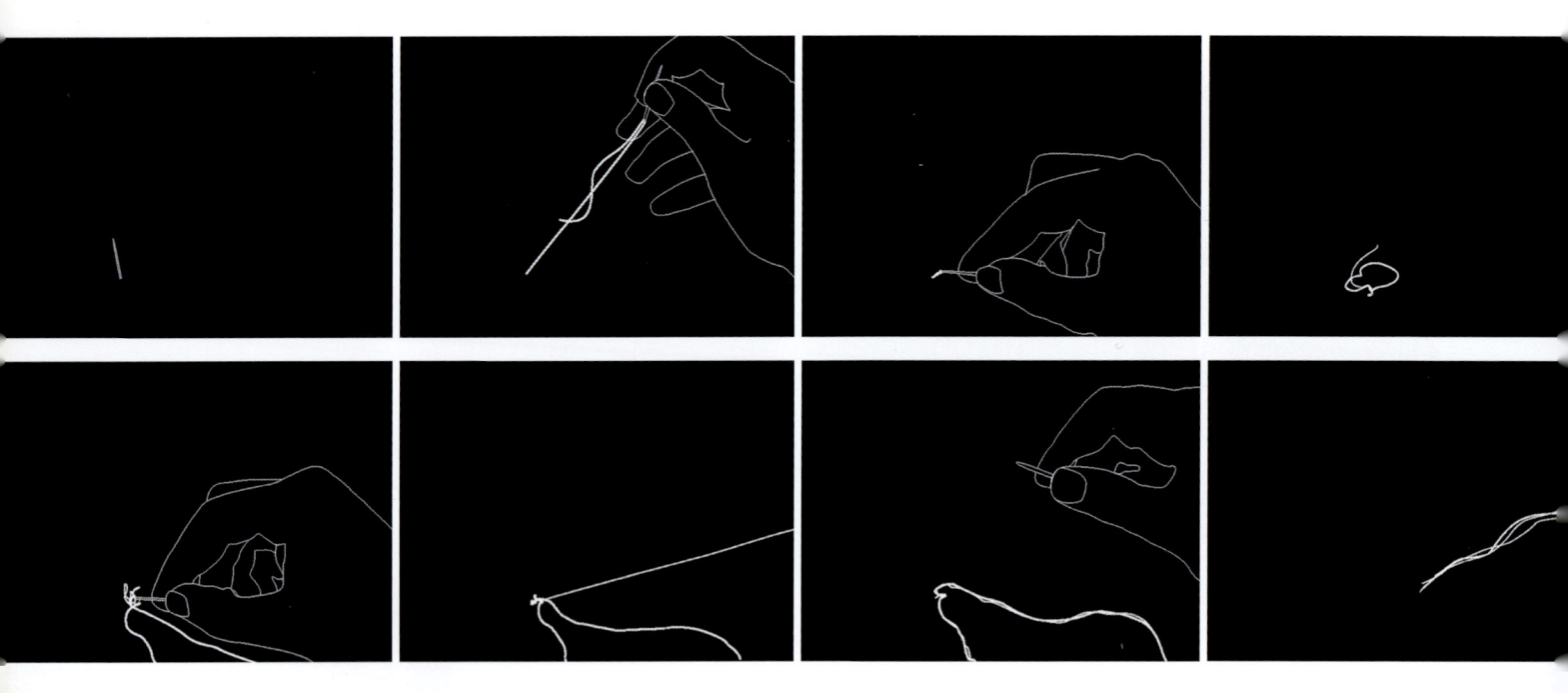

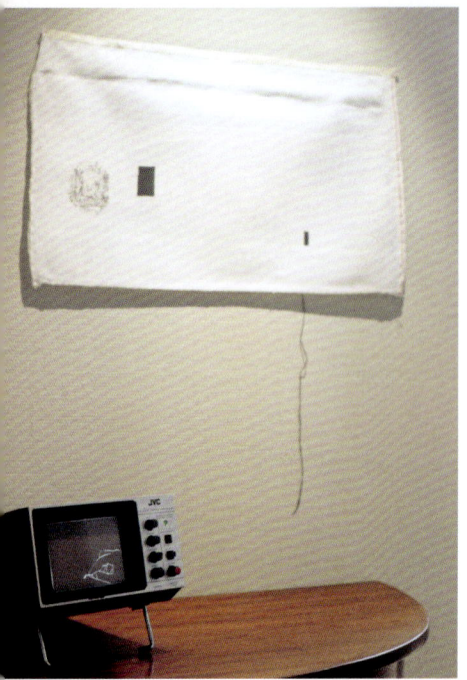

HAND STITCH: PERSPECTIVES

Sally Morfill
(*left and detail above*) *Enough* (detail), 2001. Installation comprising video, video player and monitor, woven fabric with embroidery. Purchased for Nottingham City Museums and Galleries through the Contemporary Art Society Special Collection Scheme, with lottery funding from Arts Council England, 2001. Photos: (*left*) Sally Morfill; (*above*) digital stills, Bury St Edmunds Art Gallery.

Janet Echelman
(*opposite*) *1.26*, 2010. Spectra© fibre, high-tenacity polyester fibre, lighting. Civic Center Park, suspended between the Denver Art Museum and Civic Center Park, Denver, Colorado. 70 x 19 x 9 m (230 x 63 x 30 ft), suspended 28 m (93 ft) in the air. Photo: Peter Vanderwarker.

make constantly changing patterns, which she describes as 'idiosyncratic, delicate, ephemeral, voluptuous'.[22] 'My strategy is to let my work be choreographed by nature', she says. 'It is renewed at every moment.' Janet expresses sentiments shared by all three artists: 'I want people to relate to my work not as an observer to a discrete object, but rather as a relationship between two entities that are both changing at all times.'[23]

Her works are vast thread sculptures suspended in the air, designed to breathe and move. There is no substrate of material, but simply threads of high-tensile lines knotted and wrapped around each other to form nets and webs that spin and animate the skyscape. Her interpretation of hand stitch stems from the traditional craft forms of needle-weaving and netting, where the threads link in patterns of continuous lines to become giant, complex, three-dimensional structures. Echelman has developed her own sophisticated technologies with intricate digital software programs, which configure the folding, spiralling shapes into measurable form, which it is then possible to interpret into a manufacturing process of machine-knotting and then hand-joining. It is a slow, organic, yet highly technical: 'My fabricators will turn off the machine after each knot and readjust. It allows me to have a strong, repeatable and a warranty-able piece that has the characteristics of a handmade piece. It is both industrial and handcrafted.'[24]

SOUND, LIGHT AND AIR

HAND STITCH: PERSPECTIVES

Janet Echelman
Her Secret Is Patience, 2009. Painted galvanised steel, changing sets of recyclable high-tenacity polyester braided twine netting, coloured lighting. Civic Space Park, downtown Phoenix, Arizona. 44 x 108 x 88 m (145 x 353 x 289 ft). Photo: Karie Porter.

The works are experiential, an embodied response to the vastness of the air and sky. The indoor works are delicate and responsive to the minute changes in wind current from the air-conditioning system. The outdoor works are choreographed by the patterned shades of wind and appear connected to limitless sky; they are awesome breathing entities that float like clouds. The threads are huge, interlocking circles of stitches in the air, which cast linear shadows on the earth. By day they are touched by sunlight and at night they are illuminated by rays of intensely coloured lights.

Janet Echelman's works literally shape the space. This is as a consequence of their scale but also, as with the work of sampler-cultureclash, they reach out in a dialogue with the local communities in which they are placed. Janet talks of 'stitching the city together' and 'stitching at an urban scale'.[25] The benign forms are intended to nurture relationships with the residents and embody local identity. In paying close attention to local materials and working methods, each project becomes intimately tied to its environment, serving to strengthen neighbourhood connections and promote an entirely distinctive character. Many describe the evocative nature of the forms as uplifting and spiritual. She repeats an anecdote about local businessmen lying on the grass under her work and looking into the sky to 'share the rediscovery of wonder'.

Janet Echelman learnt her fine thread knotting from fishermen on an Indian beach in the Bay of Bengal. 'I would walk on the beach and swim, just as the fishermen were bringing in their nets and it occurred to me that nets are a way of creating form without mass.'[26] The monumental net forms are a 'symphony',[27] orchestrated between Janet, aeronautical engineers, mechanical engineers, architects and industrial craftsmen. In this collaboration, she shares an interest with David and Sally: the use of digital programming of complex diagrammatic shapes and interconnected threads. For Janet this has involved the commissioning of new J-Net software, developed by a computer scientist at the Massachusetts Institute of Technology to create her specific three-dimensional geometry.

The liquid of the fishermen's water is replaced as Janet raises her jellyfish-like swimming forms into the air. If I were to offer a manifesto of words to Janet Echelman, it would be: Precise Shape, Gentle Movement, Changing Patterns, Wonder, Living and Breathing, Whispering Voices, Awe.

The works by sampler-cultureclash, Sally Morfill and Janet Echelman move between the animate and the inanimate; they intermingle the material and the experiential, which is a porous place. 'In the open world the task of habitation is to bind the weather into substantial, living forms, and in that way to participate in weaving the texture of the land. But bindings are not boundaries, and they no more contain the world, or enclose it, than does a knot contain the threads from which it is tied.'[28]

NOTES

[1] Gospel of John 20:17.

[2] Paterson, Mark, *Senses of Touch* (Oxford, New York: Berg, 2007), p. 1.

[3] Ibid, p. 76.

[4] Ingold, Tim, 'Earth, Wind, Sky and Weather' in *Journal of the Royal Anthropological Institute* (N.S.), S19–S38 (2007).

[5] Ibid.

[6] Ibid.

[7] Ibid.

[8] Ibid.

[9] Littler, David, interview with Alice Kettle, May 2011.

[10] See www.exemplum.co.uk/history.html/.

[11] Littler, David, interview with Alice Kettle, May 2011.

[12] Ibid.

[13] Rendell, Jane, 'On Thinking I Am Missing the Point', *Reveal* catalogue, (Nottingham: Contemporary Textiles Collection, Nottingham Castle Museum, 2005).

[14] Lee Knowles, Mark, September 2011.

[15] Littler, David, interview with Alice Kettle, May 2011.

[16] Ibid.

[17] Ibid.

[18] Morfill, Sally, interview with Alice Kettle, September 2011.

[19] Reveal, Contemporary Textiles Collection, Nottingham Castle Museum (2005).

[20] Morfill, Sally, *Palindromes* (2005).

[21] Ingold, T., referring to Merleau-Ponty, M. *Phenomenology of perception* (trans. C. Smith), (London: Routledge & Kegan Paul, 1964) and 'Eye and Mind' (trans. C. Dallery) pp. 159–90 in J.M. Edie (ed.), *The Primacy of Perception and Other Essays on Phenomenological Psychology: The History of Art and Politics* (Evanston Ill: North-Western University Press, 1964).

[22] Hemmings, Jessica, and Echelman, Janet, 'Net Work' in *Embroidery* (November/December 2007).

[23] Echelman, Janet, interview with Alice Kettle, June 2011.

[24] Hemmings, Jessica and Echelman, Janet, op. cit.

[25] Echelman, Janet, interview with Alice Kettle, June 2011.

[26] Echelman, Janet, 'Taking Imagination Seriously' (talk). TED 2011, filmed March 2011, posted June 2011. See www.ted.com/talks/janet_echelman.html (accessed 2 July 2011).

[27] Echelman, Janet, interview with Alice Kettle, June 2011.

[28] Ingold, T., op. cit.

KATE EGAN

Air: Off the Ground

The essential feature of quantum interconnectedness is that the whole universe is enfolded in everything and that each thing is enfolded in the whole.

— David Bohm – physicist

A COUPLE OF YEARS AGO, I CAME ACROSS an art student constructing what looked like the beginnings of a suspension bridge made of cotton threaded across the embroidery studio space at Manchester School of Art. Armed with a crewel needle and masses of bright red thread, this student looked as if she was attempting to appropriate Marcel Duchamp's threaded space, which I'd seen in his replica sketchbooks in the archive of the special collections at the University. Getting nearer to the work, my mind subconsciously decoded meaning from what was being revealed to me – from bridges to high art in 0.4 nanoseconds – and it became clear to me that the thread had become unintentionally caught around her coat button as she walked across the space threading the needle. She spoke to me, saying 'I've got this small square of red-edged Holland linen and a shisha mirror. How much cotton do I thread on to the needle?' I replied, 'The length of the thread depends on the work you are making. It's all relative! If you were constructing a suspension bridge you would need to start with 1,280 metres of thread. However, for a small shisha mirror stitch, you would use about 25 centimetres.' The work had just shrunk from monumental to 'minumental'.

Untangling the red thread and somehow getting it into a knot, we began to discuss the beauty of serendipitous mistakes. Looking at the bundled-up mass of thread, to my eyes it began to take on a new form, like a confused map of Venus's processional orbit around the Earth or one of those plasticised vein trees of Dr Von Heimlich.

The student's deviation from her initial path enriched the work considerably, and after much discussion, she recognised that mistake-making, mistake recognition and lateral thinking are the three key components on the journey of making a piece of artwork. She had understood what was happening to her work and, acting on the opportunity, she seized the moment and let the mistake take her into new territories.

In this chapter, I will be highlighting the work of two artists who use hand stitch in non-traditional and unfamiliar ways, and who are connected by the absence of cloth – they use thread and hand stitch without any ground. Kristin

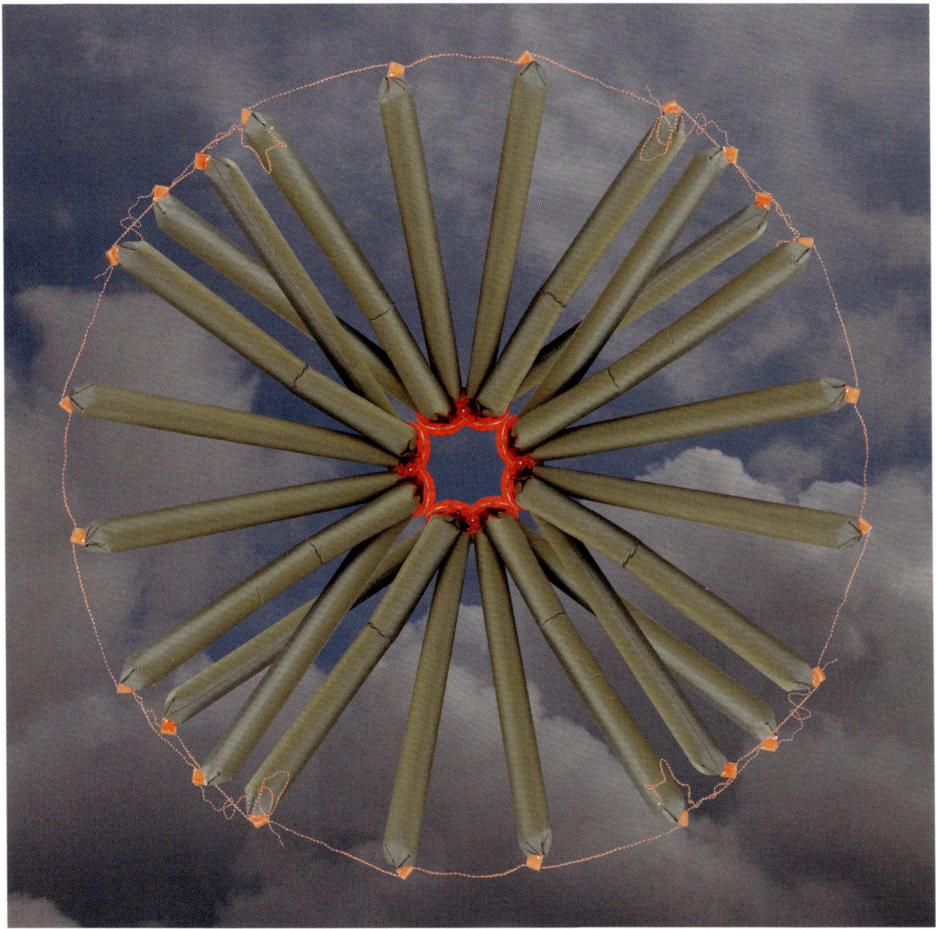

AIR: OFF THE GROUND

Kate Egan
Air, August 2011. Inflatable, open buttonhole stitch. Nylon, computer fans, laser-cut perspex, sound, jeans rivets, reflective material. 3 m x 6 m x 75 cm (3¼ yd x 6½ yd x 29½ in.) (variable). Photo: Mary Stark.

Artist unknown
Found Tangle, August 2011. Tangling, elastic thread. 80 x 40 cm (31½ x 15¾ in.). Photo: Mary Stark.

Scheving is a video artist who traverses the eastern landscape of Iceland, walking with thread. Stacy Brafield is an artist who uses videotape as thread to construct temporary pieces for exhibitions and public spaces. I will also be showing my new work, *Air*, which has been made especially for this chapter as a case study. The purpose of making the piece is to reveal my working process for this chapter, to focus my ideas towards a larger future installation using inflatable stitch, sound and geo-tagging, and also to challenge the territory of hand stitch – to provoke thought, and to offer a different perspective on hand stitch, perhaps highlighting the potential of hand stitch to others who have bypassed it as mundane and very ordinary.[1]

THE STORY OF THE MAKING OF *AIR*

As makers and artists, we are often asked, 'Why did you make that?' Or art students ask the question, 'What was the journey from "a" to "b"? How did you get there?'

We often discuss living in a hectic world where life consists of a myriad of things to do, yet for me, the one thing that binds all of these other activities together is the work I make or dream about making. Whether I'm washing up or walking through the park or beginning a tutorial group, the ideas I am working on follow me like a parallel trolleybus connected to the wire, and it is these fractured, yet interrelating rhythms that interest me and the discipline of making everything interconnect in order to make work. Before we talk about the journey, you may find it useful to read about the background to my existing work.

I use new and old technologies in my work, making reference to mass consumerism and observations of the universe (the macrocosm) in relation to the domestic (the microcosm). I often use a variety of materials in my work, for example air, soap, concrete, fabric, stitch and film. In 2002, I set up the art label 'FLOAT' as a platform for interdisciplinary and collaborative projects, in order to create new and unexpected mixes, to complement the public art I produce for interior and exterior spaces.

My work is concerned with the interconnectedness that Bohm speaks of at a sub-atomic level. All atoms are connected; however, their forms are ephemeral in the physical world. We cannot see the invisible empty air; instead, we *feel* the summer breeze or *feel* the action of breathing in the cold, wuthering wind, and we can only imagine these forms. Imagine stitching into air – into the 'stuff of the universe' or empty air – what you would be stitching into is in fact made up of oxygen, nitrogen, carbon dioxide, hydrogen and smaller amounts of argon, neon, helium, krypton, xenon and water vapour. I began imagining making *Air* in my head before I used a sketchbook or started scribbling on the ten envelopes I had collected. The inflatable structures I have created in the past have influenced this piece, and I wanted to use the inflatable form yet again and at the same time produce an ambiguous piece directly related to the marks of the stitch taken away from their ground. The journey starts here …

To begin at the beginning, before I was formally introduced to hand stitch, I remember being five years old and threading berries on long grasses, and I remember the thrill of the making process. I lived on an island near the Pacific Rim, and it was so small that you could walk around it in a day. Every morning, much to my delight, the sea washed up a series of strange objects, and my collection of sea-bleached ropes and fishing twines became my first palette of thread. At the island school, I took part in a festival making Kwakiutl Indian button blankets. I was given sequins and buttons to sew around a killer whale motif, but I found it really difficult to stitch using a needle, as I preferred the freedom of using thread without the ground and making something without the restriction of knowing what that object would become.

Years later, when I was an art student, I discovered the possibilities of hand stitch and was transported back to those childhood discoveries – something I didn't expect to find. Art school was very open and everything was possible.

Cloud-filling stitch, fly stitch and blackwork existed as embroidery stitches in their own particular contexts. However, if you strip away their cultural and social or domestic meaning, they become something else – a pattern or a mark, a new tool for new meanings and new possibilities. Take them away from their ground and they become marks open to interpretation – a grid, a pylon, a rhythm, a landscape

AIR: OFF THE GROUND

seen by the electron microscope, or something more conceptual like a map of patterns made by the never-ending noise of the Dyson between 10 a.m. and 4.30 p.m. in any street in a given town … the possibilities are endless.

The potential of taking a small, traditional hand stitch and exploiting it by freeing it from its ground and mixing it with chance makes for a fascinating and magical discovery, which we observe when the two collide.

Onwards with the journey … Ordinary events such as dreams and daydreams often provide a stimulus for my work, and I frequently start with a story. Three interconnected, non-linear dreams/stories have informed *Air*. They connect with the past, present and future – which you can fast-forward, pause or rewind to consider the wonderful history and future of textiles.

The imaginary thread of time

On my way through the 'magic' park towards the library, I found a small yellow sticky note – the kind used over and over by art students. Words of deep blue biro stared up at me. It read: 'Why *did* Carter wrap up the treasures he found in the tomb of Tutankhamen with the textiles he found in there?' Coincidence is a marvellous thing. Ever since I had re-read my 'History of Embroidery', a requirement of the Embroidery course back in 1989, I had been thinking about the role of stitch through history in its different contexts: as decoration, for status, and for depicting a moment in time as a documentary device. We can 'read' history through this special medium and yet it is also the stuff we live with every day, the interface with skin, our living spaces. Carter carefully wrapped up the treasure from the tomb of Tutankhamen with what appeared to him to be ancient but nonetheless everyday textiles (with no regard for the fact that they were thousands of years old). On contact with the bright nineteenth-century daylight, the hand-embroidered textiles turned to dust – a layer of history destroyed.

Kate Egan

(*left*) *Kwakiutl Button Blanket* (detail), 1969. Hand stitch, cotton fabric and sequins. Button blanket made at school during a Kwakiutl festival on Cormorant Island. 50 x 30 cm (20 x 12 in.). Photo: Mary Stark.

(*right*) *Air* (detail), August 2011. Nylon, computer fans, laser-cut perspex, sound, jeans rivets, reflective material. 3 m x 6 m x 75 cm (3¼ yd x 6½ yd x 29½ in.) (variable). Technique: inflatable with blanket stitch. Detail shows the edges of the inflatable threads stacked. Photo: Mary Stark.

HAND STITCH: PERSPECTIVES

This extraordinary commodity was overlooked by Carter because of its connection with the everyday; at that point in history, the idea of textiles as archaeological cloth had not yet been made. Imagine if a scrap of embroidery had been accidentally ripped and had caught on one of the sharper metal objects removed from the tomb and was taken towards the twenty-first century unknowingly.

A dream

Getting in a knot, I try a couple of hand stitches. I am interested in the very first stitch that was ever stitched: who stitched it and when and what for? Some texts say that the first type of stitch was chain stitch, others say running stitch.

A small scrap of stitch lay on the dusty floor, lonely and away from the flock. I picked up my satchel and collected this unique find to take back to the lab to look at under my 'historoscope'. Once in the lab, I could see the full history of the scrap: the bright colours, the texture of the ground, the in and out and wrapping of what I thought was chain stitch. I zoomed out with the context button and I could 'see' the maker's hands and understood that this was not what it appeared to be, which was chain stitch; instead, it was two-ply, S-twisted woollen threads couched down side by side, giving the appearance of chain stitch. I zoomed out further.

Internet jeans

The girl who had lost that sticky note scratched her head impatiently: the connection had gone down and her Internet jeans weren't functioning as they should. The knee had frayed and she had no more of the 'electro twist' to darn them with. She had also used the 'other' washing powder in the micro-wash, the kind that wasn't recommended for this type of fabric.

She had been searching for Phillip K. Dick's scramble suit, which she had read was 'Everyman and in every occasion (up to a combination of a million and a half sub bits) during the course of each hour'. She was doing initial research for the Float company, having been commissioned to come up with a textile glossary that showed every stitch known to man, with each stitch carrying a geo-tag in real time.

Sitting on the riverbank, watching the movement of the river, she began daydreaming, searching for information.

The story continues...

Air is an inflatable piece of work that comments on reality and the journey could end here. If we take another look, *Air* is a simple, inflatable group of threads, which can be made into different configurations – threads ready for sewing, either for precision, for tangling in a knot or to be couched to the summer breeze with a looped soundtrack (see *Air*, on previous page). Take a further look, and *Air* can be

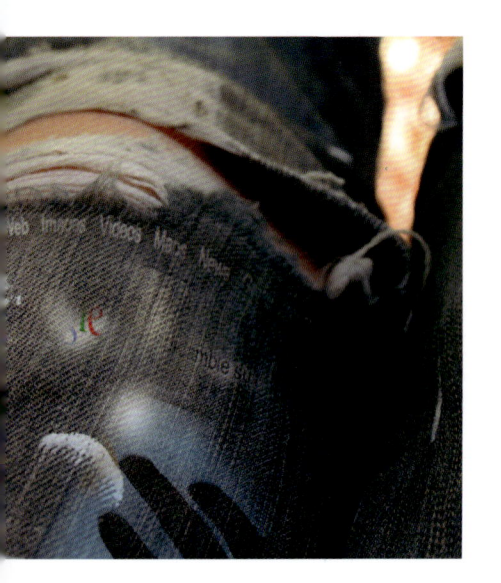

Kate Egan
Internet Jeans, 2011. Denim jeans and Google search, digital collage. Photo: Kate Egan. 'In 1997, I was listening to my father telling me the tale of when he needed to remember a particular stitch for a peculiar-shaped gash in his leg, made during a scramble in the bush in a remote part of Vancouver Island. During this phone call, we decided that what he needed was a portable interface – something he wouldn't have to hold whilst using his hand to stitch his leg. We decided that 'Internet jeans' would be the perfect solution to his problem. Internet jeans became something we talked about often and [also] something I dream about, which influences my work.'

AIR: OFF THE GROUND

seen from a new perspective – I see it as a 'dialogue textile', a piece made purely to provoke a new set of thought patterns, to act as a catalyst towards creating a new textile interface.

The works shown in this chapter are made by hand and celebrate the analogue approaches to practice; it is this analogue, handmade approach that sparks serendipitous possibilities towards future textiles. The potential application of interfaces for textile design is more potent now in this century than at any other time in history: the field of textiles sits on the brink of an explosion. Coding is one area that has a fascinating future with regard to textiles and hand stitch. Textile designers have already established good links with the medical field, architecture, nanotechnology, geo-textiles etc. As we move deeper into the twenty-first century, the everyday textile becomes the interface that is interconnected and enfolded in everything. It is this same interconnectedness that draws artist Kristin Scheving to take a walk across the northern landscape of East Iceland.

KRISTIN SCHEVING

Kristin Scheving is a visual artist, curator and director of the Culture Centre at Fljotsdalsherad, East Iceland. She has worked internationally as a curator and a visual artist and in 2005, she founded the international film and video festival '700IS Reindeerland'. EU funding has enabled the festival to show contemporary video work in various venues around the world.

The body as needle

Walking with thread across the harsh landscapes of black volcanic rock and wading through the small streams of East Iceland, sewing the landscape, is a not usually an activity we equate with hand stitch. We think instead of warmth, scale and being indoors. Kristin makes video art using the body as a needle, embroidering across

Kristin Scheving
(*left*) *Snjór*, 2006. Video (2.44 mins), snow, thread. Photo: Kristin Scheving.

(*right*) *Catwalk*, 2008. Video, water, shoes and thread. Walking in water with a ball of thread in East Iceland. Photo: Kristin Scheving.

HAND STITCH: PERSPECTIVES

the extreme black volcanic rocks flocked with brilliant green moss, and in winter couching the freezing snowscapes of her native country.

Kristin's work is largely informed by her personal quest to understand how a sense of identity is constructed through family, place and culture. As an artist and also a woman, Kristin has explored issues that indeed touch us all at one time or another – sexuality, ageing, mortality and faith. She questions the fears and comforts that continually emerge in moments of vulnerability. The personal narrative forms the raw material on which she bases her work. She relates:

My father was a fisherman and I remember him mending the nets that looked like huge, open-work embroideries when laid out across the beach against the blue sea, next to a glacier, with the red hills of iron bleeding out of the mud. The smell of the sea, his hands working away at fixing the nets – knotting – was a similar action to my grandmother's sewing. I stayed a lot with my grandmother when I was young, and do not remember her without knitting. My grandmother's influence appears in my films: she embroidered and knitted all the time. I wanted to contrast this with women now in my work. I have spent my life travelling and living in various cities in the world taking my children with me, living as an artist. Walking and sometimes running through thick snow with thread across the harsh landscapes and small streams is a physical task the antithesis of domestic warmth.

Kristin speaks about why she goes to the extremes of using thread in this way: 'Historically, people depended on making wool threads to clothe everybody to keep warm for survival. I spent a lot of my childhood with my grandmother, who was extremely resourceful at keeping her grandchildren warm. Again I was working with contrasts, a warm wool thread embroidered across the cold snow. I'm influenced by this landscape and feeling of the weather – how it controls us. I remember my mother, the fisherman's wife, listening to the weather forecast every day – looking out of the window [with a worried expression].'

STACY BRAFIELD

Stacy Brafield, an artist based in London, has completed a number of commissions, exhibitions and site-specific installations for public spaces. Stacy uses unusual yet mundane materials in her work, often giving unwanted materials and objects another chance, and so altering their value. She states:

Through the exploration of embroidery, I aim to transform the seemingly everyday object, altering the original purpose of conventional materials in order to maximise their aesthetic qualities. In the rapidly developing twenty-first century, videotapes are losing their importance and being sent to landfill sites as refuse. This work reuses and gives new life to this material by ignoring its technical qualities as a store of picture and sound. Instead, it celebrates the aesthetic qualities of a shiny black line that can travel through space. Invading architectural spaces with site-specific installations, sculptures and drawings, I aim to capture the illusion of movement through a static line. The videotape

Kristin Sheving
Eidar project, 2008. Video, fields and thread. Tying the thread and starting the walk. Photo: Kristin Scheving.

AIR: OFF THE GROUND

Stacy Brafield
(*left*) *Susie*, 2010. Videotape, copper nails. 10 x 3 m (3¼ x 11 yd). Threading and wrapping. This work was made in response to a visit to see the Northern Lights. The work shimmers and changes when viewed from different angles due to the nature of the materials and careful placement of the videotape. Photo: Stacy Brafield.

(*right*) *Aladdin*, 2010. Videotape, copper nails. 3 x 3 m (3¼ x 3¼ yd). Threading, wrapping. Commission for reception area of Beachcroft LLP, Spinningfields, Manchester. Collection of Beachcroft, Manchester. Photo: Stacy Brafield.

now records another picture and alludes to other sounds from a different time and place. As one picture is lost, another takes its place.

Reusing and recycling are key aspects of her practice and she sources her collections of raw materials from local 'suppliers' such as the tip, Freecycle, charity shops, friends and family. Of this, she says, 'I simply feel that there are so many materials already out there that are unused and derelict. So, why should I have to use a new material? When such a wide variety of objects are so ready available, I do not feel the need to use a "new" material. The challenge [is] of utilising a mundane object, something that is overlooked, and manipulating so far away from its original state.'

The titles of Stacy's works are taken directly from the 'up-cycled' videotape. A recent piece entitled *Quarter-Final*, a site-specific installation in Kurt Schwitters's Merz Barn near Elterwater, Langdale valley, aims to temporarily finish Schwitters's forgotten plans. The plans for the barn went unrealised, as Schwitters died before completing his vision. Using Schwitters's original plans, Stacy stitched across the architectural space, defining what was lost with videotape and natural light. In this commission, the videotape plays a similar role to darning, stitching across space and mending the areas which were once lost.

NOTE

[1] Scott Olsen, *The golden section, natures greatest secret*, (Wooden Books Ltd: Glastonbury, 2006), p. 28.

Places and peoples, individuals and communities

HEATHER BELCHER

Stitching a Social Fabric

INTRODUCTION

IN THIS CHAPTER, I WILL BE INVESTIGATING the use of hand stitch where it has been used as the principal element of community-based textile work. Looking at a small sample of projects, I will be exploring how it has enabled people to engage, share common experiences and voice their own stories within a group context.

Working together offers the opportunity for individuals to develop a sense of inclusion, a space to contribute. I will be looking at the structures that have been adopted in various projects and shining a light on the other activities that take place as people come together to stitch – the chatting, the exchange of ideas and techniques, and the telling of stories – and asking what it is about textiles, and hand stitch in particular, that allows people to engage so readily.

There is a long history of quilt-makers and embroiderers coming together within their communities to help each other, to keep company, and to produce beautiful pieces of cloth for their homes, families and communities. Their intentions have been numerous and include a desire to commemorate, to celebrate and to decorate, and to express individual and collective cultural identities.

'DESCONOCIDA/UNKNOWN'

I have led a number of group textile projects and am familiar with the process of bringing people together and encouraging them to participate in community-based work. But an encounter I had in 2009, in which I was unexpectedly asked to participate in a hand-stitch workshop, left me with a lasting impression of the power of this particular technique. I was attending the exhibition 'Desconocida/Unknown' and the accompanying conference, led by Lesley Millar and the artist Lise Bjørne Linnert.

As I approached the conference hall, I was met with a table laid out with names written on small pieces of paper, each attached to fabric tapes with a sewing needle. Each label listed the name of a woman who had been murdered or who

STITCHING A SOCIAL FABRIC

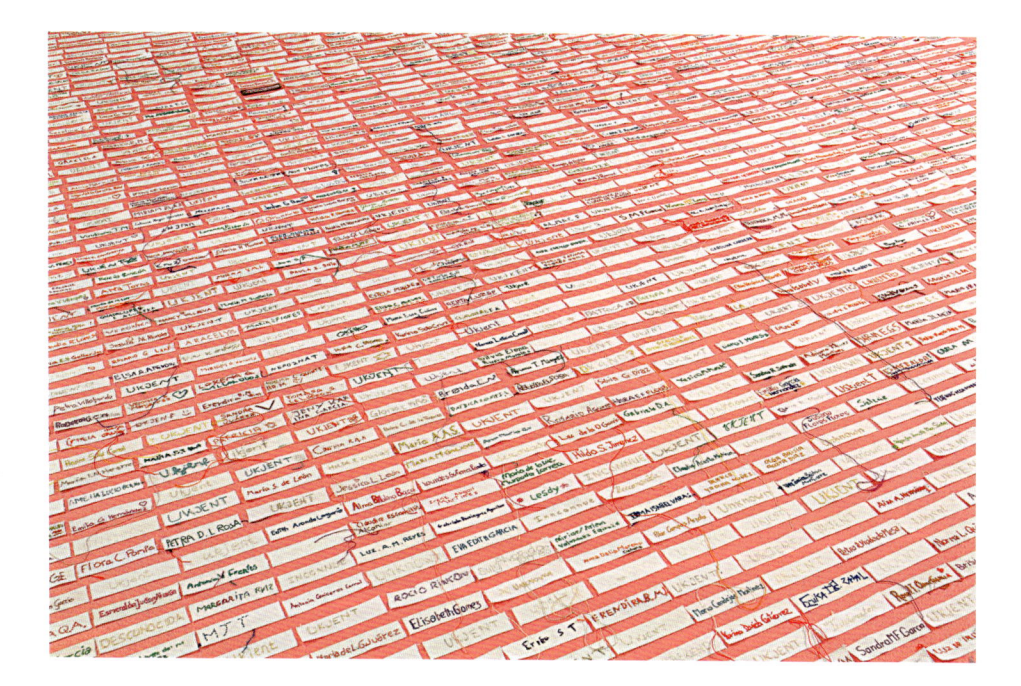

(*above*) Embroidered name tag from the project *'Desconocida: Unknown'*, 2009. Cotton web tape and thread. 2 x 10 cm (¾ x 4 in.). Photo: Lise Bjørne Linnert.

(*left*) Name tags for the project *'Desconocida: Unknown'*, 2009. Cotton web tape and thread. 2 x 10 cm (¾ x 4 in.). Photo: Lise Bjørne Linnert.

had disappeared in Juarez, a town in the 'Amexa' border area between Mexico and the USA. I was asked to select a name and then choose a coloured thread with which to embroider the name on to the fabric tag.

Immediately, I began to ask myself how I would select one name over another. How should I form the stitch – in block capitals, handwriting, or something more complex or decorative? Would I be able to stitch carefully enough? I was struck by the responsibility placed upon me to record the name of this woman, Hilda, her death and her part in this story. As the name emerged in my own handwriting, my own sense of involvement in the workshop intensified.

There was something very evocative about the physical process of stitching in that room, surrounded by others focusing in their own way on the same activity. I was distracted by my own memories of my mother teaching me 'how to' stitch and thinking of the name labels she stitched into my school clothing – in case they got lost or forgotten.

As Lesley Millar says, 'Traditionally textiles and the making of textiles have occupied territory that is both universal and intimate, one that is transitional and cross-cultural.'[1] We all have a connection with cloth, whether we are involved in the production of textiles or not. We all wear clothes and handle cloth on a daily basis. We have a familiarity with it, with the sensation of fabric next to our skins.

As others chatted and as they stitched, I was lost in a private meditation, as for me there was something very powerful about this activity that drew me in, got me involved and held my attention. Lise Bjørne Linnert, the artist responsible for the names project, says she didn't want to just respond to the situation in Juarez, she wanted to connect. 'I wanted to create something that would spread the awareness so that we couldn't stay "outside", and I wanted it to be a community project, a piece of work made together.'[2]

The physical act of stitching did this for me: I couldn't stay 'outside' and I had to become part of the protest. Although I stitched in silence in that room, I was acutely aware of the people around me. Some were chatting; some, like myself, stitched quietly, but we were all focused on the same group objective, to help commemorate the lives of these women, adding our own mark, our own voices to the communal effort.

Again, Lesley Millar notes 'Of course, central to 'Desconocida: Unknown' is that act of making, the singular ownership each participant feels for "their" name tag as it takes its place alongside the many – as Lise Bjørne Linnert comments, "This project is also about the embroiderer, who, through embroidering the name of a particular woman, is also leaving their own identity/thumbprint through the embroidery." '[3]

The intentions, aims, objectives and experiences that develop in community-practice projects vary enormously. The surrounding questions regarding emphasis are worth noting: the role or guidance of the coordinating artist in setting the parameters, structure or overall design within which the participants are able to contribute, the final outcome, the actual textile objects that are produced and perhaps shown publicly in an exhibition, or the degree to which the lives of those taking part have been affected.

NARRATIVE IN EMBROIDERED TAPESTRIES

The Bayeux Tapestry is perhaps one of the most famous of all embroideries, depicting the narrative of the Norman Conquest in the eleventh century. More recently, in the 1980s, the Quaker community took inspiration from the Bayeux Tapestry to produce a similarly large-scale embroidery depicting notable events and experiences, spanning 300 years of the Quaker Friends' history. The aim of this work was to promote community, education and opportunity. The design and structure of the 77 panels, stitched by more than 4,000 people across 15 countries, were carefully planned and coordinated to create a sense of uniformity when all the pieces came together to be shown publicly. Great emphasis was placed on the final outcome, and care was taken to incorporate elements from individuals who were encouraged to contribute research, be experimental and creative with the execution of the stitching. The work reflects the coming together and cooperation of the Quaker community as a whole and not, perhaps, of the individual.[4]

A similarly organised approach was adopted for the 'Keeping Glasgow in Stitches', a large twelve-panel banner, commissioned in 1990 by the city of Glasgow which 'became a unique fabric calendar celebrating the city with humour, poignancy, honesty and pride'.[5] Twelve artists were asked to design one panel each and lead the community groups. As with the Quaker tapestry, the final outcome was important and can be measured by the organised approach to the overall design. The intention was that the final work would be an enduring work exhibited in a public space. Ian Black, writing in *The Bulletin*, January 1991, remarked, 'This work transcends craft. In 100 years' time people will look at these and they will know who we were and what we wanted.'⁶ Clare Higney suggested that the success of 'Keeping Glasgow in Stitches' could be quantified in 'human terms, in the life-long friendship it forged between participants, the confidence and satisfaction it brought to those who took part ... and finally as a work that transcends language and local culture to speak to others as clearly as it does to Glaswegians'.⁷

HULME SWEET HULME

Lynn Setterington has a great deal of experience in working with community groups in and around Manchester and nationwide. In 2010, Lynn undertook a stitch project involving community groups within Hulme, a district a mile from the centre of Manchester. Lynn was interested in focusing on a sense of place, a sense of what 'home' meant to the people living there.

She worked with a number of organisations, including an after-school club for children, two groups of adults studying in an ESOL class (English for speakers of other languages), and Venture Arts, who worked with adults with learning disabilities.

Hulme has, in the past, been notable for its architecture; the terraced slums of the Victorian era were swept away in the 1960s, breaking up the communities that lived there. Homes were replaced with the iconic 'Crescent' flats, a great social housing experiment, only to be demolished again in the mid-1990s when the experiment had been deemed a social planning disaster. So Hulme has been a place of deprivation, change and transition for many decades and yet its community has a reputation for resilience in the face of adversity. It has a diverse and transient population. There is a large community of university students, economic migrants from Europe and beyond, and many groups of refugees seeking asylum. Alongside these groups there are people who have roots that go back many generations. For others, Hulme is a place to gather themselves before they step forward to build a new life elsewhere in the UK.

Lynn began by researching and collecting information about maps and mapping. There were old and new maps of the area and archival photographic images of Hulme. She used the maps as starting points for discussion, generating reminiscences from the older members of the community, and a sense of history for the schoolchildren and for those new to the area. She also introduced the same theme as a project for students at Manchester Metropolitan University. Some of the students would later assist Lynn, working with participants, passing on their creative and technical expertise, gaining experience themselves in working in a community setting. Many of the students also lived in Hulme.

With the two ESOL groups, Lynn was able collaborate with teacher, Neela Egan. Neela incorporated the theme into the lessons. They began to draw maps of where they had travelled from, the places they called home. They 'mapped' their journeys, the routes they had taken to arrive in Hulme. Their places of origin included Somalia, Afghanistan, Pakistan, China, Korea, the Philippines and Poland.

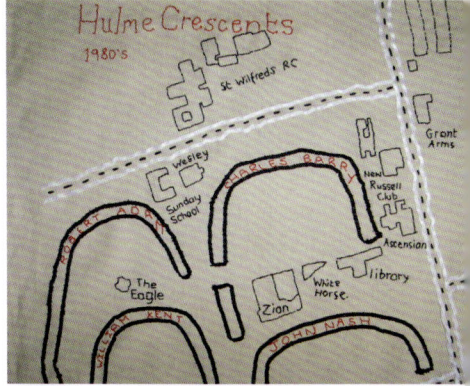

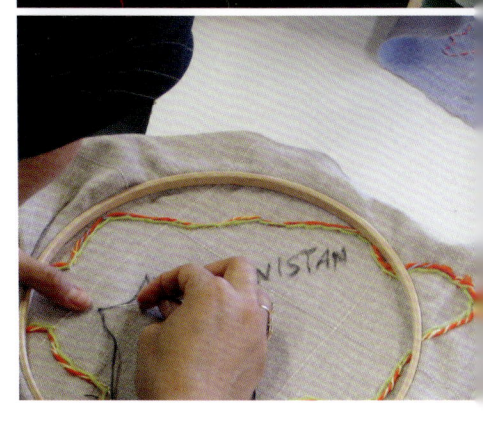

From top:
Stitched map of the Hulme 'Crescent' flats (demolished in the 1990s), 2009. Fabric and threads. Approximately 35 × 35 cm (14 × 14 in.). Photo: Lynn Setterington.

Group of ESOL students stitching their maps in Hulme, 2009. Photo: Lynn Setterington.

Woman from Afghanistan stitching her map, 2009. Fabric, thread and embroidery hoop. 25 × 25 cm (10 × 10 in.). Photo: Lynn Setterington.

HAND STITCH: PERSPECTIVES

Lynn says that many were hesitant about drawing but felt comfortable with the process of stitching. Perhaps it is the association that stitch has with 'practicalities', the making and mending of clothes and other domestic objects, that somehow feels less precious or intimidating. But the question of accessibility goes beyond that. When a group of people sit together and spend time together, they have to slow down. For groups who are unfamiliar with each other, hand-stitching acts as a focus. People can concentrate on their own stitching and they can listen to others. They can join in the conversation or they can ask for advice about the technical process; they can help one another and they can share in each other's life experiences at their own pace, getting to know one another over an extended period of time. What a fantastic vehicle for learning a language.

Lynn is interested in this accessibility of stitch in the work, describing stitch as being universal and multicultural, going beyond language. Extraordinary stories began to emerge as the students started to stitch their 'maps'. Some of the work revealed a very real sense of disorientation, socially and, more poignantly, geographically. One student had never seen a world map before and had little understanding of where Britain was, let alone Hulme, in relation to the world and the country she had travelled from. One man decorated his map with footprints, describing how he had walked for hundreds of miles to flee his country of origin.[8] In the context of these maps, stitch has become a wonderfully expressive means of communication and a beautiful 'drawing' in its own right.

Although the process of making the work and the telling of the stories was the focal point of the project, the exhibition at the end was also an important outcome for the participants. It gave the different groups involved in the project the opportunity to come together, to see and show their work in a public venue alongside the work of other members of their community. The exhibition was brief, but it demonstrated how the project had captured the stories of these individuals and communities and marked another transient but telling moment in the history and life of Hulme in the spring and summer of 2010.

'RESPECT AND PROTECT'

In 2009, MMU hosted an event to raise awareness of World Aids Day. Lynn Setterington, Senior Lecturer in Embroidery, and Jo Verran, Professor of Microbiology, had decided to get together to mark the day by organising two quite different activities that would support and complement one another. Jo runs a Bad Bug Book Club, 'where a group of scientists and non-scientists meet to discuss books in which infectious disease forms a major part of the plot. On the list was *Dorian* by Will Self, which has the additional title of *An Imitation*, since it uses Oscar Wilde's *Picture of Dorian Gray* to underpin a tale of decadence and HIV transmission in the early 1980s.'[9]

Having worked together before, Jo invited Lynn to work with the book club to make a communal stitched banner, which would involve taking the banner to a number of different venues, including two drop-in sessions in the university,

Stitched map of Pakistan, 2009. Fabric, thread. 35 x 35 cm (14 x 14 in.). Photo: Adrian Hunter.

STITCHING A SOCIAL FABRIC

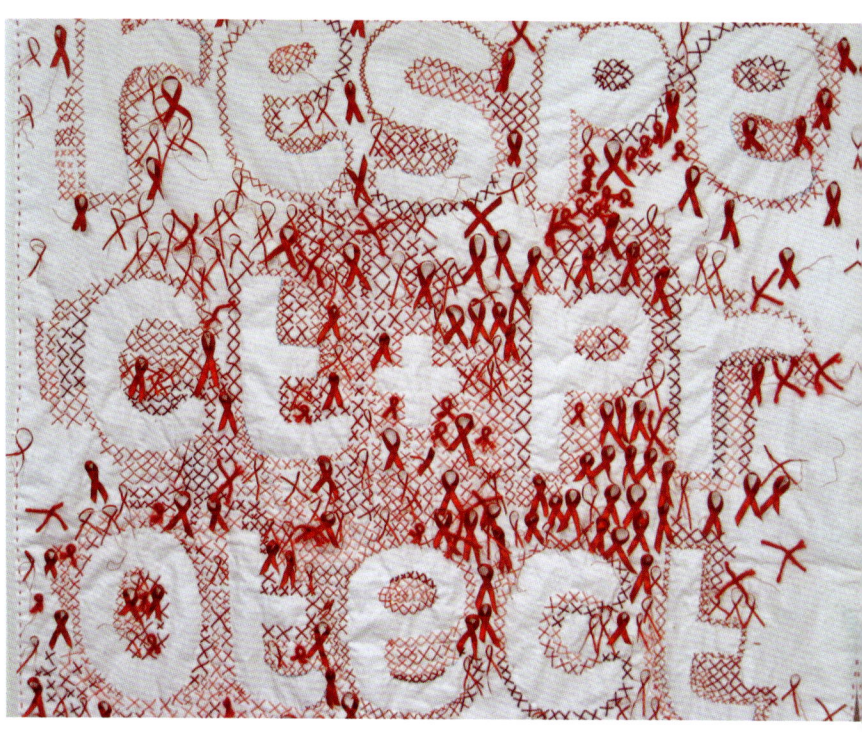

supported by some of the students, two local community group venues, one session in a school and another public drop-in session at the Whitworth Art Gallery. The banner was to be completed alongside the readers of the book club, in a pub on World Aids Day, 1 December 2009.[10]

Public engagement was a key issue of the project. In taking the banner from one group to the next, building on the work of the previous group, its message would be passed to the public and all those who contributed to the artwork. Lynn describes some of the conversations that took place while the quilt was being stitched as 'telling': at the Whitworth Art Gallery drop-in session, one of the participants recounted her experiences as a midwife working in Africa with women affected by Aids.

One of the themes for World Aids Day was 'Respect and Protect'. Lynn chose this slogan and designed it to dominate the composition of the banner. The spaces that form the shapes of the letters are left vacant, suggesting a sense of those who are now absent. The background is filled, rather exuberantly, with red cross-stitches or 'kisses' and the iconic Aids ribbons. At the centre of the quilt is a white cross representing the 'and' in the slogan, but which is also reminiscent of the symbol of the Red Cross charity.

Cross-stitch is perhaps one of the most familiar of all embroidery stitches; the beauty and simplicity of its use in the design is that of its accessibility to all. The simple cross-stitch allows everyone to make his or her mark. Indeed, people of all ages, abilities and nationalities contributed to the making of this banner. Even Jo Verran got involved, 'despite being worried about my needlework skills. It was actually a wonderfully soothing and engaging activity to be sewing and talking to people across a banner'.[11]

(*left*) Students from Manchester Metropolitan University working on the *Respect and Protect* banner, 2009. Cotton fabric, threads and ribbons. 100 x 100 cm (39½ x 39½ in.). Photo: Adrian Hunter.

(*right*) *Respect and Protect* banner, work in progress, 2009. Cotton fabric, threads and ribbons. 100 x 100 cm (39½ x 39½ in.). Photo: Adrian Hunter.

One particularly interesting aspect of the group activity was the way that the stitching began to build up and develop as it moved from one group and venue to another. Lynn described how people tended to work around the edges, nervous about venturing into the centre of the work. There were concerns about the centre remaining unfilled. Perhaps this was a matter of physical constraints, of sitting around a table and people not being able to reach into the centre, or perhaps it spoke of the polite, tentative nature of the group activity where people are initially unfamiliar with one another. Perhaps they were being careful about how they negotiated the space, not wishing to stride into the middle to take 'centre stage' or to trample over the work of others. This speaks volumes about the dynamics and characteristics of any group activity, recording the nature of how people contribute, collaborate, develop connections, build relationships and discuss ideas. Allowing the 'spaces' to remain evident in the final outcome offers a glimpse into the process of making, enriching the story of the quilt's journey from one community group to another.

There are many variations of hand-stitch community-based practice, each with its own emphasis. For some, the priority is to create a thing of long-lasting beauty; for others, the process is more important, with its purpose to empower, or act as a means of individual and/or community engagement. Community projects can support learning and develop new skills, act as a means of communication to cross cultural divides and language barriers. The projects can bring comfort to the lonely and isolated, helping to build and strengthen our communities.

In Kyrgyzstan, a small, mountainous country in Central Asia, they make boldly patterned and coloured, hand-stitched and hand-felted carpets known as Shyrdaks. Identical patterns are cut from two pieces of handmade felt. The pieces are then swapped over to make two fabrics, one the reverse of the other, often known as 'sister' felts. The pieces are stitched together with hand-spun thread and then quilt-stitched on to another layer of plain handmade felt. These are, in a sense, another interpretation of 'community-stitched works'; the tradition that informs their production is possibly a 'blueprint' for how we should evaluate other community-based projects. Shyrdaks are mostly designed and made by individuals, but they are entirely bound by a sense of real community and heritage. Traditionally, the structure of the design and the meanings of the patterns refer to the maker's relationship with his or her community, and are influenced by the animals, plants and landscape that surround them.

Shyrdaks might appear to have rigid parameters with a set repertoire of motifs, but the combinations and the juxtapositions that develop as individual makers select their colours, motifs and stitches demonstrates richly personal voices of individual lives and narratives. Masters or *ustas* are held in high esteem and are often asked to help others with the drawing of the patterns on the felt. Stephanie Bunn states that: 'Designs are not copied but improvised within a repertoire of traditional motifs which the master knows, so no two shyrdaks are the same.'[12]

Shyrdak (felt carpet) from Kyrgyzstan, 2011. Handmade wool felt and hand-spun wool cord. 150 x 350 cm (59 x 137¾ in.). Photo: Heather Belcher.

It is this freedom to explore the boundaries of the design framework, to allow participants the space to 'move around', find their place, make their own individual mark within the context of the group that is crucial in any community project. Hand stitch and quilting are hugely important elements in the shyrdak. They reveal the degree of skill and creativity of the master or *usta*. They add rhythm to the design, as well as strength and durability to the structure. They are skills that are enormously time-consuming, demanding great patience, and command great respect from the community. The Kyrgyz have a saying that 'Every stitch is a step in life.'[13]

Stitching the shyrdak together, 2003. Hand-spun wool cord is stitched in position to cover the seams of the handmade felt pieces. Photo: Heather Belcher

NOTES

[1] Linnet, Lise Bjørne, *Desconocida: Unknown*, ed. Lesley Millar (Epsom: University for the Creative Arts, 2009).
[2] Ibid.
[3] Ibid.
[4] Levin, Jennie, *Living Threads: Making the Quaker Tapestry* (Kendal: The Quaker Tapestry at Kendal Ltd, 1999).
[5] Higney, Clare, *Keeping Glasgow in Stitches*, Introduction (Edinburgh: Mainstream Publishing Company, 1991).
[6] Black, Ian, *The Bulletin* (January 1991).
[7] Higney, op. cit.
[8] Interview with Lynn Setterington, July 2011.
[9] *Microbiology Today* (February 2010).
[10] 'A Stitch in Time Saves Lives', *Microbiology Today* (February 2010).
[11] Ibid.
[12] Bunn, Stephanie, *Nomadic Felts: Artistic Traditions in World Cultures* (London: British Museum Press, 2010).
[13] Interview with Kenjekhan Toktosunova, August 2011.

JANE MCKEATING

From Hand to Hand: encounters with embroiderers from Kutch

Jane McKeating
Indian Whispers, 2011. Hand stitch with digital print on linen and silk organza. Double sided. A page from the rag book. 30 x 30 cm (12 x 12 in.). Photo: Mary Stark.

FOLLOWING A TRIP TO STUDY EMBROIDERERS IN GUJARAT six months ago, the realities of life back at home have interrupted the clarity of the vision I had in India, so now I write affected by that time lapse. Next to me are my visual diary and a small, neat pile of embroidery I brought back: suitcase-sized examples that act as triggers, stimulating memories of a different culture. In a clash of cultures, Indian and English images jumble as I make new work.

I reflect on conversations where it was just stitch that connected us, a common language, though even that needed an interpreter. I think of the handle of the cloths, the colours, sounds and smells of homes and clothes. The products I've brought back represent a tidied-up version, made for a Western market – products we say we want, but I'm not sure that we really do. What we want is the originals – to buy a bit of their culture and belief and symbolism. And they want to buy a bit of ours. The most absorbing photo is one where Jivaben sits and stitches for her design school module. Her family gathers round to meet us; the baby is dressed in a mass-produced sweatshirt embellished with multi-head embroidery, his sister is in a fleece with a logo. Work in progress is kept in a plastic bag printed with mock embroidery. Will these children eventually adopt this stitching life? Will schools value it enough to include it in the curriculum?

The examples I have brought back don't quite fit the colours of my room: something jars, so they stay in the drawer. I know that a woman sat on the floor to make them, finding time amidst the household chores to sew. As an embroiderer I can estimate that time, know the process of covering the surface of a cloth with a thread, and feel the value of the hands and the making of an object.

In Gujarat, embroidery is everywhere: it covers the floors people sit on, the clothes (which when worn out become quilts), the hung cloth of the crib and bags for everything; it covers the camel and helps carry the goats. The remnants are strewn inside and out, going back to the earth, the embroidery outliving the function of the artefact, visible after the cloth has gone.

I visited three organisations in the Kutch region of Gujarat: the SEWA Trade Facilitation Centre, the Kala Raksha Trust and Qasab. Throughout the vast desert region, the craft of hand stitch contributes to the survival of thousands of families. The density of the artisan population supported by NGO embroidery initiatives makes this region a rich contemporary source for understanding the beauty, power and currency of stitch.

The last 60 years have seen mass urbanisation and turbulence, with partition in 1947, war with Pakistan in 1971, and devastation by cyclone in 1998 and earthquake in 2001. Significant development initiatives were needed to rebuild communities and create sustainable employment. Due to regular cycles of drought, the traditional cattle-herding livelihood of these largely nomadic communities became erratic and the search for alternative sources of income started to increase. Pankaj Shah, of Qasab, elucidates:

> On one hand the borders got sealed in 1947, on the other, the roads opened up from the country to these villages. So tourists, travel writers and the researchers started coming in to Kutch, seeing the beauty of the embroidery, the culture itself, and started offering prices and slowly it started the market it was not meant for.[1]

Gujarat has a long history of professional embroidery. John Gillow states that during the seventeenth century it was 'probably the most important centre for fine commercial embroidery in the world',[2] but the mass of embroidery made by Kutchi women was not intended for sale.

> The execution of craft was not just an economic compulsion, but a sacred duty. This largely explains the very meticulous care and devotion with which the humblest work was performed. The commonest of articles were endowed with beauty for each task was a dedication.[3]

The work is described by Eiluned Edwards as 'significant markers of caste identity'.[4] It was made for dowries and personal use up until the 1950s, when Kutch opened up to the outside world. Dowry inflation led to the dowry prohibition act

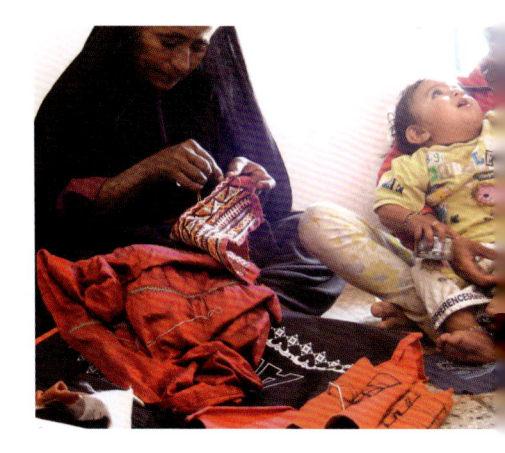

(*above*) Jivaben and family from the Debaria Rabari community at their home in Kesavnagar, in the Kutch region of Gujarat, 2011. Photo: Helen Felcey.

(*below*) A new use for an embroidered textile outside a home in Kesavnagar, 2011. Photo: Jane McKeating.

in 1961. The government of India then started promoting the craft at national level, and an international market developed. However, the infrastructure to enable the artisans to get a fair price was difficult to establish.

The mass procurement of traditional embroidery by middlemen who recognised its market value, throughout the 1970s, literally emptied villages of their heritage. Lovers of embroidery in the West were part of that process, buying it without much thought for its origins. Women were not fairly paid for heirloom embroidery or for new work. In 1968, the first NGO to address this, the Shrujan Trust, started work.[5]

Throughout the 1970s, the State Craft Emporiums bought and sold embroidery, establishing a buoyant market, but with little vision or planning for development at grassroots level. After 20 to 30 years, Shah remembers,

There was saturation, there was a stagnation that happened in the designs and the colours, the quality got affected because the middlemen would go to exhibitions, customers would start bargaining and in the end everything was getting compromised ... [The embroiderers] also wouldn't put their heart into the work.[6]

There has been a shift, from a craft at the heart of a community within which embroidery is designed, made, used and valued, to embroidery produced for economic reasons. These are very different practices.

A snapshot of some of the current activity follows, provided by interviews recorded on my visit. See the Further Reading section for recommended texts where scholars have researched in depth the techniques, traditions and cultural contexts. Whilst to some extent competing for markets, each organisation differs in objectives and philosophy, and they consciously avoid duplicating effort within the communities they serve.

SEWA (SELF-EMPLOYED WOMEN'S ASSOCIATION)

The SEWA Trade Facilitation Centre (STFC) was set up in 2003 as a commercial arm of SEWA, a women's trade union, to produce embroidery through self-reliance projects. Currently, there are 3,500 artisan shareholders in 80 villages across Gujarat.[7] The objective is to create livelihoods, with embroidery design as the secondary focus. However, design development is clearly central in order to win large orders to sustain the volume of women dependent on the work. It is the understanding of the original embroidery practice that initially created the employment, so this needs to feed into the current design development. Keen to expand beyond the traditional, the artisans are supported in the development of new approaches in order to operate in an expanded market. The debate comes in the interrelationship between the commercial concern and the traditions of the craft practice.

For the first 20 years following independence in 1947, there was mass migration to the cities, overlooking the potential within the villages and the skills within the rural home. But whilst working with the poorest communities, SEWA

Remnants put together to create quilted bags, using hooked needle chain stitch (ari) for the embroidery, to be sold in the Hansiba shop. STFC, Ahmedabad, India, 2011. Photo Helen Felcey.

found the handicraft skills passed on from mother to daughter very much in evidence, though most were unaware of their value:

> *The men thought that the women would do their cooking and take care of the cattle. They never thought that the women could bring in [a] livelihood. At first the women didn't trust the organisation, but once they started getting a good green note, which was like their husband's full month's salary, respect was created for these women.*[8]

The embroidery is flexible work, fitting in around domestic tasks, animals and fields. Samples are made in Ahmedabad; kits are created and sent to the districts, where women are grouped according to their level of skill and then make pieces that will be applied to a product once completed. The Hansiba brand,[9] named after Hansibaben, the first rural artisan SEWA worked with, has three retail outlets for the home and export market. Hansibaben, at 92, has worked with the organisation for 24 years. Hansibaben was working as a labourer when the opportunity came, through SEWA, to use the skills she learnt at the age of 12, and she exchanged travelling to construction sites for working from home.

STFC also works with international clients who understand the organisation's philosophy. A constant search for new export markets is required, due to the expanding numbers of women reliant on the work, and so international designers are invited to work with STFC. I discussed the experience with two of them.

Graham Hollick

Graham Hollick is a British designer who undertook two visits to develop a homeware collection. Open-minded from the outset, Graham wanted to understand the artisans' approaches. He describes the relationship with them as one

'Stitch by Stitch', bedding collection. Designed by Graham Hollick and stitched by members of the STFC SEWA project in 1999–2009. Photo: Beth Evans.

of balance: as a designer, you introduce something but it is a two-way process, and the artisans challenge the way you work. He stressed, 'You need to be very patient and respectful of their input and skill. [It is] hard to know the effect that will have on some of these communities, a long way down the line, but in another way it may also reinvigorate them.'[10]

Graham emphasised the importance of putting the value back into hand work, saying that if the women are to get a fair price and produce something beyond running stitch, then a sense of understanding of the source, the people, the skill and effort needs to be communicated to the buyer. Stitching needs to be valued and paid for, so that the stitcher can earn enough for survival.

Adapting the motifs he saw in traditional textiles, he experimented with scale and colour. Kutchi women took part in a workshop to develop the work, using complex stitches in different ways. To the eventual buyer in Europe, the challenges involved are not always evident. These particular women were familiar with ari (chain stitch) hooked embroidery, but found it difficult sewing unfamiliar stitches that were not made with a hook. Sometimes the base cloths and threads varied in quality, or blunt needles made it difficult to stitch. Graham designed for a white cloth, but soon saw that this was impractical. The experience was valuable to Graham and whilst the scale of production isn't suited to him currently, it has led him to use his experience in many other developing countries.[11]

Maddy Fraoli

Maddy Fraoli, a rug designer from the USA,[12] was introducing the hooked rug process to a group of Mochi artisans, simplifying a traditional Mochi embroidery design, during my visit. The rug hooking emulates the process of the ari work done with a hooked needle. She explains:

Kantaben, from the cobbler community, Gujarat, India, 2011. The women have great skill with the ari chain stitch hooking technique. Photo: Howard Peller

My input is about developing what they already have. I think that what is missing most for them is the access to contemporary markets, knowing what people's homes look like. For me to come here with a rug project was really presumptuous, because the Indian market does not use rugs ... but the European markets do need rugs.[13]

For unskilled women, the scale could help to achieve better quality than attempting intricate embroidery. The cross-referencing of craft skills introduces the viability of using rags left over from other products.

The future success of the project will require good communication with the women, quality control with the right mix of design and technical understanding, and the persistence to explore new markets. It was interesting to observe how the hooked stitch technique could so usefully be adapted, whilst being completely alien in terms of the embroidery familiar to the community. However, the importance of a volume of work to sustain the large numbers of women reliant on employment cannot be underestimated. Villoo Mirza of the STFC comments:

The flooring industry does massive work, so if we get visibility in that area we get work for about 1,000 women. For flooring, you can simplify and take the geometric patterns and textures and use recycled waste ... it is in a very nascent state just now, but we feel that if we do some exploration it would bring good revenue.[14]

KALA RAKSHA TRUST

The Kala Raksha Trust[15] was established in 1993 by Judy Frater who, as an anthropologist, had undertaken research into both Rabari and Suf embroidery in the Kutch region for 20 years, together with Prakash Bhanani and Daya Bhahani. Concerned at the effects of commercialisation upon embroidery practice, Judy was persuaded to utilise her experience, sensing the significance of this transitional

Bride's woollen shawl from Bharwad community, East Kutch, c.1976. Collection of Jane McKeating. Worn at weddings and festivals; hand-spun wool that was hand-woven, tie-dyed and then embroidered with wools. Photo: Mary Stark.

period and its effect on traditional practices. Judy's research brought insight to an organisation determined to harness an understanding of the artisan's heritage.

Starting off with 20 women in three communities, the trust now works with 1,000 artisans from diverse religions and backgrounds, many with nomadic lifestyles. Their traditions, like the people, are not static but continually evolving. Here I touch on the interrelationship between the traditional embroidery made in these communities and the embroidery they now make for sale. Judy stresses: 'Kala Raksha works on the understanding that tradition evolves, and must evolve to remain vital, that the way to preserve tradition is to nurture the creative capacity of artisans to innovate.'[16]

The reading of the embroidery is not through stitch type but through symbolic motifs with significant meanings. Specific to each community, the motifs are traditionally formed from an ingenious vocabulary of stitches. The mass of stitches in traditional work has a striking density, a surface of complex combinations, sometimes at such a miniature scale that it becomes hard to identify.

Highly skilled, embroiderers work straight on to cloth without a hoop or pattern. The work is seemingly anonymous but, like handwriting, the artisan recognises the hand of the maker. The embroiderers see the fabric and start work. 'Our [Western artists'] medium is pen or pencil, but you don't draw before you draw, so you have to think of it that way and I would hate to take that away from them, it's their vocabulary.'[17]

The work evolves through constant reinvention within a set of cultural parameters. Missing from designs by someone outside the community is the innate knowledge of the guidelines and meaning within which experimentation takes place. Now, frequently, it's oversimplified, unravelled, a minimal motif in a corner, attractive on the rail in the Fab India[18] store in Ahmedabad, but having no recognisable meaning. As Frater says:

When you do the production work, that's all gone, the hand quality; yes, it is fast, cheap, good for the customer, bad for the embroiderer. When you do fast and cheap, that's what a machine does, that's a factory and then the artisan gets more work, but less value as a creator. We do repeat, but each is a little bit different.[19]

Colour, whilst not verbalised, has huge significance. It is the biggest consideration when creating work for new markets. Understanding and valuing the sensibility of the traditional palette are important if new work is not to become a neutralised version of the exquisite cloths that fill the museums. Traditional colours are bright; there is logic to their choices. Asked to work with a different palette, they became quite adept at tonally matched substitutions. Contrast was instinctive, intrinsic to the meaning, and central to our original attraction to the embroidery. Recently, however, the colours selected are those closest to the base cloth. The artisans are not used to evaluating or articulating the impact of that change.

Patience, practice, design: all factors in making beautiful things, and if one element is removed, the balance is lost. So Kala Raksha determined that to attract customers, the artisans themselves would make the decisions about change. For there is a danger that what made the embroidery desirable could disappear, leaving no market at all. Frater remarks, 'People come to us all the time and say I want to work with your artisans, and usually I tell them, you don't – you want them to do your work – that's different, and the first thing they want to do is change it.'[20]

So, having started to collect fine examples of traditional work, a museum was opened in Sumrasar in 1997, an archive to be used as an active resource to inspire artisans,[21] both preserving and elevating the work to impact on new design. Workshops held in the museum led to the start of the Kala Raksha Vidhyalaya Design School in 2005. The school holds classes where both Indian and international tutors contribute to the curriculum with a remit to develop artisans' design and marketing skills. Frater muses:

If a Rabari woman designs a seashell, it should be a Rabari seashell ... I think also a lot about not wanting to impose a sense of what is right and wrong, which is so easy to do. I am always searching for the indigenous vocabulary ... if the concept was there; somehow they had a way to articulate it.[22]

Kuvarben, a Dhebaria Rabari and a design school graduate, met us in her home in Kesavnagar (a part of Lodai newly built following the earthquake), where she proudly displayed her own 'Artisan Design' collection. Emptying bags full of embroidered experiments, she confidently discussed her ideas through Judy as interpreter, giving an insight into her working practices.

Jivaben, also in Kesavnagar, having completed one design school module, demonstrated a mixture of old and new influences. The community's own response to a ban on embroidery is a decorative use of ribbons and braids – an irrepressible expression of colour and pattern that adorns clothes and bags.

Kuvarben (Rabari), a graduate of the Kala Raksha Vidhyalaya Design School, with her family inside her home, 2011. Photo: Helen Felcey.

HAND STITCH: PERSPECTIVES

(*above*) Kuvarben (Rabari) outside her home in Kesavnagar, 2011. She is holding a quilt made for her 'Artisan Design' collection, to be sold through Kala Raksha. Photo: Helen Felcey.

(*right*) Detail of cushion from Kuvarben's 'Artisan Design' collection, 2011. Cotton fabric and thread, appliqué, hand stitches (back stitch, interlaced stitch). 40.5 x 40.5cm (16 x 16 in.). Photo: Mary Stark.

The label 'Artisan Design' was cautiously introduced in 2010 to raise the perceived value of the creative input. There is a determination to educate the buyer to raise the status. Hand stitch could disappear in a generation if it's not seen as desirable employment by young people – who all now attend school and have little time for embroidery. Frater comments:

The words seem to matter. Craftsperson, designer, artisan, the terms have a lot of different meanings attached and relate to the ultimate value. If you are in the US or UK and you say 'hand work', you gear up for expensive and valuable. Here, you gear down a good deal! … We value the head more than the hand. In India, the whole caste system is based on that: the more you work with your hand, the lower you are.[23]

Does design have to precede making? The work is worthless without good design. There is an implied meaning that designers have knowledge and artisans have skills. The artisan's aesthetic sensibility is so integral to the stitching itself that you can't separate it. In the UK, we talk about learning through making. In the process of making, one can think and plan and change.

QASAB

Set up in 1997 by Pankaj Shah and Meena Raste following six years of preparation, Qasab is a collective enterprise of 1,200 craftswomen of eight ethnic groups, from 52 villages across Kutch. Qasab, focusing on embroidery, grew out of KMVS (Kutch Mahila Vikas Sangathan),[24] a larger group empowering women and addressing their social needs.

NGOs and government corporations met together in the late 1980s to discuss the socio-economic aspects of the crafts in Kutch. Linking preservation with new

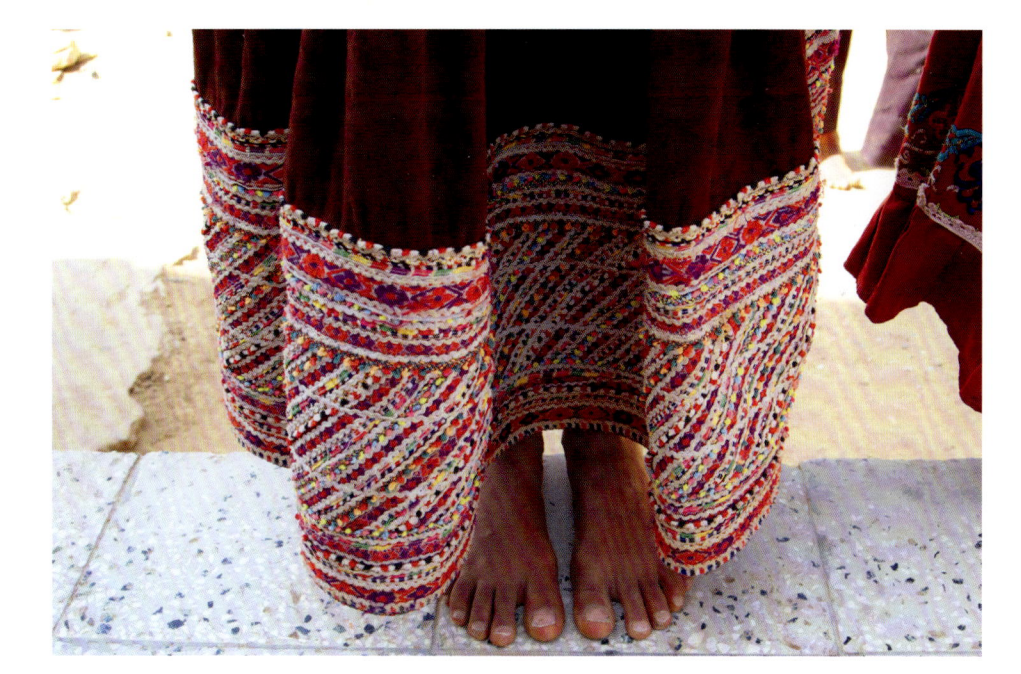

Synthetic ribbons and braids applied to various base cloths on a child's dress in Kesavnagar, 2011. Photo: Helen Felcey

opportunity is a complex process, but Qasab wanted to highlight the cultural identity of each community, not as 'job workers', but translating their tradition into a quality commercial artefact. Meena Raste asked the question, 'What were your original standards? What would you have been doing for your own dowries? What is it that you would have been proud of doing?'[25]

Previously, the fabric was covered in a three-dimensional way; the stitches frequently outlived the cloth. The women would wear a garment for ten or 20 years, then the embroidered parts would be cut off and applied to the next piece. So, acknowledging the limitations of the existing markets, Qasab aspired to address a different client, one who might value the diversity of stitch types across communities in the region. Pankaj Shah stressed that it was 'bringing the embroidery to the centre stage. It's the embroidery that has to sell it. Not the product with some embellishments here and there'.[26]

For speed, to compete with mass-produced products, embroiderers were using mirrors to reduce the quantity of stitch, producing 'mirror work' rather than 'embroidery'. The extensive stitch repertoire so admired within traditional work is difficult to maintain, with stitches disappearing from use in the last 25 years and women having to be persuaded to revive them. Inevitably, in the pursuit of big orders, work produced is through piecing and simple stitch, utilising one thread type, so losing the variety of textures. Shah explains: 'We need to pay them money to develop and revive stitches, otherwise they want to repeat the same things that are fast. What we get them to do has to develop through to production, otherwise there is no point.'[27]

Qasab's design philosophy is to let each piece reflect the characteristics of the community of origin, but bring in contemporary materials and colours, and develop it as a marketable product. The revival of traditional stitches reinforces the

HAND STITCH: PERSPECTIVES

Pakko and Kharek embroidery of Meghwar Community by craftswomen of Qasab – KMVS. Photo: Jane McKeating.

differences in each community's repertoire, with the older women contributing their technical knowledge.

The earthquake in 2001 was a huge setback, but embroidery was used as a form of rebuilding. Qasab reached out to isolated communities that had not been reached earlier. Shah remembers:

> *Organisations came and built houses, but how will you get out of the shock? Fifteen to twenty days after the quake, our operations were restarted; the women would start doing the embroideries and it became like a therapy. There was a lot of trauma, a lot of loss, and it was stabilising. If you just sat there brooding over the shock it wouldn't have helped. Initially, the women said 'Why should we start working? What are you doing, are you mad?'*[28]

Appliqué and embroidery of Dhebari Rabaris of Kutch. Produced by Kutch craftswomen for Qasab KMVS. Photo: Helen Felcey.

By starting to work, many women took control of their lives. Sustainable employment became crucial. After the earthquake, craft struggled to find its place within an increasingly industrialised environment created through an injection of new money. For embroidery to be a realistic aspiration for young people, its organisation and promotion must have equivalent momentum.

Some of the women were given a chance to make larger pieces to be promoted internationally, and an exhibition with the Vancouver Museum in Canada in 2002 demonstrated that high-quality work is not confined to historical pieces. The pieces celebrated the variety of the region's embroidery.[29]

Qasab's concern is that projects should demonstrate a long-term vision. In the West, signature crafts have a stronger market, therefore a focus on the artisan as designer and maker seems a way forward. They are seeing those who have been educated returning to the craft, understanding the value of the handmade, being part of the repositioning and re-branding. Mothers and daughters work together, thinking and talking about what works and doesn't. Qasab supports the artisans in taking risks they couldn't afford to take alone, as some of the larger pieces take more than a year to produce collaboratively. Given a palette, the artisans design the pieces, seeking advice as they progress, constantly adapting ideas.

The women soon understand how to price work, which stitches are expensive, and to include design fees. Meena emphasises that the women are smart and are starting to charge more. If the quality of the embroidery is poor, the price paid is reduced, stimulating high-quality workmanship. There is still a pressure to prove its viability in a highly competitive market against all that the digital age has to offer. 'One has to find a balance. We are talking about a sustainable market. We have to make a certain size [of] cushion covers. If you make a jacket, someone has to wear it. It's what design is.'[30]

It all takes time. As an embroiderer herself, Meena understands the artisans, which helps to build trust, 'she has to play a dual role of an evil stepmother and a fairy godmother. But that is what business is about'.[31]

Our focus has been craft excellence, not preservation, but a feeling that you want to produce the best. Giving them the opportunity to not worry about income, during the transition, and not imposing our ideas too much on what would be the meaning of conservation, not frozen in time ... It should be evolving: we cannot impose our romantic notions, but we guide them to make it meaningful, so that many of them are able to create embroidery for themselves.[32]

In Bhuj, the principal city in Kutch, stands the grand Pragmahal Palace, long deserted by princes and kings, a building which, while still lavishly furnished, is literally returning to the earth.[33] There is a naturalness in its gradual decomposition, as though the earth is reclaiming it. Throughout time some things last, while others return to dust. Of that which survives, elements get transformed, corrupted, blended and amended. In the piecing and the darning, sometimes out of the muddle comes something exciting and surprising, and a new tradition is begun.

So, six months on, thanks to the interventions and foresight of organisations in Gujarat, on my laptop I can view hundreds of digitised Kutchi embroideries collected in Sumrasar. I can purchase both artisan-designed artefacts and fairly traded hand-stitched clothing. The people I met knew the importance of capturing and valuing the past to inform the future. Not stagnant, but an evolving tradition, alive and lifting families out of poverty. The variety of approaches, both large and small scale, some purist, some less so, helps strengthen both cultural and commercial possibilities. Inspiring and supporting new generations to discover the value of handmade stitch is as crucial a debate in India as it is in Western communities. The time, patience and practice spent in crafting beautiful cloth will have currency and value as long as it adapts to a changing world.

To capture a snapshot in the transformation of one story as it evolves into another is both a privilege and an inspiration. I look at my own culture anew and feel part of my own story, which I pour into my own embroidery.

NOTES

[1] Pankaj Shah, interview with Jane McKeating, Bhuj, February 2011.
[2] Gillow, John, and Nicholas Barnard, *Indian Textiles* (London: Thames and Hudson, 1991).
[3] Chattopadhyay, Kamaladevi, *Indian Handicrafts* (New Delhi: Allied Publishers, 1963).
[4] Edwards, Eiluned, *Textiles and Dress of Gujarat* (London: V&A Publishing, in association with Mappin Publishing, India, 2011).
[5] See www.shrujan.org (accessed September 2011).
[6] Pankash Shah, interview with Jane McKeating, Bhuj, February 2011.
[7] See www.sewatfc.org (accessed September 2011).
[8] Villoo Mirza, interview with Jane McKeating, STFC Amedabad, February 2011.
[9] See www.sewatfc.org/hansiba (accessed September 2011).
[10] Graham Hollick, interview with Jane McKeating, London, January 2011.
[11] See www.grahamhollick.com (accessed September 2011).

Jane McKeating
Indian Whispers, 2011. Hand stitch with digital print on linen and silk organza. Double sided. Page from the rag book. 30 x 30 cm (12 x 12 in.). Photo: Mary Stark.

---

[12] See rosehilldesign.com (accessed September 2011).

[13] Maddy Fraoli, interview with Jane McKeating, STFC Amedabad, February 2011.

[14] Interview with Jane McKeating, STFC Amedabad, February 2011.

[15] See www.kala-raksha.org (accessed Sept 2011). Starting with 20 women from one community, the trust now has 1,000 artisan members from seven ethnic communities in 25 villages.

[16] Judy Frater, in interview with Jane McKeating, February 2011.

[17] Ibid.

[18] See www.fabindia.com (accessed September 2011).

[19] Judy Frater, interview with Jane McKeating, Sumrasar, February 2011.

[20] Ibid.

[21] See www.kala-raksha-museum.org (accessed September 2011).

[22] Judy Frater, interview with Jane McKeating, Sumrasar, February 2011.

[23] Interview with Judy Frater, Sumrasar, February 2011.

[24] See www.kmvs.in (accessed September 2011). Set up by a group of women from urban areas: Sushma Iyengar, Alkan Jani, Meera Goradia, Lata Sachde and Meena Raste, along with women from the rural interior, Parmaben, Fatmaben, Niyamatben, Hakimaben and Nanduba.

[25] Meena Raste, inteview with Jane McKeating, Bhuj, February 2011.

[26] Pankaj Shah, interview with Jane McKeating, Bhuj, February 2011.

[27] Ibid.

[28] Ibid.

[29] Maiwa and Kutch Mahila Vikas Sangathan, *Through the Eye of a Needle: Stories from an Indian Desert* (Canada: Maiwa Handprints Ltd., 2003).

[30] Meena Raste, interview with Jane McKeating, Bhuj, February 2011.

[31] Ibid.

[32] Ibid.

[33] Pragmahal Palace was built in 1865 in the Italian Gothic style. Since the earthquake in 2001 and subsequent neglect, it has fallen into disrepair. Still open to visitors, it contains a large collection of decaying taxidermy.

ALICE KETTLE

Outside, Inside and In Between

YOU CAN TAKE UP A PIECE OF HAND STITCH ANYWHERE. Its portability is part of its magic. This chapter looks at the closed space where hand stitch can be made and persist. For some makers, containment is forced upon them as a physical circumstance; for others, a choice is made to be singular and solitary; and for yet others, space occurs within the mind, a separation from the accepted patterns of society or the established processes of learning. In circumstances such as these, the following individuals have chosen to make creative companions of needle, cloth and thread. Often, stitching is a private and intimate practice which helps to address the reality of life or the monotony of a separate, distanced existence. In some cases, stitch is used to confront the chaos of the outside world or the interior of the mind and to stitch life back together; whilst in others, it is simply a wondrous process of creating and making.

These stitchers can be described in different ways, such as naive, self-taught, primitive, visionary, marginalised or as outsiders.[1] The stitchers have an alternative view from mainstream culture, standing alone and mirroring a particular and personal view of their immediate world. Their work is often informed and directed by an extraordinary life story or experience of place. There are recognised categories of practice used to describe these makers, such as 'outsider art', but the emphasis here is on the autonomous space of each as an artist/maker, the perception of the outside world from within, or the interior world manifested in the form of hand stitch.

OUTSIDER ART

I first encountered the work of 'outsider artists' in two remarkable exhibitions: 'The Fabric of Myth' at Compton Verney, UK, in 2008, which showed textile work informed by 'cultural and personal myth',[2] and 'Intuition' at the Whitworth Art Gallery, Manchester, in 2010–11.[3] 'The Fabric of Myth' showed 'outsider' work alongside mainstream art practice and I share the view of the director of the Whitworth Art Gallery, Maria Balshaw, that these works help us to challenge definitions around categories of art.[4] I was struck by the positioning of these works at the edge of fine art, outside of recognised practice, much in the manner that textile and applied art also occupy an outside fringe. There are projects such as the Barrington Farm Art Barn, the Pallant House Gallery's 'Outside In' programme, and the Creative Growth Center USA, which seek to encourage opportunities for creative practice and promote such work. Collections such as the Musgrave

Kinley Outsider Art Collection, an important acquisition within the Whitworth Art Gallery, provoke critical questioning about the fundamental character of art practice.[5]

'Outsider art' emerged in the first half of the twentieth century, a term coined by the art historian Roger Cardinal in 1972[6] and originally from Art Brut (a French term that is translated as 'raw art'), as defined by Jean Dubuffet in the 1940s. It is a contested term commonly used to describe those outside the art establishment, whose art expresses their own inner contradictions and hidden desires. An appreciation of a different creative impulse from the orthodox Western art tradition emerged in the first half of the twentieth century, which looked at the unconventional, the self-directed and those on the edge, with Dubuffet's particular interest in creativity and madness.

The way I make use of this term acknowledges the difficulties of 'designation and its relationship with the art world'.[7] I shall concentrate on particular artists' and makers' work in hand stitch which 'emerges in their inner world and imagination. The purpose of the work is in its own creation',[8] and the impact of separateness and internment in a particular circumstance. Many of these individuals have a background of stitch within their professional lives or within the family, or they see stitch as providing the creative material and process to mediate their inner world in the context of their particular location.

I shall start with the voice of James Gladwell (1953–), who is one of a group of self-taught artists at Barrington Farm on the north Norfolk coast.[9]

I dreamt this picture, I just saw it and the next morning I had to put it on the cloth.

James Gladwell
Mermaid (detail), 2010. Cotton thread and pen on cotton sheeting. 84 x 122 cm (33 x 48 in.). Photo: Ruth Whitten.

HAND STITCH: PERSPECTIVES

I do cross-stitch; I use white sheets that I get from charity shops and different coloured sewing cottons. It's just ordinary sewing cotton; I don't think thicker thread would work. It can take a whole year to do one piece.

I sewed at school (that was a long time ago); I enjoy it more than painting. I relax better when I'm doing needlework, it keeps your mind going and you think of something else. I sew when I'm not here, too. I sew at home and I do it if I can't sleep. If I start I can't put it down until it's finished.[10]

Alongside the emergence of Art Brut at the beginning of the twentieth century was the parallel development of a new understanding of alternative realities and theories relating to the unconscious mind, spearheaded by Sigmund Freud and the psychiatrist Carl Jung. In the 1920s and next to this new psychoanalysis, work took place with patients in mental institutions to examine the place of art within the realm of the 'insane'.[11] Dr Hans Prinzhorn of the Heidelberg Psychiatric clinic in Austria published a study of the drawings and other visual materials that he had collected from patients throughout Europe,[12] arguing that the creative urge is present within all of us from childhood, and the artistic insight from the mentally ill stemmed from the same creative roots.

Agnes Emma Richter (1844–1918)
Handmade jacket embroidered with autobiographical text, 1894. Thread on hospital linen. Prinzhorn Collection, Centre for Psychosocial Medicine, University Hospital Heidelberg. Sammlung Prinzhorn, Inv.-Nr 743. Photo: Prinzhorn Collection.

Amongst the Prinzhorn collection I have picked two works and their makers in hand stitch. The first is the embroidered jacket of Agnes Richter (1844–1918), made in 1895. The jacket is the uniform of the asylum, on which she has stitched graffiti inside and out. A former seamstress, the intense word stitching is 'untamed writing' of interlocking sentences and layers of words, which transform the jacket into a compelling narrative and intensely beautiful customised garment. Through the stitching, Agnes Richter has reclaimed her voice and individuality within the confines of an institution, even transcribing the printed laundry mark '583 Hubertusburg' into an embroidered motif. The jacket has become a celebrated testament to Agnes Richter.[13]

The enclosed secured space is shared by Johanna Natalie Wintsch (1871–1944), who was born in Poland and became a patient within a psychiatric institution at the beginning of the twentieth century. Her stitch work is ordered and mannered, containing text, numbers, charts and theosophical symbolism.[14] She depicts the interior/private and exterior/public world, the real and the perceived, which are embroidered in red, blue, yellow and mauve on a neutral cloth with the stylistic sense of art nouveau – that is, the curved lines and the bringing together of the natural environment in images of flowers and plants with other symbols.

Johanna Natalie Wintsch (1917–44)
The God of the Bride, 1923. Coloured embroidery. Prinzhorn Collection, Centre for Psychosocial Medicine, University Hospital Heidelberg. Sammlung Prinzhorn, Inv. -Nr.6044. Photo: Prinzhorn Collection.

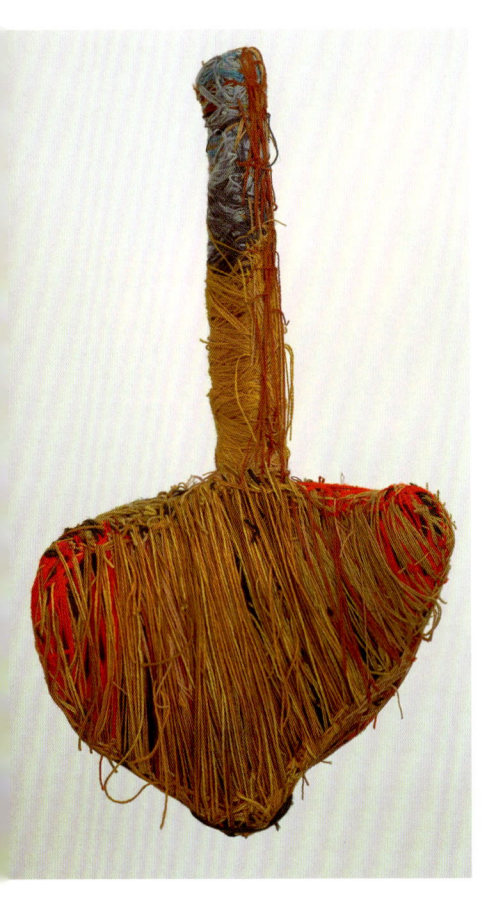

Judith Scott
(*left*) *Untitled*, c.1990s. Bound object in thread. Collection of the Musgrave Kinley Outsider Art Collection, Whitworth Art Gallery, Manchester. © Creative Growth Art Center, California, USA. Photo: Whitworth Art Gallery.

(*right*) *Untitled*, 1991. Bound object in thread. 122 x 25 x 51 cm (48 x 10 x 20 in.). © Creative Growth Art Center, California, USA. Photo: Johann Feilacher

Judith Scott and Elzbieta Harbord both use the significant relationship with a twin sister as the subject of their work. Both women were divided and separated from their sisters and relocated into different worlds. The works appear as metaphors for isolated separation and of binding together. Scott's pieces are often worked as pairs and companion pieces, whilst Harbord's complete focus is directed to her twin.

Judith (1943–2005) was an American artist recognised internationally for her textile/fibre work.[15] Her remarkable sculptures are formed using threads, torn cloth and wools, which are wrapped around objects like swaddling until they are completely covered. The metamorphosis of the object through the process of thread binding is completely transformative; it is often impossible to imagine what the object within actually is. Like cocoons, the works are defined by their invisible content and interior space. Scott was introduced to textile at the Creative Growth Art Center in California, on whose website she is described as 'a visual artist isolated from outside influences as a result of the impact of deafness and Down's syndrome. She was independent and self-directed'.[16, 17]

Elzbieta Harbord trained as a seamstress and tailor on Savile Row, where she learnt to hand-sew on her knee, a technique she uses today in her stitching. Elzbieta's work mostly references the life of her twin sister, a nun in a closed order in France, and as with Judith Scott's work, it is infused with the close association between herself and her sister alongside a sense of profound separateness.

At the moment I am researching my wonderful, dearest to my heart, twin sister Wanda, now known as Sister Marie-Aniela who is a nun. She joined the convent when she was almost 17 years old. She used to live in England and is now living in France at the Visitation Convent. She is a great genius of an artist in her own

OUTSIDE, INSIDE AND IN BETWEEN

right and has also made her own nun's habit and is able to keep the measurements and working pattern in her head.

I studied tailoring many years ago. I trained as a tailoress and cutter at The Tailor & Cutter Academy, Gerald Street, London (ladies' and gents'.) As time went by, I moved around London and ended up working in Savile Row at a tailor's shop, Douglas Bunn, who made riding jackets (as well as other garments), which I had the pleasure of finishing using hand stitching.

One particular old, traditional tailor's method of hand sewing was using invisible stitch (prick stitch). I also used back stitch, long stitch and running stitch in making the garments. I learnt the original way of hand-stitching, sitting on a table or chair and crossing your leg and resting the garment on your knee whilst hand-sewing. Thanks to my training, I am able to improvise, design and incorporate my skills within my art. I had to give up the tailoring trade as it affected my back due to my spinal problems and other health issues.

In some of my recent sewn work, I have used back stitch and running stitch on my tracing paper. I wanted to experiment, as I find the delicate transparent paper a challenge and a change from using fabric.[18]

The inner creative world offers both the subject and impetus for some work. Two key and celebrated exponents are Madge Gill, who looked to a spirit world, and Arthur Bispo do Rosário, whose preparation for the final Judgement provoked a remarkable series of works. Madge Gill (1882–1961) was a self-taught artist whose reputation was acknowledged within her lifetime.[19] She showed her work publicly, although much of her later life was spent in self-imposed exile within her home, drawing, painting and stitching. Her work is obsessive in its repetitive mark-making and in its prolific quantity. She was an exponent of mediumistic art, her work driven by the spirit world as she acted as the conduit for Myrninterest, the name she gave to her artistic 'self'. The stitching has an obsessive density of mark, crosses and zigzags. Madge was brought up in a children's home in Canada until she was 19, when she returned to the UK and married her cousin Reggie Gill, with whom she had three sons and a stillborn daughter. The impact of her daughter's death (which almost led to her own death and the loss of one eye) was the catalyst for her starting to draw. Much of her work was often made in bed by oil lamp and in semi-darkness. When she died, many hundreds of drawings were discovered all around the house.[20, 21]

Arthur Bispo do Rosário (1909–89) was a Brazilian artist. He was diagnosed with paranoid schizophrenia while a patient at the Juliano Moreira Colony for the mentally ill in Rio de Janeiro, where he went in his twenties, and stayed periodically for almost 50 years. He is considered to be one of the key Brazilian artists of the twentieth century, and his work is represented in various collections, exhibitions, programmes and films.[22] He began his works in the 1960s, using found materials to make miniatures out of daily ephemera. He also worked in embroidery, making ceremonial cloaks covered with insignia, stitched motifs and 'messages on

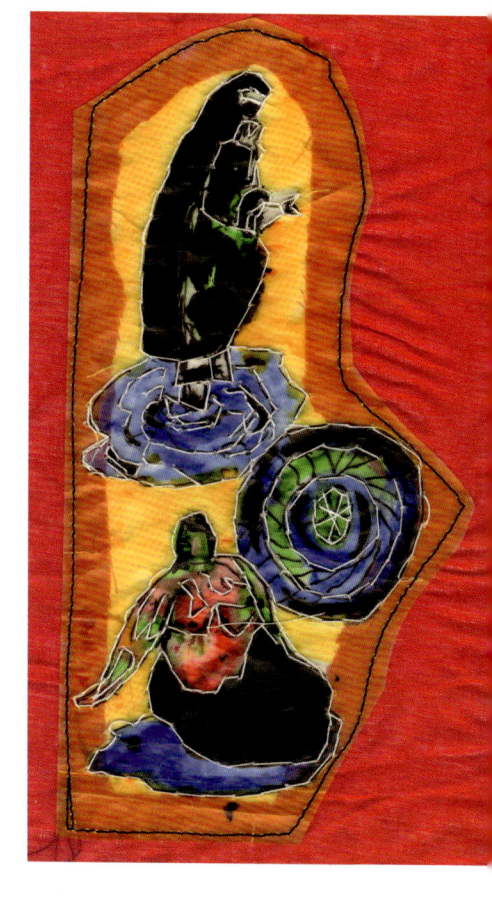

Elzbieta Harbord
Freedom and Restriction, 2011. Cotton thread and Indian ink on cotton and tissue paper. 20.5 x 29.7 cm (8¹/₁₆ x 11¾ in.). Collection of the artist. Photo: Pallant House Gallery.

HAND STITCH: PERSPECTIVES

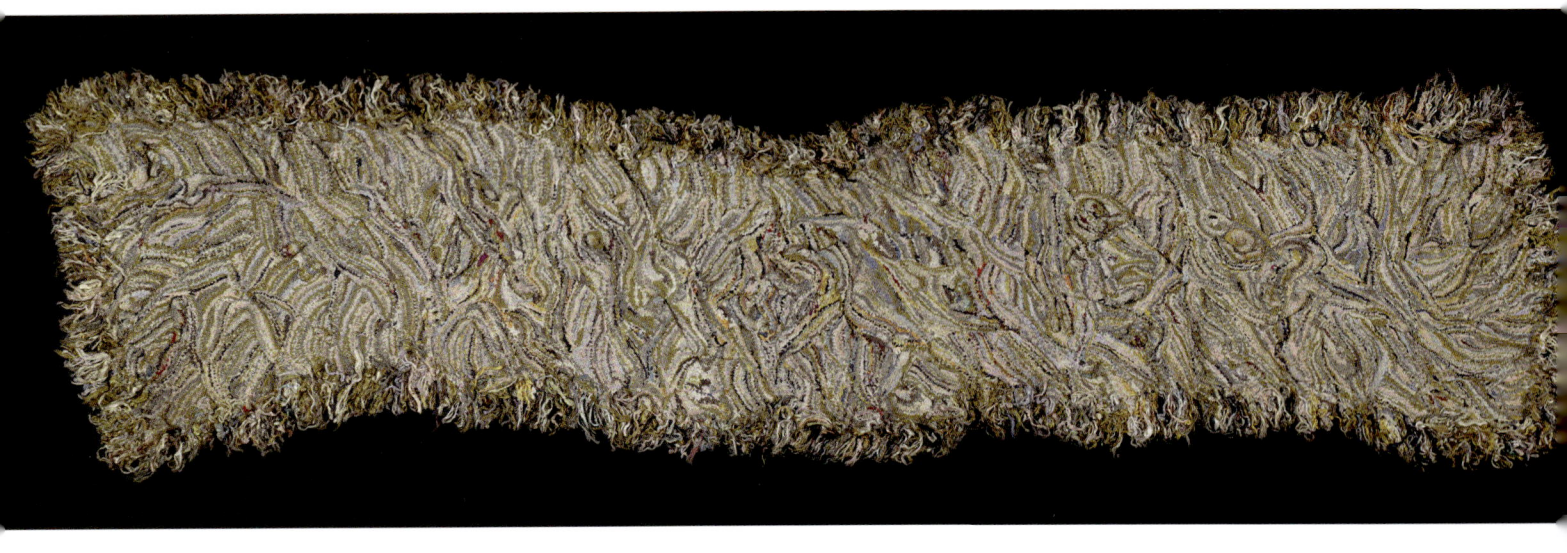

Madge Gill
(*above*) Untitled, undated. Collection of the Musgrave Kinley Outsider Art Collection, Whitworth Art Gallery, Manchester. Image courtesy of Newham Heritage and Archives. Photo: Michael Pollard, Whitworth Art Gallery.

(*below*) Drawing in black ink on calico. Image courtesy of Newham Heritage and Archives. On billiard table in her sitting room, London, *c*.1936. Photo: unknown.

those materials which he could find where he lived: bedsheets, bedspreads, old uniforms, asylum clothing'.[23] Regarded as a visionary artist, he created over 1,000 works 'motivated by a request for God to rebuild the universe and record the divine passage by land',[24] and in preparation for the Last Judgement.

The support and interest in outsider and alternative art has enabled networks and organisations to nurture individuals and promote works that need to discover a sense of place within the wider artistic frame. I have previously mentioned some current examples, but will focus briefly on the 'Outside In' programme of the Pallant House Gallery in Chichester, which is a project that provides a platform for artists who find it difficult to access the art world and who see their creativity as hidden. Like many of the non-traditional creators in the project, Chaz Waldren's (1950–) work reflects the closeness of home and community, in his case shown through his strong Christian belief, his wife Sally and his home town of Bognor Regis. He works from a small bedroom with a dedicated workstation littered with biblical quotes and inspirational messages. Whilst stitch is not his primary medium, the work has deep connections with textile in its patterning and surface quality. The deeply personal is shared by the work of Valerie Potter,[25] whose work takes the form of an emotional diary which she began after a period of trauma in her life. She describes her work as 'a footprint (not a handprint) in time'.

Finally, I would like to look at confinement of a different kind, which nevertheless provides the condition for creative stitch. Ray Materson was incarcerated in a high-security prison in the USA for armed robbery. He began to unravel his socks and to stitch tiny badge narratives that either echo the hardcore reality of the streets he inhabited whilst outside, or represent a dream-like other world. His work carries an intoxicating mixture of delicately beautiful tiny stitch work and tough subject matter, such as prostitution and drug-taking. Hand stitch, for Materson, started with the throwaway material to hand and became a process of rehabilitation. I shall let him speak for himself:

My work grew out of a need – a most desperate need – to do something positive in a very negative environment. I can't begin to express how truly hideous prison life can

OUTSIDE, INSIDE AND IN BETWEEN

Arthur Bispo do Rosário
Manto da Apresentação (presentation cape), date unknown. Fabric, thread, paper and metal. 118.5 x 141.2 cm (46¾ x 55½ in.). Coleção Museu Bispo do Rosário Arte Contemporânea/Prefeitura da Cidade do Rio de Janeiro.
Photo: Rodrigo Lopes.

HAND STITCH: PERSPECTIVES

Valerie Potter
(*above*) *Ma Pauvre*, 2007, detail. Stranded cotton thread on unbleached calico. 50 x 30 cm (20 x 12 in.). Photo: Julia Elmore.

Chaz Waldren
(*below*) *Prayer*, 2009. Gel and felt pen on paper. 30 x 42 cm (12 x 16 1/2 in.). Pallant House Gallery Collection. Presented by Jackie and Steve Street (Purchased from 'Outside In' Biennial Competition, 2009). Photo: Pallant House Gallery.

OUTSIDE, INSIDE AND IN BETWEEN

Raymond Materson
(*opposite*) *Involuntary Blue*, 1995. Thread from socks on cotton. 5.5 x 7 cm (2¼ x 2¾ in.). Photo: American Primitive Gallery, New York.

be. It can be little more than sheer, frightful existence for many. The fear is relentless ... there is monotonous ongoing routine. Doors open at specific times ... marking moments of continual tedium. Days, weeks, months, seasons ... years ... Once I discovered embroidery, I learned I could escape.[26]

Both his grandmothers were seamstresses and embroiderers.
My mom would tell humorous stories about home life and the sewing was always a part of that. My father's mother, Grandma Hattie, sewed as a hobby. It was the memory of Grandma Hattie and her sewing basket that first inspired me to try my hand at sewing when I was in prison. I recalled how peaceful the act of embroidering made the elderly woman.[27]

HAND STITCH: PERSPECTIVES

The following anonymous works share the impulse of the monotony of time, but in this case related to entrapment at sea. These works of the nineteenth century are from the National Maritime Museum, London, and are sailors' stitched pictures made on voyages under sail. The long duration of the periods at sea meant that the ship's crew had to be entirely self-sufficient and skilled in stitching in order to mend clothing and sails. During the lengthy periods of leisure time, the sailors stitched for their own pleasure, illustrating pictures of ships, rigging and flags, which were stitched with Berlin wool. Each piece is different, a portrait of the ship with emblems and motifs, and made in long running and short darning stitches, all in one direction. These stitched works are private views and a visual historical record of the seafaring of this period.

'Outside, inside and in between' are words I have used to explore the space, location or condition in which each of these works was made or where each artist works. They serve to enquire into the circumstances of making, the confined space, the compulsion to stitch and the unrestricted imagination, with materials that are immediate, creative and most importantly to hand.

Henry Robert Fisher
A woolwork picture depicting a schooner under sail at sea, part of a coast seen to the left, *c.*1895. Wool, canvas. 54 x 71.2 x 3.5 cm (21 x 28 x 1½ in.). © National Maritime Museum, Greenwich, London. Object number TXT0003m. The vessel is flying a Red Ensign and has a clipper bow. A red, swallow-tailed house flag with a white saltire is shown at the mainsail.

88

NOTES

[1] These terms are hotly debated and some of them have been criticised for reinforcing prejudice.

[2] Harrison, Antonia, and James Young, *The Fabric of Myth*, exhibition catalogue (Warwickshire: Compton Verney, 2008).

[3] 'Intuition' exhibition of outsider art at the Whitworth Art Gallery, Manchester, June 2010–February 2011.

[4] Balshaw, Maria, 'Intuition Symposium', Whitworth Art Gallery, Manchester. See www.youtube.com/watch?v=06lsFf4MnSk (accessed 21 August 2011).

[5] Ibid.

[6] See http://en.wikipedia.org/wiki/Outsider_ar/(accessed 2 June 2011).

[7] Thompson, Jon, 'Intuition Symposium', Whitworth Art Gallery, Manchester. See www.youtube.com/watch?v=06lsFf4MnSk/(accessed 18 August 2011).

[8] See www.outsider-artworld.com/(accessed 2 August 2011). Outsider art; Demirel collection.

[9] A portrait of one of the artists at Barrington Art Barn, *Beautiful Colour* by Amanda Ravetz, can been seen at http://vimeo.com/16386572/(accessed 22 August 2011).

[10] James Gladwell, in conversation with Antonia Riviere, Barrington Farm's art facilitator, 2011.

[11] Maizels, John, *Raw Creation: Outsider Art and Beyond* (London, New York: Phaidon, 1996), p. 15.

[12] Prinzhorn, Hans, *Bildnerei der Geisteskranken* (Berlin: Springer-Verlag, [1922] 1994), translated into English by Eric von Brockdorff as *Artistry of the Mentally Ill: A Contribution to the Psychology of Configuration* (Vienna, New York: Springer-Verlag [1972] 1995).

[13] See http://www.fudgethefacts.com/?p=10 MAR 22, 2008 Writing On A String* //notes for an exhibition //Agnes Richter's jacket: hypertext before hypertext (accessed 17 August 2011)

[14] See www.frieze.com/shows/review/search_for_the_spirit/(accessed 7 July 2011).

[15] Brut Connaissance and Diffusion Collection (Paris and Prague), Museum of American Folk Art (New York), INTUIT – The Center for Intuitive and Outsider Art (Chicago, IL), L'Aracine Musée d'Art Brut (Paris, France), Musée d'Art Brut (Lausanne, Switzerland), and the American Visionary Art Museum (Baltimore, MD).

[16] Nieves, Evelyn, 'Artist Emerges With Works in a "Private Language"', *New York Times*, 25 June 2001.

[17] See http://hidden-worlds.com/judithscott/'Judith Scott – artist extraordinary 1943–2005' (accessed 8 August 2011).

[18] Elzbieta Harbord 'Outside In' programme, Pallant House Gallery, Chichester.

[19] Her work gained recognition in the 'Outsider Show' at the Hayward Gallery, London, 1979.

[20] See www.newhamstory.com/node/2191/(accessed 8 July 2011).

[21] Musgrave Kinley, Outsider Art Collection, Whitworth Art Gallery Manchester.

[22] Bispo's output was featured in journalist Samuel Wainer Filho's TV programme, *Globo's Fantástico*, broadcast in 1980. In 1982, Frederico Morais curated the exhibition *À Margem da Vida (At the Edge of Life)* at the Rio de Janeiro Museum of Modern Art (MAM/RJ) and included Bispos's work. Bispo's work can now be seen at the Bispo do Rosário Museum, formerly known as the Nise da Silveira Museum (http://unconsciouskoine.tumblr.com/post/5908112812/arthur-bispo-do-rosario-japaratuba-sergipe: accessed 3 August 2011). Also see: Luciana Hidalgo, *Arthur Bispo do Rosário: o Senhor do Labirinto* (Rio de Janeiro, Editora Rocco Ltda: 1996).

[23] 'Preparing for Eternity', from interview with Wilson Lázaro in November 2008. Author: Katrin Bettina Müller, culturebase@hkw.de.

[24] See http://www.google.co.uk/url?sa=t&source=web&cd=16&sqi=2&ved=0CH4QFjAP&url=http%3A%2F%2Fportalliteral.terra.com.br%2Fartigos%2Farthur-bispo-do-rosario-o-ilustre-desconhecido&ei=Fb8_TsPUGoOZhQf39KCZAg&usg=AFQjCNFGTF6OIEQvcZH3YRqh_C2pFN5vAw/(accessed 11 November 2011).

[25] She is not part of the 'Outside In' programme at Pallant House Gallery, Chichester.

[26] Ray Materson, interview with Alice Kettle, 2011.

[27] Ibid.

Capturing time, moments and narratives

ANNE MORRELL

From Madras to Manchester: a narrative on the desire to hand-stitch

HAND STITCHING TAKES TIME. That is not only the time it takes to complete, but also one's own time spent in learning how to make stitch act as a mark to develop a concept. There are probably other craft activities that can claim the same degree of commitment, but certainly hand-stitching is labour-intensive and not necessarily the comfortable pastime, physically or mentally, that it was once considered.

My own journey has taken a long time, a lifetime, learning about embroidery and becoming comfortable in the language of stitch. For me, as for anyone moving from one culture to another, it could be said that the difficulties in understanding one culture or language led to a better understanding of the other. Certainly this applies to my time with hand stitch.

As a child, one had to learn the British Victorian methods, some of which are still in use today. In 1979 I produced an encyclopaedia[1] and more recently I wrote on the migration of stitches,[2] separating the very different needs of makers and curators in museums. It took all this for me to finally see that there really is no need for the maker to learn through the naming of stitches. Rather, we should seek an understanding of the relationship between fabric and thread, and how stitch can be used to push ideas and concepts.

The journey I will describe reflects my need to understand and sort out conflicting methods, determined to find a path through that which interests me. I needed a language I could use and be confident with to pursue my ideas and concepts through line, colour and surface textures. There is no real reason why my research led me to use hand stitch in my studio work, except that it is the most comfortable for me at this point in time. As stitching cannot be separated out, in my view, from other embroidery techniques, it suits me to call what I do in my studio 'embroidery' and then wonder what that means. This takes me back to the start of my journey.

I was born and brought up in India and my experiences there have remained a major influence on my thinking and research. I came to England to finish my education and this included going to art school. Drawing was the major skill required to enter art school. The National Diploma in Design (NDD) was a four-year course. For two years, all students followed a general art and design education and selected a craft, ending in an examination. This was followed by two years of specialisation (in my case, in hand embroidery) culminating in a project that was sent off for examination. Numbers of students were low and the common education we all undertook meant that any specialisation in the final two years was underpinned by what we had learned previously.

My journey with hand embroidery started when I transferred to Goldsmiths College in London to take machine embroidery – only to find that Goldsmiths was not accredited to award a diploma in machine embroidery – it had to be hand embroidery. In the late 1950s and early 1960s, visits to France, Germany and Italy made us aware of what was happening through the work of artists such as Luciano Fabro and the Arte Povera group. That is the direction I chose to take and there seemed to be no place for that in the fine art departments in England; textiles was the area where one could encompass that kind of work and thinking. But I had left school unable to sew; at least my teacher Miss Baines had told me so. I guess my domestic science apron hem was sewn at the 'wrong' angle, though I was never quite sure what was 'wrong'. I have to thank Christine Risley,[3] who helped me to move on from machine embroidery by showing me that hand embroidery, like my machine work, need have nothing to do with sewing skills. So I took hand embroidery as my speciality.

The postgraduate teaching course in those days was the ATC (Art Teachers Certificate). On this course, we taught in schools and were given lectures that really expanded our ways of communicating with and through practice. At this time, changes were being introduced: domestic science was being phased out and needlework moved into the art room. Some of us worked at the V&A, being shown how to make use of the museum for any classes we brought to see objects or exhibitions.

For me, hand embroidery seemed a boring subject then, and I agreed with Rebecca Crompton[4]:

It is undesirable that a beginner should first spend too much time in becoming acquainted with a large variety of the stitches used by the needlewoman. Some knowledge of stitches, must, of course, be acquired at an early stage, but many people start by working a series of stitches mechanically in rows, overlooking the desirability for this kind of information to be acquired gradually. A teacher of embroidery need not teach too many stitches at once – although they may all have to be learnt eventually. A doctor may intend that a bottle of medicine should be taken, but not all at once![5]

Alongside Victorian attitudes about right and wrong, particularly with regard to needlework, embroidery was positioned then as a women's craft, which was typical of the attitudes towards women prevalent at that time. However, people

HAND STITCH: PERSPECTIVES

Grandma Butler's student teacher books and sampler, 1899. Collection of Anne Morrell. Photo: Michael Pollard. Primary school teachers were taught through books like these while they taught in a school. As soon as they were married, they had to leave their post.

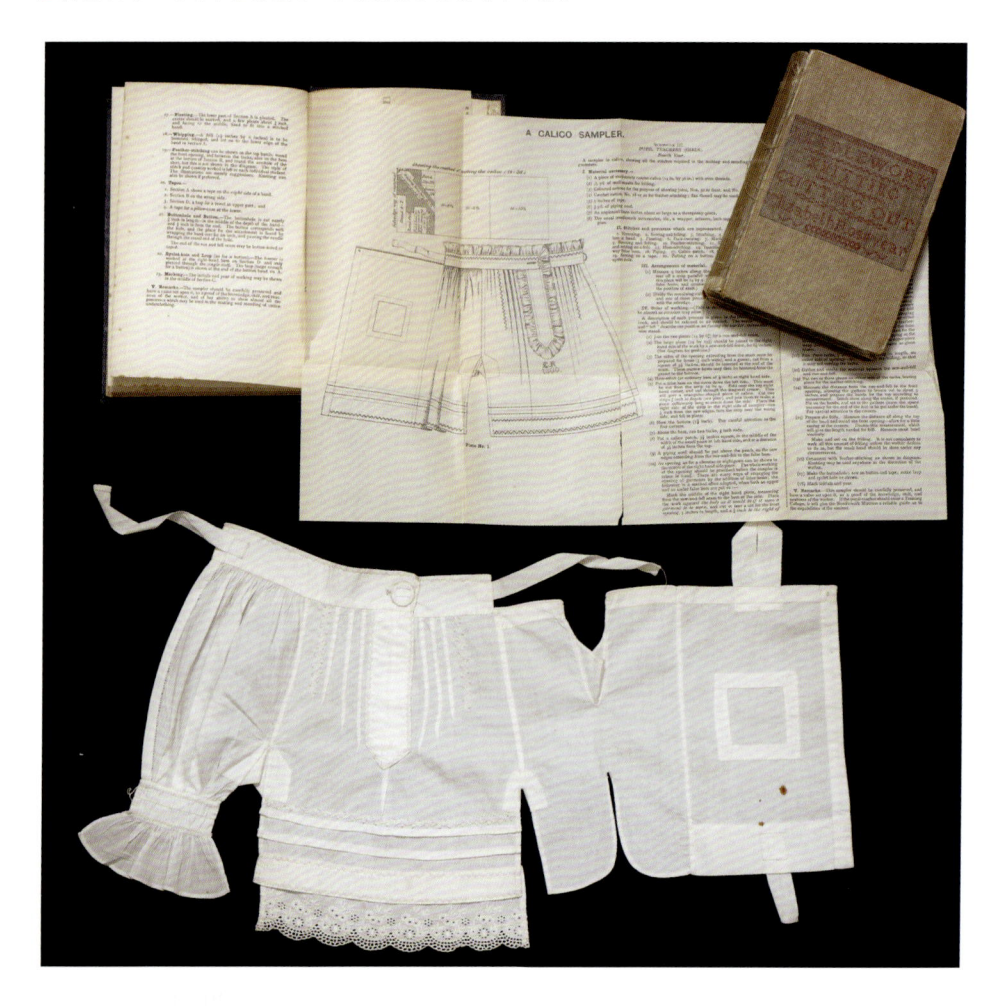

like Rebecca Crompton had sought to encourage the development of freer hand embroidery, moving on from the kind of teaching that was in place at the turn of the twentieth century. My grandmother's teaching book[6] and a sampler dated 1899 are an example of the latter. Here the teacher is told over three pages how to conduct needle drill with the lower and upper division of infant classes.

> *Needlework drills are of great use and value ... The purposes of these drills are manifold.*
> *1. To interest the children, and make them obedient and attentive.*
> *2. To make the children's hands supple and dexterous.*
> *3. To make the children quick and industrious, without any undue excitement.*

The role of museums and the task of collecting and educating through collections always fascinated me, though how works were selected and the value and quality of the collected works did puzzle me. Whose values were being applied? How were they applied? These were constant questions to which I could find no answer.

Through studying the work of Louisa Pesel (1870–1947)[7] and Alfred Bühler (1900–81)[8] it became clear to me that all embroidery stitch techniques are

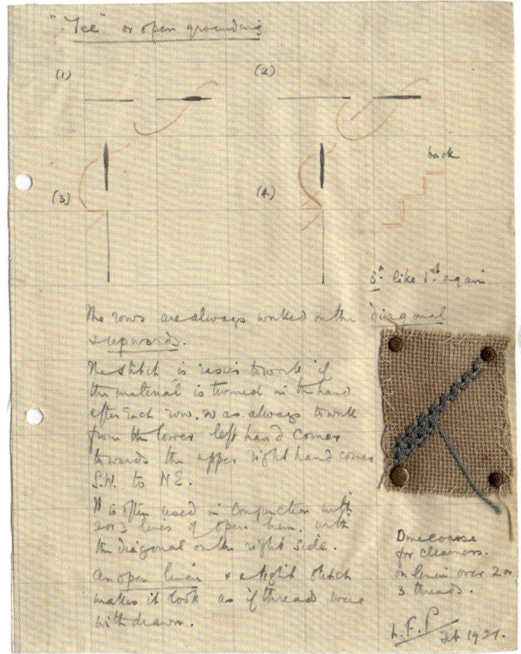

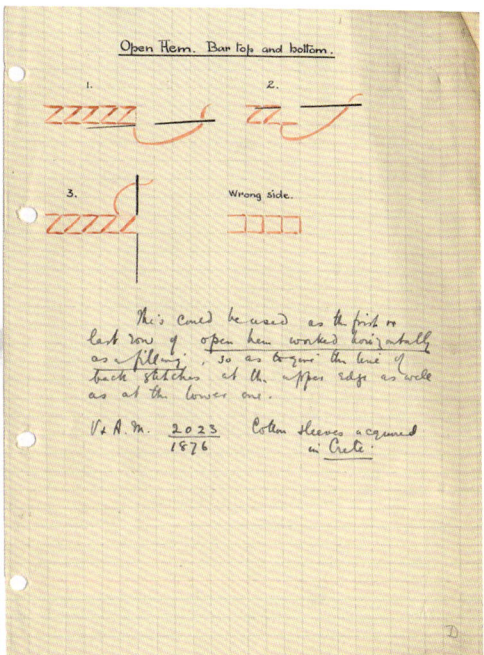

FROM MADRAS TO MANCHESTER

Louisa Pesel
Pages from working notebooks, 1921.
Collection and photo: ULITA.

Left-hand page reads:

'Yee' or open grounding.

Stage (1) (2) (3) (b), fifth like the first again, back. The rows are always worked on the diagonal and upwards.

The stitch is easier to work if the material is turned in the hand after each row, so as always to work from the lower left-hand corner towards the upper right-hand corner (south-west to north-east).

It is often used in conjunction with two or three lines of open hem, with the diagonal on the right side.

An open linen and a tight stitch makes it look as if thread has been withdrawn.

Done coarse for clearness in linen over two or three threads.
L.F.P. /Feb 1921.

Right hand page reads:

This could be used as the first and last row of open hem worked horizontally as a filling, so as to give the line of back stitches at the upper edge as well as at the lower one.

interconnected. That is the interconnections not only of one stitch to another, but also through the relationship with, and outcomes from, other textile techniques. I arrived at this thought, which I considered a bold statement at that time, thanks to the work of Louisa Pesel. I could feel the impact of her work as I stood looking, fascinated, at her hand-stitch samples in the V&A's Textile Study rooms. Then, later, in the 1980s, I felt the same fascination while working on her notebooks. I realised that this work, undertaken earlier in the twentieth century, was vital to the understanding of hand stitch. Pesel's hand stitches were described, drawn and painted, with stitched samples. I was interested in the methods she employed, such as looking at both the front and the back of the stitching. She worked on embroidery from several cultures, showing us, amongst other things, how to understand the objects and the stitching.

It is vital to recognise the crossover between different crafts, cultures and techniques. It is possible to find the earliest examples of hand stitches, now classified as 'embroidery', in historic and modern basket-making, sewing and weaving. In these examples of a Roman Egyptian sock of the second century AD, an Australian string bag of the late 1990s and English contemporary baskets made by Mary Butcher, we see the embroidery stitches called stem stitch, Ceylon stitch and open buttonhole stitch. Textiles, as we know, are not made of materials that survive well in most ground conditions, but there are exceptions to the rule and hand stitching has been found in several ancient sites.

In the 1920s, excavations in the Altai Mountains uncovered fifth-century Iron Age material that is really exceptional,[9] giving us a glimpse of the wonderful embroidery being produced at that time. An example is the shabrack[10] a saddle cover.

93

HAND STITCH: PERSPECTIVES

It is covered by Chinese silk of cream colour and an embroidered pattern. The material is a kind of tussore woven from raw silk, while the pattern, formed from multicoloured silk threads, shows Wu T'ung trees with various kinds of pheasants. The shabrack is trimmed with a narrow band of blue felt, within which is a strip of reddish-brown felt with tridenticulate leather cut-out decoration. The latter is pasted over with gold-leaf and tinfoil.[11]

The stitch used is chain stitch, probably using a regular needle, but this stitch can also be made with a hook called an ari, not unlike a rug or crochet hook, that has, from earlier times, been used when making a chain stitch on leather. A similar hook is used on fabric as well and this is called tambour or ari embroidery.

Does the change in tool with the use of a hook, not a needle, then exclude this from hand embroidery? This work is the hand stitch that is the forerunner of the Cornely machine. To me, there is no real division between hand and machine embroidery, machines being developed to make much of the work, previously carried out by hand with a needle, faster. Traditionally, stitches are produced by the needle[12] and the thread is inserted and brought out of the fabric at specific intervals. This action, the repetition of such actions and the grouping of threads, can produce an endless variety of surfaces and combinations of effects.

However, the use of a needle by a weaver to work on the warp when it is on a loom blurs the line between embroidery and weaving, as the needle is used for both activities. Needles are also used for medical purposes, making one question again the fact that it is the tool that is used as the reason to draw a line between activities that use a needle, but a line there is, though it does not stop one making hand stitches with whatever needle one wants to use.[13] A wide range of needles is available for upholstery, skins and leather, which can be used for hand stitches and embroidery. The variation in the 'fabric', the material being embroidered, is also something to consider. It does not have to be a woven, felted or printed material.

(*above*) Shabrack (horse saddlecloth). Silk (tussar, tussore) fabric, multicoloured silk thread, chain stitch. 226 x 62 cm (88 x 24½ in.). Collection of the Hermitage Museum, St Petersburg, Russia. Photo: Michael Pollard, from a drawing in the book *Frozen Tombs of Siberia*. Pazyryk burials of Iron Age horsemen, barrow 5, Siberia, Russia.

(*right*) Child's sock, Roman Egypt, Oxyrhynchus, second century AD. Wool thread, knit-stem (a stem stitch movement worked to resemble knit), also called Ceylon stitch and needle coiling stitch in embroidery, length 11.7 cm (4½ in.). Collection of Manchester Museum, University of Manchester. Acc. no. 983. Photo: Geoff Thompson.

FROM MADRAS TO MANCHESTER

Face and reverse, front and back, right side and wrong side. These are words usually used when describing a finished object, the embroidery stitches being seen as surface stitches, implying that one side only is to be seen. However, some pieces require both sides to be seen and sometimes the 'wrong' side is facing the worker while the right side, the other side, will be the one that is to be seen. I often work with the reverse facing me. There is nothing more humbling than to find a stitch (the use of colour alerting one to something extraordinary) that is producing, at one and the same time, one pattern on one side and a different pattern on the other side.[14]

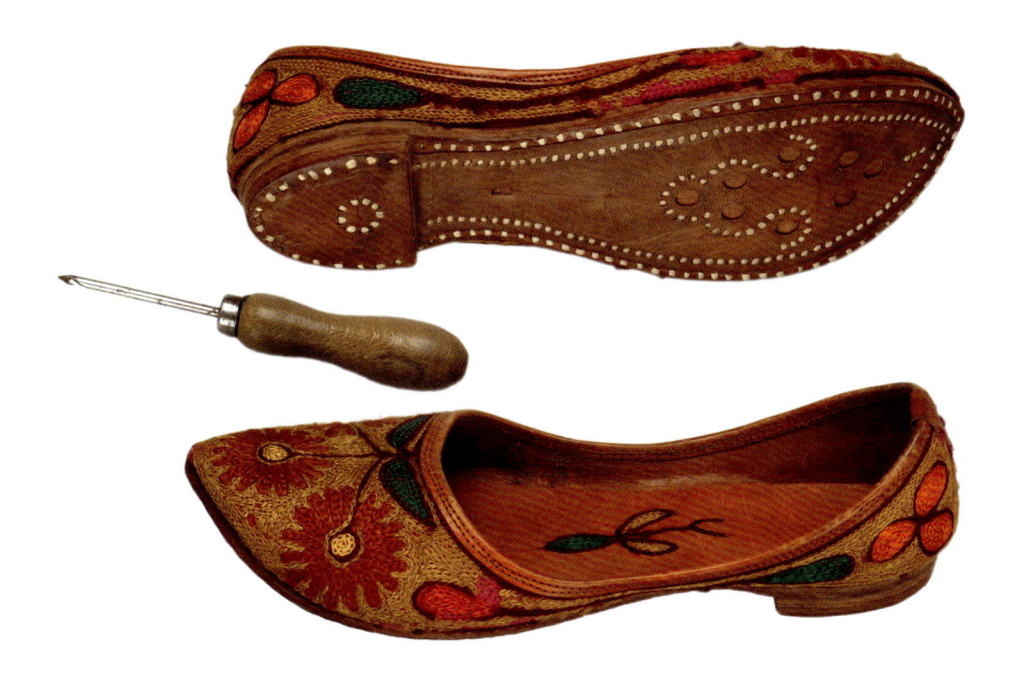

Mary Butcher
(*left*) *Wall Pocket 1* and *Wall Pocket 2*, 2011. Each 10 x 18 cm (4 x 7 in.) with tails 24 cm (9½ in.) and 30 cm (12 in.). *Wall Pocket 1*: vine rattan or Alabama supplejack (*Berchemia scandens*), ash (*Fraxinus excelsior*).
Wall Pocket 2: willow bark (*Salix triandra* and *Salix purpurea*), rattan vine (*Berchemia scandens*). Collection of Anne Morrell. Photo: Michael Pollard. Looping is a basketry technique, called open buttonhole filling stitch (worked left to right) in embroidery.

Alice Gandaburrburr
(*above*) *String Bag*, 1998. *Brachichiton diversifolius* fibres. 67 x 40 cm (26⅜ x 15¾ in.). Collection of Mary Butcher. Photo: Michael Pollard. Looping is a basketry technique, called open buttonhole filling stitch (worked left to right) in embroidery.

(*left*) Ari and a pair of embroidered shoes. Leather, wool thread. Kutch, Gujarat, India, 1998. Collection of Anne Morrell. Photo: Michael Pollard. These shoes have been embroidered with a hook (ari) used for leatherwork. The chain stitch is worked in several colours.

95

HAND STITCH: PERSPECTIVES

Detail of a Hazara prayer cloth, Afghanistan, early 20th century. Cotton fabric, cotton thread. Counted thread work. 23 x 25 cm (9 x 10 in.). Collection of Anne Morrell. Photo: Michael Pollard.

Child's wool tunic, 8th–10th century AD. Height of tunic: 46 cm (18 in.). Collection of the Whitworth Art Gallery. Acc. no. T.8505. Photo: Michael Pollard. Small side gores, applied trimmings and darned in at least ten different sewing threads.

FROM MADRAS TO MANCHESTER

The stitches found in early archaeological finds include embroidered pieces, and these stitches are still used today in contemporary work for a multitude of outcomes from the practical to purely decorative, or used as a metaphor in fine art. Finds in Egypt (up to AD 1000)[15] show hand embroidery that uses a number of stitches which are still familiar, including chain stitch, back stitch, diagonal filling stitch and form stitch[16] or running stitch to create a decorative fabric such as a child's woollen tunic with a number of different coloured threads.

The running stitch is a wonderful example of a stitch or mark being used across embroidery techniques. Here it is used in a vertical and horizontal direction, and when the stitches cross, they form a pattern rather like a plain woven pattern. Running stitch is a basic stitch and movement, used for a multitude of expressions in most cultures. The use made of the stitch as a base on which to float patterns and designs by the Banjara[17] combines practical purpose and decorative effect.

Over the years, I have taken great delight in seeing hand stitch used by others who shake the very core of preconceptions about hand stitch – artists such as Joan Beadle, Kate Egan and Belinda Pollit. When seen together, their work shows how various materials, alongside the scale of the stitch/mark itself, can create vastly different outcomes.

Joan Beadle takes stitches through grass and soil, often deliberately and obviously made to look like stitches in fabric. Her work in the early 1980s took stitch out into the landscape. Buttonhole stitch, taken from side to side, forms a Cretan stitch and the same stitch, when used to link two pieces of fabric together, is called insertion stitch. In her work, it appears that the stitch 'sews' two edges of soil together. Work like this is, by its very nature, temporary and perhaps only finally

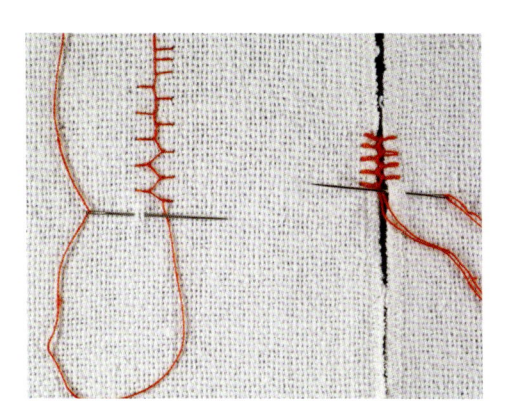

Detail of an interlaced pattern on a running stitch by the Banjara (Lambani), Deccan, India. Mid-20th century. Collection of Anne Morrell. Photo: Michael Pollard. The white running stitches are made as a base on which to hold two or three pieces of fabric together, and these in turn are then used as a base on which to float patterns. A thread is passed under the running stitch and only goes through the fabric at the start and finish. There are many interlaced patterns on the embroideries of the Banjara.

(*above*) Sample: Cretan stitch and insertion stitch. Collection of Anne Morrell. Photo: Michael Pollard.

Joan Beadle
(*right*) *Stitched Trench*, 1982. Here the stitches in the sampler have been used to appear to 'stitch' a trench together. Photo: Joan Beadle.

HAND STITCH: PERSPECTIVES

Joan Beadle
(*left*) *The Process of Stitching*, 1982. Cross-stitch. Collection of Joan Beadle. Photo: Joan Beadle.

(*right*) *Burning Stitches*, 1982. Cross-stitches set alight. Photo: Joan Beadle.

exists in the photography of the journey. In *Burning Stitches*, the cross-stitches are deliberately destroyed so, it could be argued, reinforcing the temporary nature of stitch. Hand stitch is often part of the pieces, as she describes:

Looking back through old notebooks which almost 30 years on are still strangely relevant to many aspects of my current practice, I note that this collection of investigations into stitch were in some way inspired by an interest in the physicality of stitching – and the idea of stitching into impossible things – the ground, blocks of snow, pigskin, my own skin! I remember trying to hammer long sacking needles into curves to attempt to 'stitch' into the ground: they didn't work! And so I had to make do with the illusion of stitching instead.

Some of this interest was prompted by a book of instruction to teachers of needlework in elementary schools dating from 1882, which I had found in a jumble sale.

My interest in instruction … [has been] resurrected and continues in a recent work, Cut One On Fold, an artist's book exploring the idea of things going wrong! In making mistakes – in things where the unintentional is valued – it is informed by so many of my encounters with sewing, both well and badly! Sometimes [I was] following instruction and sometimes following a deliberate and temperamentally unavoidable dissent from instruction in the drive to find personal alternatives and 'other' solutions.

Kate Egan combines new technology and hand processes in her textile work. She works with a number of different materials; hand stitch is often used to echo and play with its more usual place on a textile. On this occasion, buttonhole stitch is worked on an edge that does not need to be secured. Of *I Can See*, a recent piece, she says,

FROM MADRAS TO MANCHESTER

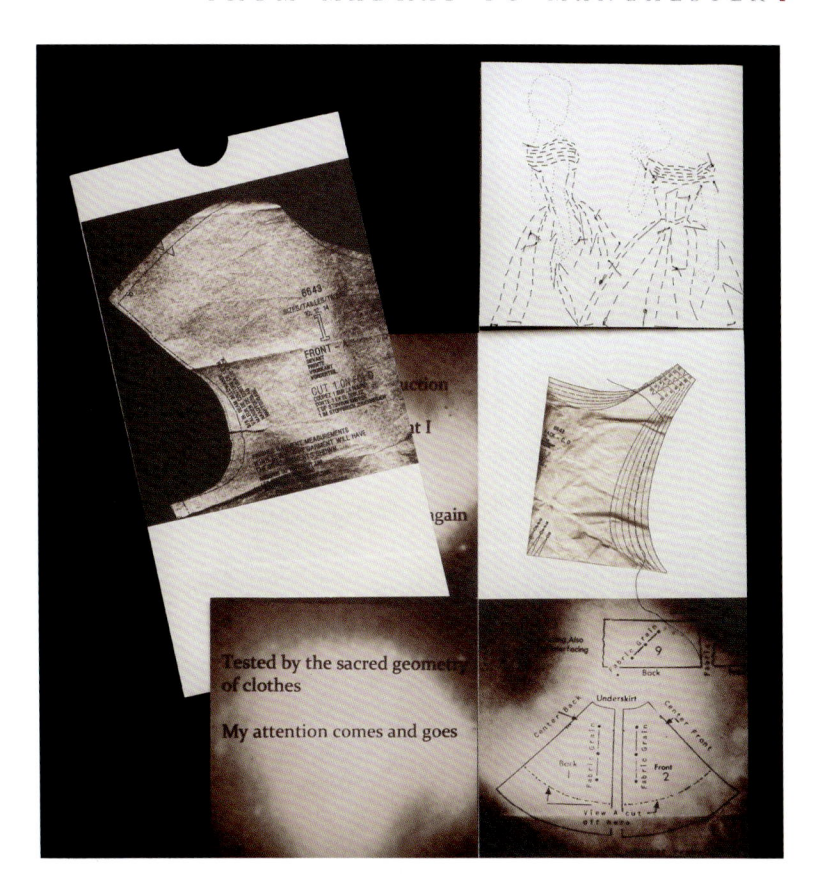

Joan Beadle
Cut One On Fold, 2010. 48 x 24 cm (19 x 9½ in.). Paper, cotton thread, running stitch. Digitally printed artist's book with stitching and perforations, featuring the 'wrong' side of the stitching. Photo: Michael Pollard.

Kate Egan
I Can See, 2011. Laser-cut wood, high-visibility thread, yellow LEDs, buttonhole stitch. Circle diameter: 16 cm (6¼ in.). Photo: Michael Pollard.

The stitch is worked around the piece using precut holes to highlight the edge, which gives it an industrial aesthetic. I am interested in mimicking machine processes using hand stitch: I collect tents, hoarding covers, tarpaulins etc. to understand how these industrial artefacts are constructed.

I Can See questions notions of 'reality' i.e. if we were shrunk down to subatomic level, what would we see? We would see that all the stuff that surrounds us – the chair, the air, the wall, the LED, the buttonhole stitch – is made of the same basic particles.

Belinda Pollit[18] shows how hand stitch can be taken to a micro level: stitch that is hardly visible without a magnifier. The process of making these portraits changed once the work started, as she explains,

When I began each roundel, I had an idea of what I wanted to produce, but each embroidery had a will of its own, as a slight change of stitch angle often completely altered a facial characteristic or expression, and as a hairstyle evolved, it had a big impact on the portrait. It was only when the last stitch was completed [that I] would I know what character I had produced. This made the process much more fun and interesting, if a little nerve-racking.

These approaches require an ability to think beyond the conventional, beyond the known, to push an idea and to make a statement.

Since 1993 I have been working in India at the Calico Museum of Textiles.[19] This has allowed me to further explore and understand embroidery in a region of the world – a region encompassing several countries now – that I would say has had a long and wonderful history in the use of stitch as identity and language. It was possible, in the early to mid-1980s, to travel to villages in Kutch to observe and record, with text and video, the way in which stitches were made and spoken about as identity and language. It was possible from the stitches and patterns to tell which village a wearer was from and something of their status. Stitches – hand stitches – were not named; rather, the whole motif, not the stitch alone, was given a name. This was perhaps one of the last places one could study hand stitch in this way.

Judy Frater documents the embroidery of the Rabari in Kutch, and her time with them understanding the use and meaning of the pieces. She says:

Embroidery style identifies its user. Lachhu was seeing more than the stitches, patterns and colours in my collection. What she unfailingly recognised in embroidery styles were the peoples who make and use them. Stylistic differences become critical; they signal peoples of different communities and simultaneously imply relationships among them.[20]

The peoples of Kutch are an example of how the increase in literacy mitigates against the use of embroidery as part of a language.[21] After literacy has come to the village, the stories in the patterns are gradually forgotten. Some of the old textiles find their way into other projects, and are thus recycled.[22] I like the fact that embroidery/textiles do not last, that they disintegrate and that parts live on through recycling and in doing so, find another life. In time, the light will decay

FROM MADRAS TO MANCHESTER

Belinda Pollit
12 Miniature Portraits, 2011. Each portrait 3 cm (1¼ in.) in diameter. Photo: Michael Pollard. Most of the textile materials that I use have been acquired over the years from friends and family. It is a good feeling to follow in the footsteps of generations of family stitchers from both sides of my family. A large variety of hand stitches have been employed in these pieces. The portrait that is shown on its own is of Ann, born in 1963. It is constructed using distorted fly stitch, back stitch, couching and detached chain stitches.

the thread and fabric. Light has been something I really miss in Britain compared to India, and I like lighting to add to my work when it is up on a wall. The ripples and shadows, the changes light makes to the finished piece, can only be fixed in a photographic image.

The work that I produce now, started in 2008, uses stitch to convey the message of the way I see, and relays what I am interested in. It was developed from experimental work undertaken with David Green,[23] printing on stitch and removing stitch, working in boxes and making wall pieces with a variety of materials that collaged surfaces together. I still look at the same sources in nature, from a trip to frozen white Alaska to skies and changes in surface of water and land through the seasons.

Looking at shapes, the square seems to have followed me through my work, as does light,[24] impermanence and change. I like my work to be taut and stretched, but not exclusively, which often means that I use cloth as a means to an end, not as a textile that I am embellishing or adding to. The cloth becomes mine to change and do with as I will. I like secrets and being 'unconventional', defying Miss Baines with my 'bad' sewing, which puckers up the fabric and uses techniques I know were considered 'wrong'. The use of an ancient symbol for water across the work could be seen as merely a line or pattern: I see it as a form of graffiti.

My research in India has had an impact on the way I see and use stitch. Through challenging the subject and oneself it is a journey, like any other, where ideas move and develop and change and one becomes more confident. It would be wonderful if a word could be found to describe this lateral thinking about stitch – but then perhaps not, or we are back to Victorian mindsets.

Anne Morrell
Untitled, 1972. Felt and various threads. Felt over card, card piece and leathers, inset canvas work using a tent (petit point) stitch. 56.5 x 33.5 cm (22¼ x 13¼ in.). Government Art Collection (UK). Acc. no. GAC13523. Photo: John Hunnex.

NOTES

[1] Butler, Anne, *The Batsford Encyclopaedia of Embroidery Stitches* (London: B. T. Batsford, [1979] 1982; paperback 1983); *The Arco Encyclopaedia of Embroidery Stitches* (USA: Arco, 1979).

[2] Morrell, Anne Butler, *the migration of stitches & the practice of stitch as movement* (India: Sarabhai Foundation, Ahmedabad, 2007).

[3] Christine Risley (1926–2003) taught machine embroidery at Goldsmiths College at this time.

[4] Marsh, Gail, *Early 20th Century Embroidery Techniques* (Lewes: GMC Publications, 2011), pp. 112–14.

[5] Crompton, Rebecca, *Modern Design in Embroidery* (London: His Majesty's Stationery Office, 1936).

[6] Rosevear, Elizabeth, *A Text-Book of Needlework, Knitting and Cutting Out with methods of teaching* (London: Macmillan, 1896), p. 15.

[7] Marsh, Gail, *Early 20th Century Embroidery Techniques* (Lewes: GMC Publications, 2011), pp. 92–94.

[8] The recording methods of today can be photography and the moving image, but previously, the investigation had to be as thorough as that undertaken by Pesel. My early inspiration was through her work and that of Alfred Bühler, anthropologist and director of the Ethnographic Museum in Basel, where the textile technology gallery was of particular interest. A similar gallery can be found today at the Calico Museum of Textiles.

[9] On view at the State Hermitage Museum in St Petersburg, Russia.

[10] A saddlecloth made from various fabrics.

[11] Rudenko, Sergei I., *Frozen Tombs of Siberia: The Pazyryk Burials of Iron Age Horsemen* (Berkley and Los Angeles: University of California Press, 1970), pp. 174–79, colour plate 178.

[12] Andere, Mary, *Old Needlework Boxes and Tools* (Newton Abbot: David and Charles, 1971), p. 55.

[13] A medical student loaned me a (medical) curved needle to work the stitches on the piece for the Design Centre London, 1967.

[14] Bucherer, Paul, and Cornelia Vogelsanger, *Gestickte Gebete* (Bubendorf: Stiftung Bibliotheca Afghanica, 2000). See also *the migration of stitches & the practice of stitch as movement*, p. 14.

FROM MADRAS TO MANCHESTER

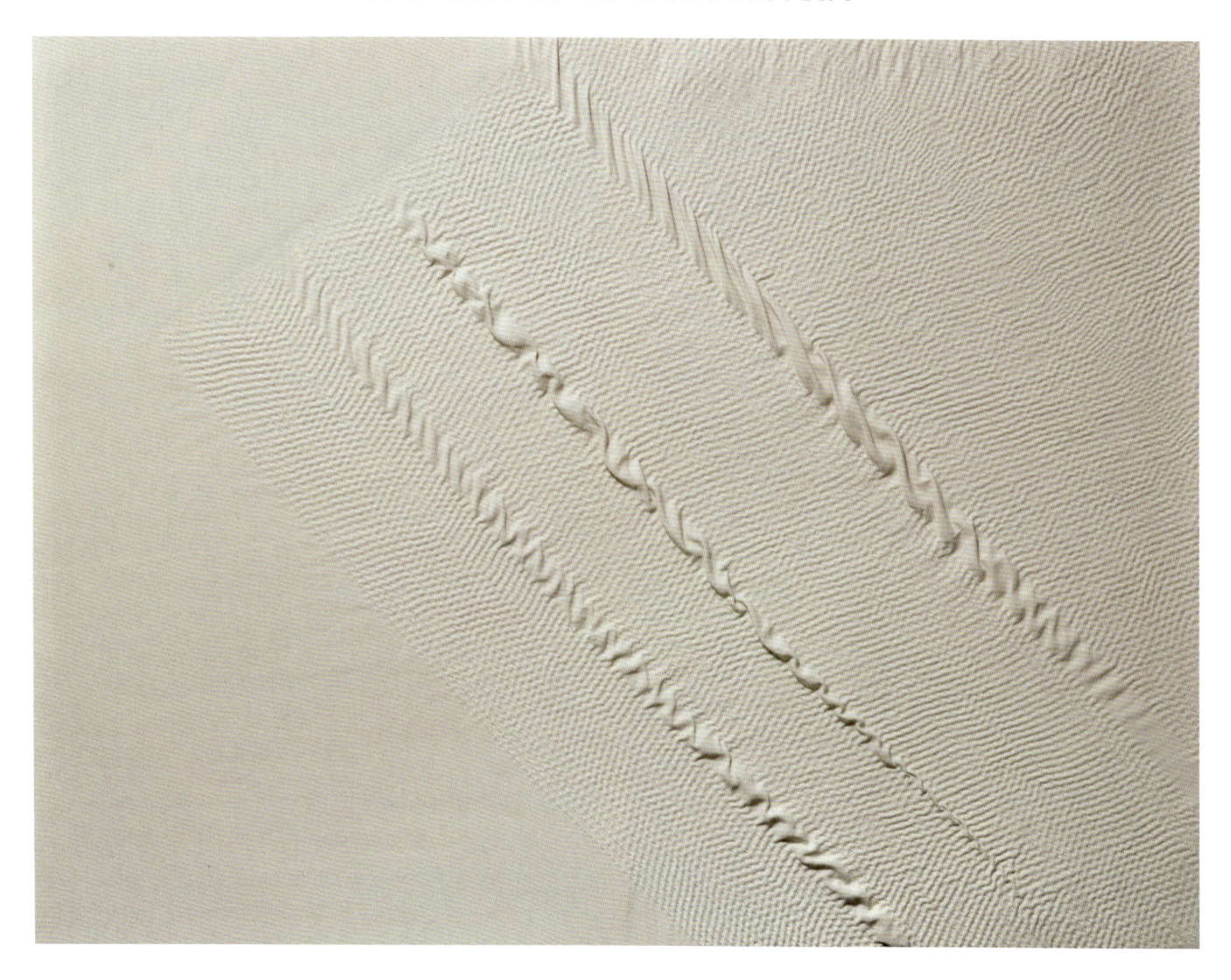

Anne Morrell
Incline, 2011. Cotton fabric, various threads, running stitch. 86 x 115 cm (34 x 45¼ in.). Photo: Michael Pollard.

[15] Pritchard, Frances, *Clothing Culture: Dress in Egypt in the First Millennium AD* (Manchester: University of Manchester, 2006).

[16] Shrujan Trust, *Under the Embroidered Sky – Embroidery of the Ahirs of Kutch*, 2010. This stitch (maakhi) can be seen in use in India today.

[17] Banjara, or Lambanis, gypsies of India.

[18] Belinda Pollit, *The Family and Its History Are Fictitious*.

[19] See www.calicomuseum.com

[20] Frater, Judy, *Threads of Identity: Embroidery and Adornment of the Nomadic Rabaris* (Ahmedabad: Mapin, 1995), p. 17.

[21] Shrujan Trust, *Under the Embroidered Sky – Embroidery of the Ahirs of Kutch*, 2010.

[22] Norris, Lucy, *Recycling Indian Clothing: Global Contexts of Reuse and Value* (Bloomington: Indiana University Press, 2010).

[23] David Green, lecturer at Goldsmiths College, 1960s. We published a book together: *Pattern & Embroidery* (London: Batsford, 1970). See page 94.

[24] I have been made so aware of light and so often the lack of it here in England. To me it feels like 'living under a stone' many days of the year.

JUNE HILL

The Length of a Needle

TWO YEARS AGO, I WAS INVITED TO CURATE AN EXHIBITION on Beryl Dean to mark the centenary of her birth. I was familiar with the name but knew little about her practice. My reply was equivocal: I asked if I could first learn more. This was agreed, and I was put in contact with numerous people who either knew Beryl or had worked alongside her. I listened to their recollections, then was introduced to some of her work and finally to all of her archive.

I discovered early on that the name Beryl Dean was a form of synonym for ecclesiastical embroidery. Over the months, I came to know her as a formidable and controversial figure; someone who attracted deferential respect and fierce criticism and remained unfazed by both. I became as fascinated by the woman, as by the artist. As I read her diaries, lecture notes, scrapbooks and annotated reading lists, I found myself responding to preconceptions of her work with the words: 'But there's so much more to Beryl Dean than her ecclesiastical embroidery.' Yet, even as I assumed the role of defender, I realised the folly of my stance, for ecclesiastical embroidery was the field Beryl had chosen to transform. This was her specialism, something she had made her own whilst simultaneously encouraging others to take up the cause. Who was I to take that away from her? My task, I realised, was not to deny her achievement, but rather to contextualise it for those who did not as yet know its full extent – those who had not been able to reflect on her personal papers or have her life's practice unveiled before them.

So I set out to do precisely that. In the process, I seemed to absorb elements of her persona. I grew atypically assertive and refreshingly forthright: a dispute at the supermarket was followed by another with a colleague. I stood my ground. Beryl would have done the same. She was, after all, seated on my shoulder. I became a form of amanuensis. I worked obsessively, late into the night as, of course, had my subject. People spoke of hearing Beryl teach as they read my text for the catalogue. I quoted her writings to others and illustrated my arguments with points she had made or experiences she had endured. There was no hope: I was a woman possessed by a spirit that was not my own.

If I had to justify this behaviour, I would explain that this was not a crisis of identity, but rather the unexpected outcome of a desire to understand someone different from myself, whom I had grown to admire. I wanted to share that person with others. This was about setting a record straight. You see, if Beryl Dean were seated beside me, rather than on my shoulder, I would want to ask her one simple question: 'What would you be doing if you were practising today?' And I do not know what her answer would be. I am not convinced she would take the same path again. There are so many concerns articulated in her work: all underpinned by her fervent conviction that the expression of ideas is integral to creative practice and her belief that in order to communicate those ideas, work must address the issues of its day and be grounded in a process of making.

The desire to pose that simple question, and the sense of uncertainty surrounding her hypothetical response, convinced me of the need to look afresh at Beryl Dean and to re-examine the contribution she has made to contemporary embroidery.

THE BERYL DEAN ARCHIVE

We are just stepping into a wider world and need not feel lonely, except in the way that pioneers feel lonely. Life is easier for married people but I think it ought to be if anything richer for us, so long as we take it with full hands and not with the inferiority sense which has often ruined the lives of spinsters ... The knowledge I think that the secret of life does lie in our own hands and need not elude us unless we ourselves allow it to do so.[1]

Those words by Freya Stark were transcribed in longhand in a small notebook Beryl Dean kept of quotes from texts she had read. That notebook is part of a substantial archive the artist maintained on her work and thinking. It is a rich and varied resource that documents Beryl's career as it developed over seven decades and, in so doing, offers insights into both her practice and the field in which she worked.

Reading through an archive without the person at hand to question and probe can be a perilous business. Alongside the inherent danger of projecting oneself on to the material and taking an overly subjective reading, there is also the issue of not knowing the weight attached to particular elements. What is central and what is peripheral? Where are the nuances?

We can assume the material in this archive was significant to Beryl: it is something she has chosen first to keep and then to leave for others to learn about her work. It is part of her legacy. But how do we assess the significance of that legacy? More importantly, a decade after Beryl Dean died and 82 years after she embarked on her career, how do we now perceive the significance of her work?

A dominant figure in embroidery from the 1950s onwards, Dean's position waned in the latter years of her life. While Constance Howard – a contemporary whose career ran in parallel with Dean's – continues to be highly esteemed, Beryl Dean has become a more marginal figure, at least in terms of public awareness. This may in part reflect the current status of her chosen area of practice – church needlework – as much as her approach to work. Perhaps more crucially, it suggests an oversight of context. In order to assess the import of Dean's work, we need to understand how the field developed during her lifetime and analyse the contribution she made to that process. And it is here where the Beryl Dean Archive comes into its own. It is primary source material.

Beryl Dean in her studio, 1974. The Beryl Dean Archive. Reproduced with permission of the Executors of the Beryl Dean Estate. Photo: W. Taylor.

HAND STITCH: PERSPECTIVES

Royal School of Needlework, Exhibition Road, 1929. The Beryl Dean Archive. Reproduced with permission of the executors of the Beryl Dean Estate. Photo: William E. Gray.

PIONEERS

That quote from Freya Stark is a reminder of the circumstances in which Dean and her contemporaries developed their practice. It is taken from 'Beyond Euphrates', an autobiographical account of the author's travels in Iraq and Persia during the 1920s and 30s. Freya Stark was one of those indomitable female figures who literally blazed a trail that future generations would make their own.

Beryl Dean was a trailblazer in a different field: one of a small cohort of pioneering women artists. They faced the same decision that Freya Stark had and, like her, chose to take hold of their own destiny. Independence was not an easy course for a woman in the 1920s. Less so for those who elected to pursue art. Beryl Dean's parents disapproved, but she would not be deterred. Art school was not considered an option, so she chose to study needlework: a subject she loved and practised daily.

> *I was determined to have a career [in art] at a time when it was not usual ... Some neighbours of ours ... who were artists, persuaded my parents that I ought to be trained, and they set about finding out the possibilities. They discovered the Royal School of Needlework. As it seemed the next best thing to doing art I went there.*[2]

Beryl Dean emerged from the RSN as a teacher determined to explore the creative potential of embroidery. She went on to study at Bromley School of Art and the Royal College of Art, all the while working part-time in education to support herself. Rebecca Crompton and Elizabeth Grace Thomson were her mentors; Constance Howard, Kathleen Whyte, Sylvia Green and Margaret Forbes her peers.

As practitioners, educators and advocates, these women helped to establish a new movement in stitch. Their efforts were paralleled by others active in ceramics, glass, weave and print. In examining their relative significance, it is therefore important not to view work in isolation but rather in the context of the whole. The world was different in their day, and it was they who helped precipitate that which has come to pass.

HISTORY, TRADITION AND THE CONTEMPORARY

The relationship between past and present practice was one that exercised Beryl Dean a great deal. She studied the traditions of her craft and encouraged others to follow suit. Extant work was, she maintained, a source of both information and inspiration. She knew well the early British embroideries at the V&A and the glories of Opus Anglicanum (1250–1350). 'I have been influenced in many ways, but especially the history of the craft', she commented. 'In Britain we have such a splendid heritage.'[3]

She drew on that legacy in her making. Renowned as an exceptional needlewoman – 'Miss Dean's technical knowledge and dexterity are as nearly perfect as possible', wrote her tutor at the Royal College of Art[4] – her work was distinguished by the creativity with which she used those skills. She was fascinated by goldwork – partly for the challenge its execution presented and, perhaps more importantly, as a means of 'drawing with light'.[5] She relished whitework for the potential it offered to experiment with texture, tone, surface and structure. She became renowned for combining techniques that otherwise remained distinct: in one instance whipping drawn thread work with weaving chenille to create a sense of luminosity. In another, exploring the raised line by juxtaposing Italian and English quilting.

Much as she valued the history and technicalities of her medium, however, Dean refused to be restricted by either. She was adamant that in order to be relevant, work must be rooted in an understanding of its day. It could – perhaps even should – reference the past, but it must not live there. The hackneyed and derivative were always roundly condemned. Equally, whilst command of one's medium was vital, it was the expression of ideas that was of fundamental importance. Technique – and decoration[6] – was a means to an end, not an end in itself: it was how one turned the idea into a reality.

> *Too often designs adapted from familiar styles continue to be repeated long after that decorative period has been superseded by another. This results in lifeless, watered-down variations lacking the vitality of the age which gave it birth. It is the idiom which is a living and vital expression of the present which can be sincerely felt and understood.*[7]

The need for, and value of, modern design was the underpinning principle of her work as an artist, teacher and writer. It is thus necessary to understand her definition of the term. She is not using it in reference to something that could be produced separate from its originator. Rather, design is for her 'a creative activity of self-expression',[8] and 'an intellectual process which not only requires thought but observation and imagination'.[9] It is part of the process of making art, a means of visual communication. She wanted to express her own ideas in stitch and cloth, and her entire career was centred on the twin aspirations of doing that herself and enabling others to do precisely the same.

CLOTH, TIME AND THE PROCESS OF MAKING

Beryl Dean's life was totally absorbed by her creative practice. She never stopped making: always pushing her medium, her skills and those of others. As her projects grew in ambition, she came to work on a monumental scale: frontals 260 cm (102 in.) long and 100 cm (39½ in.) high; a series of five wall panels each 270 x 120 cm (106¼ x 47¼ in.). Unable to make in any way other than meticulously by hand, she would frequently stitch for 20 hours at a stretch. Every piece was 'progressed by the length of needle',[10] measured not by stitches to the inch, but by the months – even years – it had taken to make.

> *I build up so much from [the material and] the technique because I love doing it so much, I build the colour up as I go along because I think you get excited by the unexpected … combinations. It's the inventiveness that keeps it alive while you are doing it … It's in your mind all the time, you're adding to it in your imagination even while you're not working on it.*[11]

Cloth had been important to Dean since childhood. She valued both its haptic and its textural qualities. Encouraged by her aunt, she had collected scraps of fabric and thread since the age of seven or eight. These were stored in a box under her bed and she would escape school to blissfully sew all day long. It was a habit that informed her making as an adult. Wherever she went, she would seek out unusual pieces of cloth or yarn. Synthetic fabrics, handwoven cloth, real gold thread, sari material, Thai silk, Swiss furnishing fabric, kid, cellophane, parachute string, raffia: all were incorporated into Dean's work. That she could recollect the details of their acquisition and usage decades afterwards is indicative of the potency textiles carried for her.

FREEDOM, DISCIPLINE AND ART

Dean's approach to embroidery was largely informed by the innovative practice of Thomson and Crompton, whom she met whilst a student at Bromley School of Art (1933–35). There she was encouraged not only to experiment with stitch, texture and form, but also to place her work in the context of contemporary culture.

> *Miss Thomson decided that my outlook on life needed broadening, so she took me to Paris where we visited the Louvre, the Luxembourg and many galleries and museums … I learned a great deal, it was all a revelation … The impact made by Rebecca Crompton was tremendous at the time (imagine using buttons). It elicited praise, also strong criticism from traditionalists. Yet those who understood what she was doing put*

Beryl Dean
Embroidery in the style of Rebecca Crompton, 1930s. The Beryl Dean Archive. Reproduced with permission of the executors of the Beryl Dean Estate. Photo: Iveta Olekjova. 'Freedom and movement contributed to the liveliness of [Rebecca Crompton's] embroideries, and an original use of fabric and thread was characteristic. This was the time when everything was very functional, decoration embellished structure and romanticism was out' (US Museum Lecture Notes, 1962, The Beryl Dean Archive).

on an important exhibition of her work at the V&A which was unlike anything one had ever seen. And it was also shown with modern sculpture at the Leicester and other galleries.[12]

Crompton's visionary approach to embroidery was one with which Dean had a natural affinity. The very materiality of her craft informed every aspect of her practice. She had a tacit understanding of her medium and developed work in accord: layering, overlapping, juxtaposing weight and texture, stitching through and over, couching, knotting, interlacing and darning. Her style verged on iconoclasm. The only limitations she acknowledged were those of context and the nature of the discipline itself.

> *[Designers] should feel themselves to be free from the conventions ... they should not allow themselves to be bound by any particular colour sequence, nor should they feel obliged to use any specific kind of material ... or feel under obligation to use traditional symbols which are obscure, trite or meaningless ... This liberation needs to be tempered, however, by a reasonable discipline ... The integrity of artists lies in their honest use of the materials of their own day to serve and express contemporary understanding and belief.*[13]

ECCLESIASTICAL EMBROIDERY

In 1952, after a period working in education, fashion and theatre design, Dean resolved to focus her energies on the revitalisation of ecclesiastical embroidery. This, she concluded, was a means to help stitch to prosper and to pursue the zeitgeist.

> *I had a longing to go back to doing embroidery. This coincided with the realisation that with the rebuilding of churches after the war, unless something was done about it new [textiles] would be made to the same outworn designs, whereas on the Continent exciting new ideas were in use.*[14]

Dean's training at the RSN had grounded her in the heritage of British ecclesiastical embroidery. She knew the language of its forms, its seminal works and the status accorded it during the Opus Anglicanum period, when it was perceived as the finest needlework in Europe. She had also been taught that, historically, the relationship between religious and secular stitch had been both open and fruitful – one influencing the other. By the mid-twentieth century, however, there was an evident disparity between the two. '[Ecclesiastical embroidery] was just dead', she explained. 'No new ideas had been introduced since the end of the last century.'[15] In contrast to its earlier vibrancy, church needlework had come to be dominated by commercial textiles – largely woven brocades, damasks or linen – with Victorian Gothic the dominant style.

Beryl Dean
Festival of Britain, 1958. Fine whitework using pre-war thread on layered organdie. The Beryl Dean Archive. New Hall Art Collection, Murray Edwards College, Cambridge. Photo: J. E. Lowe. Reproduced with the permission of New Hall Art Collection and the executors of the Beryl Dean Estate.

THE LENGTH OF A NEEDLE

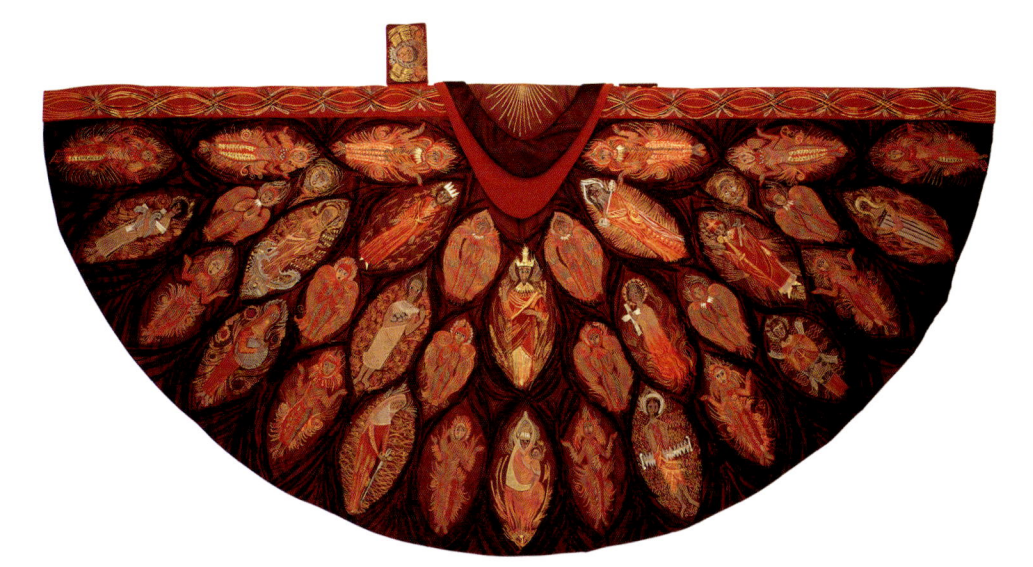

Beryl Dean
Hammersmith Cope, 1968. Silk with appliquéd medallions depicting martyred angels and saints. Coloured metal threads, spangles and pearl purl. 305 x 152 cm (120 x 60 in.). Photo: Beryl Dean Archive. Reproduced with the permission of the executors of the Beryl Dean Estate. Designed by Susan Riley and made by Beryl and 40 students at Hammersmith College along with a set of five other copes. It represents 5,000 hours' work.

(*below*) Annotated sketch of cope design, 1968. Photo: The Beryl Dean Archive. Reproduced with the permission of the Dean and Chapter of St Paul's Cathedral.

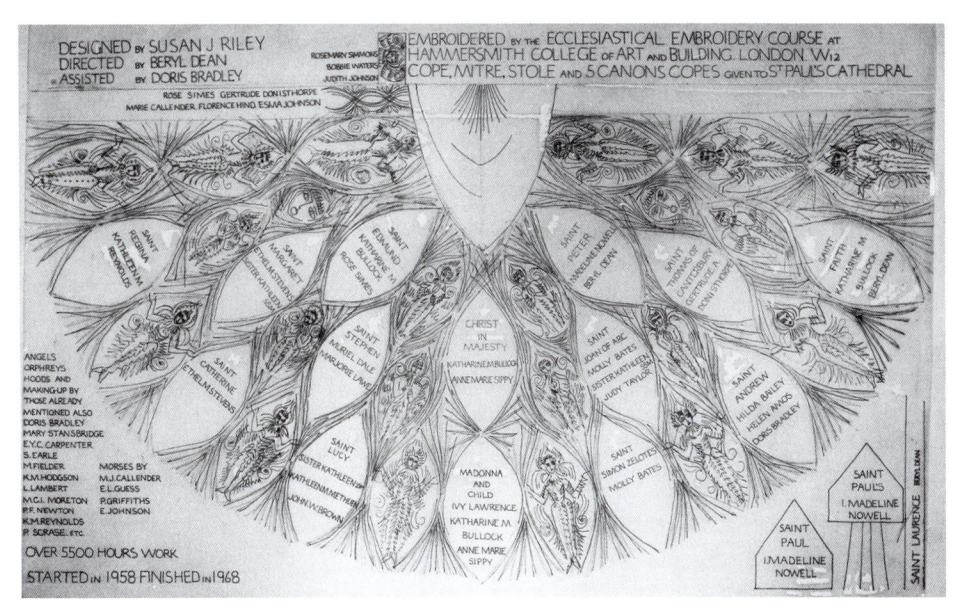

The post-war reconstruction of Britain presented a unique opportunity to introduce modernist art and architecture into the sector: a sector that was itself being influenced by the radicalism of the Liturgical Movement. There were significant implications from both these developments: the latter placed new demands on internal spaces as the relationship between clergy and laity was transformed; the former provided a means to express that through innovative design and the use of modern materials, including the more plastic medium of concrete. The planning of iconic new buildings – notably at Coventry and Liverpool – made reform seem all the more imperative to Dean. 'I was afraid that our churches … would spend their war damage money on terribly commercial, old-fashioned things', she explained.[16] She had seen the work done by Le Corbusier at Ronchamp and Matisse at Vence: these were her sources of inspiration and the benchmarks she referenced.

111

The potential benefit to modern stitch in pursuing this strategy was considerable. The Church had been a long standing patron of art practice and was then still central to national life. Textiles, colour and symbolism were perceived as integral to its expression of ideas and emotion. Banners, altar frontals, vestments, palls: all had a place in its ministry. Liturgical seasons were identified with a palette of white, gold, red, purple and green. Key concepts were conveyed by images of the elements, the natural environment and cross forms. Here was a seemingly apposite means of giving modernist stitch a major platform.

CONTEXT, COLLABORATION AND ENGAGEMENT

In her first substantial publication on the subject, Dean wrote: 'Interior design offers lucrative opportunities, but church work is still often regarded as the best, because it offers the strongest challenge.'[17]

The element of challenge was one of the aspects that Dean found most compelling about ecclesiastical embroidery. It came in many forms. There were the restrictions within which work had to be developed – those markers of colour, form and symbolism. Then there was the context in which each piece would be used: a term that covered its architectural setting, daily usage and liturgical significance. Beyond that, there was the issue of expectation. 'I feel very strongly that there should be some body of informed opinion that only the best should be used in the house of God',[18] she asserted. It was a comment on the passive acceptance rather than active commissioning of work, yet it reveals a profound conviction. This was a field in which the finest of artists had worked. That was the implicit challenge presented to herself and her peers: they had to pursue excellence.

'It could be', she mused in 1968, 'that embroidery … may make an important contribution [to] Church Art as a whole.'[19] It was not idle speculation. Dean's practice was recognised as having a pertinence that extended beyond stitch. Her work was exhibited alongside that of Eric Gill,[20] Graham Sutherland, Barbara Hepworth, Marc Chagall[21] and John Piper.[22] Her books had equal standing and were viewed as authoritative texts by a wide spectrum of practitioners. An early article noted:

> *Although it may be strange to review* Ecclesiastical Embroidery [*in* The Glassman]*, there are so many points held in common, especially where contemporary work is concerned, that we feel this book is of great value to a stained-glass craftsman.*

Dean actively encouraged collaboration between disciplines and herself worked closely with the influential architects Sir Basil Spence, George Pace and Anthony Blee. The latter made a significant contribution to her groundbreaking publication *Ideas for Church Embroidery* (1968). Acclaimed as a postmodernist visual primer, the book was also an argument for the value of creative partnerships.

Perhaps the most profound of her collaborations, however, was the one Dean established with her students. Although she positioned herself outside academia, her teaching – as a sessional tutor, public lecturer and writer – was highly influential. The weekly classes she led at Hammersmith College of Art (1952–76) and the Stanhope

THE LENGTH OF A NEEDLE

Beryl Dean
Windsor Panels, 1974. 120 x 270 cm (47¼ x 106¼ in.). Collection of Windsor Castle. The Beryl Dean Archive. Reproduced with permission of the executors of the Beryl Dean Estate. Photo: W. Taylor. Made for the Rutland Chantry Chapel, Windsor Castle, the panels depict the life of the Virgin Mary and the early life of Christ. Ground of linen and lurex woven by Jack Peacock to Beryl Dean's specifications. Hand-embroidered in goldwork with drawn and filled work, appliqué in fabric and leather. A total of 1,490 hours was spent on each panel: five years' work in total.

Institute (1962–79) had a widespread impact. Dean's students worked alongside her on several major commissions and themselves became influential figures in ecclesiastical embroidery. The substance of all she taught them was documented in nine major publications. Practical yet imaginative, these books sought to equip a wide readership in the principles and practice of modern design. Dean developed a strategy of launching each new publication with a linked exhibition. It proved highly effective. Grassroots involvement in stitch grew significantly. It became a form of movement: one that echoed the lay participation promoted by the Liturgical Movement. 'Most far-reaching has been the trend she has encouraged towards parishes making their own [textiles]', wrote one commentator. 'Out of Hammersmith and the Stanhope Institute in Bloomsbury have grown a network of voluntary groups trained to work to a commissioned design.'[23]

A NEEDLE LENGTH

In 1968, Beryl Dean curated 'New Ecclesiastical Embroidery' at St Paul's Cathedral, with the assistance of Constance Howard. The first of several major survey exhibitions Dean would organise, it attracted national media coverage and, in so doing, significantly heightened the awareness of stitch as an expressive medium. One reviewer reported:

> *My illusions of gentlewomen bent over their petit point were shattered. There's a revolution in embroidery generally. You don't have to work your stitches evenly or perfectly any more: you do what you wish, to achieve the effect you want.*
>
> *'Cut a great big hole in your canvas if you feel like it', said the assistant from Goldsmiths College cheerfully. 'Have courage and experiment.'*[24]

One of the criticisms made of Dean's work is that it is dated. It cannot be denied that some is of its time. If Beryl Dean were to take up her place with me here, she would probably concur. She was always her own sternest critic. Yet this is as much an affirmation as a criticism of her work, for being pertinent to her time was precisely that which Dean desired. She strove to establish a contemporary idiom in embroidery and that is what she did. Her practice was prescient rather than visionary. She understood that another generation – and other artists – would imagine things differently. 'I'm not Graham Sutherland – I'm not so forward-looking',[25] she said of herself. Beryl Dean was a modernist artist who loved to work in stitch and cloth, and valued the honest making of those who did likewise. 'The secret of life lies in our own hands', Freya Stark had written. The significance of that phrase did not elude Dean: she never allowed it to do so.

NOTES

[1] Notes from Freya Stark, *Beyond Euphrates: Autobiography 1928–1933* (London: Century Travellers, 1951. The Beryl Dean Archive.

[2] Lecture notes, Hampton Court, 1990. The Beryl Dean Archive.

[3] Rye lecture notes, 1970s. The Beryl Dean Archive.

[4] Reference, 14 March 1939, Kathleen M. Harris, Teacher of Embroidery, RCA. The Beryl Dean Archive.

[5] Dean, Beryl, *Ideas for Church Embroidery* (London: B. T. Batsford, 1968). Anthony Blee, architect (Blee worked with Sir Basil Spence on Coventry Cathedral) and contributed an article to *Ideas for Church Embroidery*, p. 15.

[6] Ibid., p. 35.

[7] Ibid., p. 27.

[8] Ibid., p. 34.

[9] Ibid., p. 27.

[10] Excerpt from transcript of lecture at St George's Chapel, Windsor Castle, 28 November 1988. The Beryl Dean Archive.

[11] Extract from radio interview on 1974 exhibition 'Beryl Dean and Her Students', St Andrew's Holborn. The Beryl Dean Archive.

[12] Extract from a handwritten tribute to Grace Thomson, The Beryl Dean Archive.

[13] Dean, Beryl, *Ideas for Church Embroidery* (London: B. T. Batsford, 1968), pp. 21–22.

[14] Rye lecture notes, 1970s. The Beryl Dean Archive.

[15] Extract from handwritten notes entitled, 'Book by Joan Edwards'. The Beryl Dean Archive.

[16] *Forum World Features,* 'World of Women', vol. 24, 1975, Elizabeth Taylor's interview with Beryl Dean. The Beryl Dean Archive.

[17] Dean, Beryl, *Ecclesiastical Embroidery* (London: B. T. Batsford, 1958).

[18] Lecture notes. The Beryl Dean Archive.

[19] Dean, Beryl, *Ideas for Church Embroidery* (London: B. T. Batsford, 1968), p. 100.

[20] Crafts Centre of Great Britain, Hay Hill, 1958–65, featured the *Madonna and Child* banner alongside works by Gill.

[21] 'Artists Serve the Church: An Exhibition of Modern Religious Work' organised by the Exhibition Committee of the Coventry Cathedral Festival 1962, Herbert Art Gallery and Museum, Coventry.

[22] John Piper and Beryl Dean both designed copes for St Paul's Cathedral to mark the 1977 Silver Jubilee of Queen Elizabeth II.

[23] Hatts, Leigh, 'A Change From Off-the-Peg Church Vestments', *Catholic Herald*, 30 March 1990. The Beryl Dean Archive.

[24] Newspaper clipping – article by Violet Johnstone on the exhibition at St Paul's crypt, 1968.

[25] Extract from radio interview on 1974 exhibition 'Beryl Dean and Her Students', St Andrew's Holborn. The Beryl Dean Archive.

Beryl Dean
Cope, Canterbury Cathedral (detail), 1975–80. Photo: The Beryl Dean Archive. Reproduced with permission of the executors of the Beryl Dean Estate. Design worn by the Dean and Chapter at the enthronement of the Archbishop of Canterbury.

MELANIE MILLER

Embroidery and the F-word

THIS CHAPTER PROVIDES A SUBJECTIVE, GENERALISED OVERVIEW of feminism and embroidery. Feminism is a fiendishly complicated subject. An introductory section sets the scene, followed by a discussion of communal art practice and craftivism, and then four contemporary practitioners are looked at in more detail, arthur+martha, Deidre Nelson, Lynn Setterington and Caren Garfen. Finally, there is a consideration of the current position of stitched textiles within the art world.

The relationship between embroidery and feminism today is complex. As Karen Rosenberg writes, in a review of 'Pricked: Extreme Embroidery', held at the Museum of Arts and Design in New York in 2007:

In the 1970s, artists who swapped their paintbrushes for a needle and thread were making a feminist statement. Today, as both men and women fill galleries with crocheted sculpture and stitched canvases, the gesture isn't quite so specific. Some contemporary artists gravitate to the retro-kitsch factor; others seize on the exacting technique, or the association with sweatshop labor, or a personal memory of Aunt Gladys's afghans.[1]

For reasons fully explored in Rozsika Parker's seminal book, *The Subversive Stitch: Embroidery and the Making of the Feminine* (1984),[2] embroidery has long been an appropriate vehicle for women making artistic and political statements with needle and thread. Historically, with a few notable exceptions, such as Artemisia Gentileschi, Elisabeth Vigée Lebrun, Angelika Kauffmann, women were mostly denied access to the fine arts and so had to express their creativity through mediums such as textiles and embroidery, which they did have easy access to. The subject of why there have been so few great women artists has been extensively debated, a key source being Linda Nochlin's groundbreaking essay from 1971.[3]

1970S FEMINISM

The feminist art movement began in the late 1960s/early 1970s, reflecting general developments in feminism, and as a response to the male-dominated hierarchical art establishment. Amongst many other early key figures were Judy Chicago, Miriam Schapiro and Faith Ringgold, who was challenging the under-representation of black artists as well as female artists. Feminist working practices collapsed the hierarchy between high and low art, embracing the use of previously undervalued and overlooked processes such as domestic crafts. Collaborative working practices were encouraged; the idea of the lone genius creating masterpieces was challenged.

The concept that art could be used for a social or political purpose was embraced; art wasn't only for the art gallery. Subject matter frequently reflected women's lives and experiences.

Judy Chicago was responsible for the creation of what is probably the most iconic feminist artwork of the twentieth century: *The Dinner Party*. This consisted of a vast triangular table, with 39 place settings commemorating 39 women of history. Each place setting consisted of a ceramic plate, an embroidered table runner and a chalice. The making of *The Dinner Party* was a collaborative exercise. Hundreds of women – and some men – were involved in making the separate components, utilising traditional 'low art' forms such as ceramics and textiles. The table was set on a marble floor inscribed with the names of another 999 women. The aim of *The Dinner Party* was to both celebrate the achievement of women, and to reiterate the validity of alternative processes for making art. The meaning of the work and its process of making were totally integrated within *The Dinner Party*.

One of the most controversial elements of *The Dinner Party* was the use of 'central core imagery': the flower-like or butterfly-like images of genitalia on the ceramic plates. Judy was endeavouring to reclaim and celebrate the marker of women's otherness; it was intended as a powerful symbol of female identity.

FEMINIST THEMES?

The following artists illustrate some of the key themes that can be seen to be 'feminist': the use of specific mediums or processes; the selection of particular subjects such as domesticity, sexuality, femininity and women's history. However, 'feminist art' is not a static, defined entity; some art can be seen as feminist because of how it is made or because of its subject matter. Some artworks I consider to be 'feminist' may not be viewed that way by their makers; it could be said that 'feminist art' is in the eye of the beholder.

Elaine Reichek

Elaine is a contemporary of Judy Chicago. Most of Elaine's vast body of work is stitched; she has developed her own language to critique modernism.

> *When I was growing up and was a student, painting was the dominant art form, really the centre of a cult, and the members of that cult were historically mostly male – there was very little room for women there. And I have to say I love painting, but I also feel, what's the big deal? I can make these same images using knitting, using embroidery – using media traditionally associated with women. But if I make them that way, of course their meaning changes, since the meaning of an artwork is always bound up with its media and processes and their history. Following through those changing meanings is one of the basic pursuits in my work.*[4]

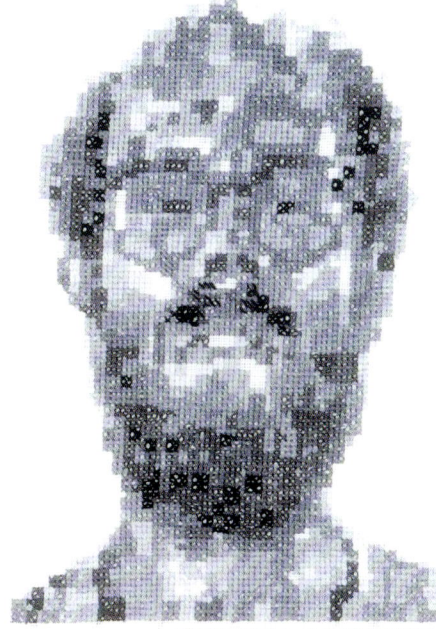

Elaine Reichek
Sampler (Chuck Close), 1997. Hand embroidery on linen. 21.6 x 27.9 cm (8½ x 11 in.). Photo: Adam Reich.

HAND STITCH: PERSPECTIVES

Orly Cogan
East of Eden, 2008. Hand-stitched embroidery, appliqué and paint on vintage linen. 203 x 61 cm (80 x 24 in.). Photo: Adam Reich.

Orly Cogan

Orly creates an interesting tension between her subject matter and her medium: representations of women (many of them naked), exploring their roles and identity, are stitched in outline on to traditional hand-embroidered tablecloths and table runners, creating a playful dichotomy.

> *My art deals with history, tradition, mythology, fairy tales, nature, humour, irony and intimacy. I create a dialogue using the vintage fabrics as two-way mirrors into the like-minded fantasies of competing generations. I add to these a layer of attitude (such as hand-sewn, thick pubic hair), which updates what was once considered an old-fashioned womanly craft with a kind of happy-go-lucky postmodern perversity. The fabric becomes the foundation for a fantastical, exotic dialogue between the old and the new.*[5]

Andrea Dezsö

Andrea uses a range of processes and mediums within her practice. For a stitched series called 'Lessons From My Mother', she has called on her native Hungarian background to stitch 50 contemporary cultural myths and create a series of humorous cautionary proverbs. Many of them relate to female sexuality, female health, or the relationships between men and women. The words 'My mother said' precede each statement: 'You can get hepatitis from a handshake'; 'If you let a man fuck you he'll leave you because every man wants to marry a virgin'. Each statement is accompanied by a (sometimes explicit) drawing.

COMMUNAL PROJECTS

Working collectively, rather than independently, was one of feminism's strategies. Feminism also encouraged the idea that art could/should be used for a social or political purpose, not just for the art gallery.

Textiles and stitch have frequently been used to create small and large-scale artworks to raise awareness of particular issues. One of the most well known is the *Aids Memorial Quilt*. This is an ongoing project. Each panel, 90 x 180 cm (35½ x 71 in.) in size, memorialises an individual who has died from Aids or an Aids-related illness: eight panels are then sewn together to make a 'block'. These blocks are then displayed alongside each other, making up huge quilts. Each panel is very individual, created in a way to represent or celebrate each person. To date, more than 45,000 individual memorial panels have been made. The quilt is a collective act of mourning, a way to raise awareness of the Aids pandemic, and a way of raising funds for those affected by Aids. It is also a demonstration of how 'the personal is political'.

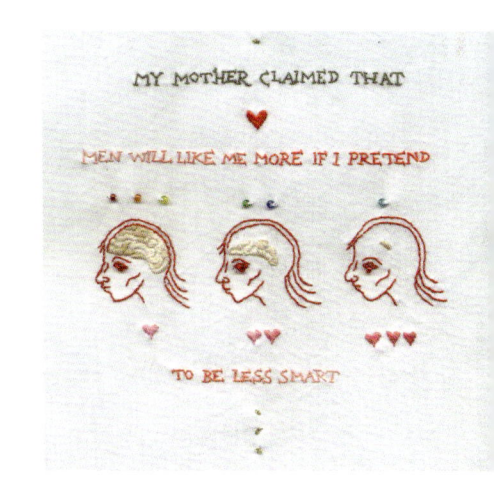

Andrea Dezsö
'Lessons From My Mother' series: *Men Will Like Me More*, 2006. Cotton and metallic floss embroidery on cotton fabric. 13 x 13 cm (5 x 5 in.). Number of pieces in series: 50. Photo: Andrea Dezsö.

HAND STITCH: PERSPECTIVES

Homenaje a los caídos (Homage to the Fallen Ones), Chilean arperilla, late 1970s. Maker unknown. Hand-stitched appliqué using different weights of fabric scraps. Approx. 45 x 36 cm (18 x 14 in.). Courtesy of Fátima Miralles, Spain, with thanks to Roberta Bacic. Photo: Colin Peck. The Arpillera has been made using an appliqué technique using a wide variety of fabric/scrap material of different weights, types and colours. These fabrics are attached onto a cotton background, using a herringbone stitch. Details such as faces, hair and more, are added with embroidery using woollen yarn. It is lined with cotton and finished around the edge with blanket stitch in red wool and finally a round crochet, also in red. Black dominates the foreground.

In the background, poor villagers tap into the mains power supply because they cannot afford to pay. The road is lined with candles in remembrance of the disappeared. The central figure carries leaflets protesting against torture. Some women lie in the road. In all, the arpillera gives voice to the sorrow and loss felt by so many.

Chilean arpilleras are small, brightly coloured appliquéd panels stitched by Chilean women during Pinochet's oppressive military dictatorship in Chile. During Pinochet's regime, thousands of people were imprisoned without trial and tortured, and many disappeared without trace. Most, though not all, were men, leaving families with no means of support. Chilean resistance to the dictatorship took many forms. Mothers, wives and daughters of the disappeared came together in groups and stitched testimonies of what was happening in Chile; this enabled them to meet with other women and share information, and since these arpilleras were sent out of the country (through charities) and sold, the women received an income. It also provided a way of disseminating information about what was happening in Chile, spreading the women's demands for truth and justice. Arpilleras were originally made as a weapon of resistance; they continue to be made as an act of remembrance.[6]

Projects such as the *Aids Memorial Quilt* and Chilean arpilleras provide a public forum for individuals to make their concerns known. The time-consuming, repetitive nature of embroidery can provide a meditative, therapeutic space; the stitching can become a part of the grieving process.

CRAFTIVISM

The *Aids Memorial Quilt* and the Chilean arpilleras can be seen as early examples of an activity now known as 'craftivism', which is where craft and activism are combined. The strategies of craftivism are used to address a range of issues; however, several key themes do emerge: there are concerns around environmentalism and sustainability; globalisation of clothing production and sweated labour; and war and violence. Craftivist activities take many forms. For example, to protest against the war in Iraq, Marianne Jorgensen created a vast pink knitted 'tank cosy' from thousands of pink squares created by knitters from around the world.

The term 'craftivism' was coined by Betsy Greer who, to demonstrate her opposition to the United States' involvement in wars in Iraq and Afghanistan, started making cross-stitch pieces based on anti-war graffiti from different parts of the globe. She states:

I decided to cross-stitch them for two different reasons: (1) to put 'dangerous' graffiti in a 'safe' context, [and] (2) to further elucidate that while their countries may fight, there are many citizens who remain opposed to war.[7]

Betsy Greer defines craftivism as:

the practice of engaged creativity, especially regarding political or social causes. By using their creative energy to help make the world a better place, craftivists help bring about positive change via personalised activism. Craftivism allows practitioners to customise their particular skills to address particular causes.[8]

For a project in the autumn of 2011, to highlight the vast discrepancy between the wages of models at London Fashion Week and the wages of garment workers in Vietnam, members of the UK-based Craftivist Collective created 'mini protest banners' and sited them in appropriate public spaces near to where the shows were being held. The manifesto of the Craftivist Collective is 'To expose the scandal of global poverty and human rights injustices through the power of craft and public art. This will be done through provocative, non-violent creative actions.'[9]

The whole area around crafts and activism is a vast and complex field. Key issues are comprehensively discussed in Kirsty Robertson's chapter 'Rebellious Doilies and Subversive Stitches' in Buszek (2011).[10]

ARTHUR+MARTHA

The term 'craftivism' could be applied to some aspects of the experimental arts organisation arthur+martha, run by artist Lois Blackburn and poet Philip Davenport. Based in north-west England, they help 'marginalised people to discover their creative voice, through eye-catching, engaging artworks with positive social outcomes. We push at boundaries of poetry and art, collaborating with people at the edges of society to create intricate patchworks of memory, humour, playfulness and sadness'.[11]

They have worked with elderly patients in hospital, excluded schoolchildren, young carers and the homeless, amongst others. They are mostly concerned with allowing people who often aren't heard in our society to be heard, and in the process create artefacts and poetry that are often poignant and thought-provoking. For the participants, the actual doing is as important as the physical outcomes in terms of raising self-esteem and creating avenues for social interaction. By exhibiting the

HAND STITCH: PERSPECTIVES

arthur+martha
Tea party at Four Acre, St Helens, 2011. Photo: Lois Blackburn. Wherever possible, Lois shares her extensive textile skills as part of the workshops: in 'Art of the Unexpected' she encouraged older people to explore creative ways to share memories – icing them on to cakes, stitching them into tablecloths and writing them on ceramics.

results, attention is given to some of the under-represented groups and issues in our society.[12]

Lois and Phil work in tandem with a range of strategies to draw out thoughts and feelings. By working with people over a number of weeks, or even months, the participants get to know and trust Lois and Phil. A long-term project with hospital patients, staff and visitors resulted in the creation of *Patience: An Insider's Guide to Surviving Ill-Health*, a gentle, but powerful reminder that all individuals can contribute creatively.[13] 'Patience' shows the positive impact that art can have on health, and shows how, even within challenging situations, art can engender humour and joy.

The aim of the 'Art of the Unexpected' project in St Helens was to encourage older people to explore creative ways to share memories:

We have been inviting older people in the community to make a mix of poetry and art, celebrating their lives and visions. We're trying to reach those who might not normally join in with art activities, by taking our workshops to the local bingo night, housebound people's homes, the doctor's surgery, Tesco's, a day centre for people diagnosed with dementia, a local library … The pieces layer together the everyday poetry of conversation and the act of memory: childhood nostalgia, saucy postcards, teatime gentility, skipping songs ('All in, a bottle of gin …'), oral history, humour, anger, celebration, commemoration. The teacloths, tea cosies, tablecloths, napkins and ceramics are a coming together of many individuals. They mark a shared past, not only that of people in Four Acre, but of working people across a whole century in all their tragedies and triumphs.[14]

DEIRDRE NELSON

Humour also plays a key part in Deirdre Nelson's work. Deirdre uses her textile practice to highlight little-known areas of social history, frequently informed by museum collections or the history of a specific place. Deirdre frequently works with groups of local people, enabling them to inform the work she creates, and sometimes participate in the making process.

Extensive research around her subject matter is crucial for Deirdre's practice: for *The Dangers of Sewing and Knitting*, Deirdre trawled through museum archives and interviewed textile workers; the resulting exhibition presented 20 'dangerous' facts connected with the history of textile-making.

> *Alongside the humorous dangers are more sinister ones: Thimbleknocking, a pair of Victorian bloomers with numerous thimbles stitched around the waist, is a reminder that many needlewomen turned to prostitution to augment their incomes. A knitted shoe refers to the life of a 90-year-old Shetland knitter, who having bartered a year's worth of knitting for a wedding outfit, could not find any shoes to wear. While acknowledging that textile work which addresses social issues invites feminist critique and perhaps an assumption that this is her point, Nelson says, 'My work is not intended to be overtly feminist. But when you do this kind of work it's always there in the history. For me it is the positive side, the humorous side that appeals.'*[15]

Four key themes emerge in Deirdre's work: a profound interest in social history, engagement with the public, a fascination with hand work, and a playful, subtle approach to humour.

Deirdre Nelson
Contentment, 2011. Silk on ribbon. Photo: Alison Marr. For the project 'wordbespoke', after a period as artist in residence at the Wigtown Book Festival, Deirdre gathered favourite words from festival-goers and curated a collection of 30 words, hand-embroidered them on to ribbons, and then sold the ribbons through a charity auction on eBay to raise funds for Ganet's Adventure School in Malawi.

LYNN SETTERINGTON

Lynn has also created a significant body of work with community groups discussed on pages 59–62. This chapter focuses on her individual outputs. She is well known for her hand-stitched quilts, which she has been making since 1988:

> *Quilts produced predominantly over the last 15 years possess a strong autobiographical content, which refers to the changing domestic, economic and social position of women within contemporary society in the West. These concerns are juxtaposed with a constant celebration of the ordinary; of the skills and activities which cannot be replaced by technology and gadgetry.*[16]

More recent work has utilised different processes, moving away from the traditional quilt format in terms of materials, but still exploring the concerns of everyday life. One body of work has utilised plastic bags to comment on consumerism; another uses safety pins to explore home and identity. A theme that can be seen to run through all of Lynn's work is a desire to highlight the overlooked, whether that is the familiar domestic object of daily life, such as washing ephemera and DIY tools, or the experiences of people who are often denied a voice, such as refugees, or people with learning disabilities.

In 1988, an exhibition took place in the Whitechapel art gallery in London called 'Woven Air', and it had a profound effect on Lynn. This exhibition displayed textiles, known as kanthas, made by Bengali women. These textiles were made from pieces of old saris patched together, stitched over their entire surface with figurative designs. Kanthas were originally made only by women, as gifts for special occasions. The images depicted were 'a harmonious composition of a host of heterogeneous objects like the comb, mirror, candelabra, nutcracker, umbrella, pitcher and other items of everyday use'.[17] The kantha format and technique suggested a way that Lynn could produce something that was both decorative and thought-provoking, providing an appropriate vehicle for her ideas. The subject matter depicted on the kanthas spoke directly to Lynn: she could identify with the fact that the makers of the kanthas had 'stitched their lives into their work'.[18]

Soon after visiting 'Woven Air', Lynn made her first piece using the kantha technique of stitching layers of fabrics together with running stitch, *In the Kitchen*. Since then, she has developed the technique further, making a vast number of large- and small-scale pieces, incorporating techniques from North Country and Welsh quilts.[19] Within this body of work the technique of making and the subject matter are fused into an integral whole – the way the work is constructed, as well as the selection of images depicted, play a part in communicating an idea. There is humour and irony in Lynn's work. The last large-scale hand-stitched quilt she made was *Mums Are Heroes* in 2005, depicting carrier bags from nine supermarkets. This piece is about consumerism, the power of supermarkets, the ubiquity of the plastic bag and the role of women.

Lynn Setterington
(*opposite*) *Mums Are Heroes*, 2005. Hand stitch on cotton. 170 x 135 cm (67 x 53 in.). Photo: Stephen Yates. This piece represents the transition to a new way of working for Lynn: the concerns explored in *Mums Are Heroes* became both the subject matter and the vehicle for a subsequent body of work.

Safeway
www.safeway.co.uk
Somerfield
Raising money to
TESCO
MORRISONS
More reasons to shop at Morrisons
PLEASE RE-USE THIS BAG AND HELP TO PROTECT THE ENVIRONMENT
Iceland
...because Mums are heroes!
Quality Foods
CO OP
The Community Retailer
www.coop.co.uk
Customer Careline 0845 7000100
are you standing next to one?
our mystery shoppers ensure you're getting the best...
Sainsbury's
making life taste better
ASDA Price
Always LOW PRICES
www.asda.com
KWIK SAVE
100% Degradable
www.kwiksave.co.uk

Lynn Setterington
Been Shopping, 2005. Suffolk puffs made from plastic bags. 122 x 108 cm (48 x 42 in.). Photo: Stephen Yates.

A change of direction

Lynn had become particularly known for her stitched quilts, but by the mid-2000s she was beginning to feel that the kantha technique was no longer appropriate: 'People saw the technique and not what it was about … working by hand was also very time-consuming and slow, and there were things I wanted to say that I wasn't able to voice with that particular technique.'[20]

In the early 2000s, Lynn ran an allotment arts class for adults with learning disabilities. Due to lack of funds for buying materials and a growing awareness of environmental issues, the group started using plastic bags as a material. This in turn led to creating 'Suffolk puffs' from the bags. Lynn then went on to create a series of quilts using this technique: *Been Shopping* is one example, made up from bags amassed as a result of personal shopping trips. She comments, 'In common with early quilt-makers, if you unpicked the quilt, you could tell something of the background and social class of the maker by the "fabrics" employed.'[21]

Lynn's newest projects, both personal and collaborative, focus on identity and the use of signatures, again highlighting an aspect of the overlooked and familiar in all our lives.

CAREN GARFEN

Caren translates her interests in gender politics and women's issues into witty, beautifully executed artworks. Her subject matter is the role of women in the twenty-first century. She works around specific themes, such as women and housework or women and dieting, researching a subject methodically before embarking on meticulous, carefully considered finished pieces that provide a humorous critique of contemporary society.

The work usually consists of screen-printed images, with tiny details or accompanying labels exquisitely embroidered with minute stitches. Humour is injected with Caren's clever juxtapositioning of sayings and homilies with everyday objects – but a consideration of serious issues underlies the humour.

The form of the finished artwork is appropriate to the subject matter, which emphasises the ideas behind each artwork. *Womanual – All Done and Dusted* is a ridiculously long tea towel dealing with women and housework. Caren originally intended that the piece was to be displayed folded, so that the viewer could not see all of the work that had been done inside, to mirror the unseen, never-ending and unappreciated ritual of housework.

The research that Caren does before embarking on a piece of work is extensive, and key to the outcome. Before commencing *How Many Times Do I Have to Repeat Myself*, a quilt commissioned by the Victoria and Albert Museum for their landmark exhibition 'Quilts 1700–2010', Caren compiled a vast body of material comprising questionnaires, archive research and interviews. For Caren, 'The practice is the embodiment of the research'.[22]

Caren is particularly concerned with the way that messages are propagated through the media either overtly or subliminally. Reflecting on the media

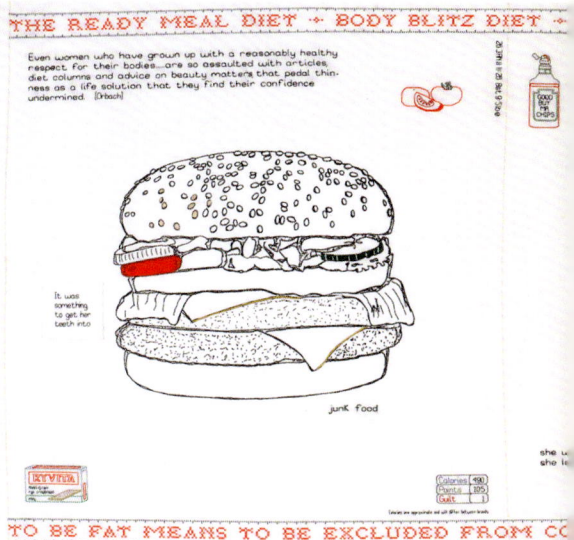

EMBROIDERY AND THE F-WORD

Caren Garfen
(left and detail above) MAIN COURSE –
Wafer Thin, 2012. Cotton, silk threads,
SF20 binder, pigments, kitchen towel
holder. 10 m x 31 cm (394 x 12 in.).
Photo: Sussie Ahlburg. A study on the
role of fat.

manipulation of women's views of their bodies, Caren decided to make a triptych reflecting the prevalence of dieting solutions to help women to achieve 'that perfect figure': Part I, *STARTER – Don't Make a Meal of It*; Part II, *MAIN COURSE – Wafer Thin, A Study of the Role of Fat*; and Part III, *DESSERT – She Had Her Cake and She Ate It*.

'Wafer Thin' takes the form of a 'kitchen paper towel roll', made up of 40 sections on a continuous ground of white cotton. The concept behind the 'paper towel roll' was that the roll starts out 'fat', but gets progressively thinner as it is unrolled. 'Wafer Thin' is a complex work; each sheet carries multiple components

127

Caren Garfen
Cleaner –Wait Until the Dust Settles, 2010 (detail). Silkscreen printing and hand stitch. 16 x 16 cm (6½ x 6½ in.). Photo: Caren Garfen.

informed by Caren's extensive primary and secondary research. Each 'sheet' carries an image of food, starting with the most calorific, the 'double burger', and works through ice creams, cakes and chocolates, to fresh fruits, diet products and, finally, diet pills.

The upper border has an exhaustive list of different diets taken from four women's weekly magazines over the course of one year,[23] including 'the ready meal diet, the body blitz diet, the age-defying diet, the chocolate diet, the beat the bloat diet'. The lower border has text taken from *Fat Is a Feminist Issue* (1978) by Susie Orbach.

The relationship between time and hand stitch is an integral component of this piece; although she loves hand-stitching, Caren did find that having to embroider all along the ten-metre border (twice) was slightly tedious – she described it as being like trying to get to the end of a never-ending diet.[24]

I'll leave the last word to Caren. When interviewed about her work for *Design Week*, she was asked, 'How did (you) think of making a silk organza teabag and stitching it with gender humour?' 'I embroider the truth', she replied'.[25]

Tracey Emin
To Meet My Past, 2003. Multimedia installation: bed, blankets, sheets. Approx. 300 x 170 x 215 cm (118 x 67 x 85 in.). © Tracey Emin. All rights reserved, DACS 2011. Collection of the Saatchi Gallery. Courtesy of White Cube Gallery. As well as being notorious for using all aspects of her life as the source material for her art, Tracey is well known for her appliquéd blankets; the Tate Gallery in London owns 19 of her artworks, only one is a stitched textile.

CONCLUSION

So, what is the position of feminism and embroidery today – remembering that 'There never was a Feminism; there were only feminisms'?[26] Things have moved on in the last 30 or so years; textile mediums and craft practices have become much more integrated into the mainstream art world. Textiles are increasingly employed by male and female artists. Grayson Perry, Michael Raedecker and Tracey Emin are all Turner prizewinners or nominees whose work utilises so-called craft processes such as pottery and stitch. However, it should be noted that they all undertook degrees in fine art rather than textiles or other craft areas.

Female artists are more firmly in the fold today: the Venice Biennale in 2005 was headed by two female directors, and an unprecedented number of women artists were included.

> *Reviewing women's participation in the 2005 Venice Biennale, Linda Nochlin concluded that, 'What I find particularly admirable about the wide array of women's art at this year's Biennale is not only the high quality of much of it, but the fact that I cannot make any striking generalisations about it.'*[27]

To some critics, feminism is the most significant art movement of the twentieth century, and they consider that it permeates almost all art practice today:

One thing is certain: feminist art, which emerged in the 1960s with the women's movement, is the formative art of the last four decades. Scan the most innovative work, by both men and women, done during that time, and you'll find feminism's activist, expansionist, pluralistic trace. Without it identity-based art, crafts-derived art, performance art and much political art would not exist in the form it does, if it existed at all. Much of what we call postmodern art has feminist art at its source. [28]

Blake Gopnik stated that feminist art is 'The most important artistic movement since World War II' in his review of 'Wack! Art and the Feminist Revolution', and cited other critcs who hold similar views:

Feminist creativity has brought about 'the most far-reaching transformations in both artmaking and art writing over the past four decades,' says Stanford scholar Peggy Phelan.

Feminist art of the 1970s was 'the most influential international movement of any during the postwar period,' declares Jeremy Strick, director of the Museum of Contemporary Art in Los Angeles.

It helped make possible 'the very terms of current artistic practice,' says Cornelia Butler, chief curator of drawings at the Museum of Modern Art.

The best American artists of the last 30 years 'are as interesting as they are in part because of the feminist art movement of the early 1970s. It changed everything,' writes New York Times *art critic Holland Cotter.*[29]

So, is the situation better for current female artists, and do they have the same opportunities as male artists? Are they equally represented in galleries and museums? Judy Chicago's view is that the art establishment is still male dominated.

A double standard continues to exist ... the way in which the art world is controlled is through permanent collections and solo publications on artists. It continues to be the case in major museums around the world that permanent collections are only about 3–5% women. In terms of publications in the 1970s, 1.7% of art books were focused on single women artists ... 40 years later and the percentage is 2.5. When I was doing The Dinner Party *I thought that... I was going to overcome the erasure of women's achievements ... What I've now understood is that we are still in the cycle of erasure.*[30]

Sue Prichard contends that women artists, and 'by extension any practice connected with the feminine' continue to suffer from marginalisation.

Women artists who choose to work with fabric and stitch often find themselves marginalised in the fine art arena ... Despite the diversity of approaches to contemporary practice, however, many women who work with fabric and stitch continue to face obstacles when seeking to exhibit their work.[31]

Labelling work 'feminist' can be problematic. Feminism is still seen as a controversial word, possibly the kiss of death to some people: 'Big museums have treated art by women, whether expressly feminist or not, as box-office poison. On the market, feminism is a label to be avoided.'[32] I invited a friend to the Whitworth Art Gallery in Manchester to see a Mary Kelly retrospective. He asked what it was about – and no sooner had the word 'feminist' left my lips than he declined the invitation.

But feminism is not a style, or a formal approach. It is a philosophy, an attitude and a political instrument. It is more important than Pop, Minimalism or Conceptual art because it is by its very nature bigger than they are, more far-reaching and life-affecting.[33]

NOTES

[1] Rosenberg, Karen, 'Needling More Than the Feminist Consciousness', *New York Times*, 28 December 2008.

[2] Parker, Roszika, *The Subversive Stitch: Embroidery and the Making of the Feminine*, first published by the Women's Press in 1984; new edition published by I. B. Tauris, London, 2010.

[3] Nochlin, Linda, 'Why Have There Been No Great Women Artists?', first published in *Art News* Vol. 69 January 1971; reprinted in Nochlin, Linda, *Women, Art, and Power and Other Essays* (London: Thames and Hudson, 1989).

[4] Elizabeth A. Sackler, Center for Feminist Art, online digital archive. See http://www.brooklynmuseum.org/eascfa/feminist_art_base/gallery/elaine_reichek.php/. Accessed 12 September 2011.

[5] Elizabeth A. Sackler Center for Feminist Art, online digital archive. See http://www.brooklynmuseum.org/eascfa/feminist_art_base/gallery/orlycogan.php. Accessed 20 September 2011.

[6] Further information about Chilean arpilleras can be found in Brett, Guy, *Through Our Own Eyes* (London: GMP Publisher Ltd, 1986), and the website http://cain.ulst.ac.uk/quilts/exhibit/chilean_arpilleras.html.

[7] Betsy Greer's website is http://craftivism.com/.

[8] Ibid.

[9] See http://craftivist-collective.com/about/.

[10] Robertson, Kirsty 'Rebellious Doilies and Subversive Stitches' in Buszek, Maria Elena, *Extra/ordinary Craft* (Durham and London: Duke University Press, 2011).

[11] For arthur+martha blog, see http://arthur-and-martha.blogspot.com/.

[12] More information can be found on arthur+martha's extensive and eloquent website: www.arthur-and-martha.co.uk/.

[13] *Patience: An Insider's Guide to Surviving Ill-Health*, by arthur+martha CIC, 2010.

[14] arthur+martha blog, op. cit.

[15] 'Deirdre Nelson' by Penny Jones, a-n.co.uk, June 2008. See http://www.a-n.co.uk/artists_talking/artists_stories/single/429714/.

[16] See www.62group.org.uk/artist/lynn-setterington/.

[17] Chattopadhyay, Kamaledevi, *Indian Embroidery* (New Delhi: Wiley Eastern, 1977).

[18] Interview with Lynn Setterington, October 1994.

[19] A number of these quilts were exhibited at Oldham Art Gallery in a one-person exhibition, 'Out of the Ordinary', in 1994.

[20] Interview with Lynn Setterington, 11 July 2011.

[21] Ibid.

[22] Interview with Caren Garfen, 1 July 2011.

[23] *Best*, *Bella*, *Woman* and *Woman's Own*, 2010–11.

[24] Interview with Caren Garfen, 1 July 2011.

[25] See http://www.designweek.co.uk/. Published 17 July 2008.

[26] Cotter, Holland, 'The Art of Feminism As It First Took Shape'; review of 'Wack! Art and the Feminist Revolution', *New York Times*, 9 March 2007. See http://www.nytimes.com/2007/03/09/arts/design/09wack.html?pagewanted=all.

[27] Chadwick, Witney, *Women, Art and Society*, 4th edition (London: Thames and Hudson, 2007).

[28] Cotter, Holland, 'The Art of Feminism As It First Took Shape'; review of 'Wack! Art and the Feminist Revolution', *New York Times*, 9 March 2007. See http://www.nytimes.com/2007/03/09/arts/design/09wack.html?pagewanted=all.

[29] Gopnik, Blake, 'What is Feminist Art?' *Washington Post*, 22 April 2007.

[30] Judy Chicago on *Woman's Hour*, BBC Radio 4, with Jenni Murray, 17 June 2011.

[31] Prichard, Sue, *Quilts 1700–2010: Hidden Histories, Untold Stories* (London: Victoria and Albert Publishing, 2010).

[32] Cotter, op. cit.

[33] Smith, Roberta, 'They Are Artists Who Are Women; Hear Them Roar', review of *Global Feminism*, *New York Times*, 23 March 2007. See http://www.nytimes.com/2007/03/23/arts/design/23glob.html?pagewanted=1.

JAMES HUNTING

The Professional Embroiderer?

THIS CHAPTER IS A REFLECTION ON THE IDENTITY OF a professional embroiderer, his role, his knowledge and his current and future working patterns. It is written as my own opinion and not as the definitive and sole function/persona of the professional embroiderer. The particular emphasis of the chapter will be on the use of embroidery within the fashion arena; as a skill, it needs to be far more comprehensive than simply an ability to technically make work to a high standard.

Within this chapter, the term 'hand' is used to describe any work not produced on a machine, free-arm or otherwise. I use the term 'professional embroiderer' to refer to an artisan who is able to use his or her skill and knowledge of hand-embroidery techniques in order to produce work for a third party or commissioning client. Within this second definition, there is a distinction to be made, since there remain a few embroiderers who are wedded to technical skill. They are experts in their field but they do not involve themselves in any of the design process. They may be from the older generation of embroiderer and have worked as employees of embroidery or couture houses. For such artisans, the work may not be to their taste, but this is not a question that they pose, since their job is to execute the work professionally within any given time constraints and to any budget.

The embroiderers of today are more often artisans who can apply their knowledge to resolve ideas and design concepts, innovate with materials and techniques in order to remain economically viable, and display an individual approach to their skills that can integrate and complement the aesthetic considerations of their clients.

The term 'embroidery' is generally synonymous with the act of using needle and thread on a cloth base. The term, however, is now open to a multitude of activities that include beading, the addition of sequins, and all embellishments to an article of clothing which lie outside other specific disciplines such as knit, weave or print. Economically, within the reality of the current fashion world, it is rare to produce any hand-stitched work other than samples (which will be translated into mechanical outcomes, and the wedding market, which I will discuss later).

I am not including here designer-makers who sell their own products or artworks. They may be professional but do not fall within the focus of this chapter, which is the application of skill in the artisan world.

My own professional identity lies where skill is mixed with a strong design element and an awareness and knowledge of the wider context, history and potential of embroidery, together with an ability to look beyond the technical precedents and constraints of tradition.

James Hunting
Sample, 2000. Stranded cotton embroidery on silk tulle. Photo: James Hunting. I produced a range of wedding veils for a client. I used soft-coloured cottons rather than the traditional cream. They are stitched with two strands of cream cotton and one other colour, which runs through. This is an aspect of stranded cotton: you can blend colours through mixing strands.

The profession of embroiderer is under threat in the UK. We have to recognise that we cannot compete with the market leaders in the making of hand embroidery. Freelance embroiderers in the UK have a set of fixed charges and expenses that specify a higher hourly rate of pay, and given the time-intensive manner of hand embroidery, we cannot be as cheap as the current market leaders, China and India.

The haute couture tradition of hand embroidery in France could be said to be superior. The French have a proactive approach to the retention of traditional craft, of artisanship and of regional knowledge, which means that embroidery continues to maintain its status as a serious profession. In France, training is financially supported by both the Ministry of Culture and the Ministry of Education, since embroidery is identified as a national skill. They train people to work with the couture world to a very high level of technical speed and finish; however, I have observed that the one thing that appears to be absent in their training is the achievement of a personal, individual, artistic approach. The cultural rules in France are so well established that although lip service is paid to the idea of the individual the individualists seem to be frowned upon.

My own particular area, whilst working in the couture houses in Paris, was finished or nearly finished dresses, so I would often be contacted late in the collection to produce work. This would mean working in the main studio of the couture house, unlike the French embroiderers, who stitched on framed-up work in the studios of the embroidery companies, the dresses being delivered for fitting. The work was focused and time was of an essence: there is no way you can be late for a catwalk. Often, dresses were finished just before the show, and by the word 'just', I mean five minutes beforehand.

Work was often interrupted by fittings and design developments, which could alter the work and outcome. These changes had to be absorbed and reacted to – this too is the reason that an embroiderer has to be able to apply knowledge and skills in order to achieve; designers are not interested in 'how', just 'when'. The greatest advantage was to work in the proximity of the '*petites mains*', the artisans of the ateliers who have an incredible skill base, can fit a garment by eye, and can produce exquisitely made and resolved pieces quietly and efficiently, the storm of the creative team passing over their heads. Fabric and couture techniques demand their own respect. I was more interested in gaining the respect of the *petites mains* than the designer himself or herself: for me, the ultimate in a good job is the respect of other artisans and experts in their field.

One of our skills in the UK is our ability to innovate, to take ownership of techniques and skills, to rework and approach them in a different way. This is a vital and essential part of our economic viability that should be celebrated (look at the 'Cool Britannia' label and how much cultural and creative activities bring into the UK). The embroidery world needs innovation, it needs to constantly build on tradition, rather than simply reworking seventeenth-, eighteenth- or nineteenth-century models in order to preserve the skills. I believe that we need to continue to acquire technical knowledge and to understand the *mechanics* and *gesture* of

James Hunting
Samples, 2010. Silk thread, hand-stitched on to silk duchesse satin. Photo: James Hunting. The brief these samples were made for was to change the texture of the silk duchesse and lose the join between the fabrics. The client had a very strong image of her look and needed the fabric to look less wedding-like and pristine. I had been looking at self-coloured embroidery and was interested in the geometric look, an extension of seeding stitch worked on the surface.

HAND STITCH: PERSPECTIVES

James Hunting
(*left*) Sample, 2004. Photo: James Hunting. A sample for couture. A traditional turkey knot stitch using silk thread, destroyed and teased into fluff, on a silk organza background.

(*right*) Sample, 2004. Oversized shisha, silver and gold threads, silk organza. Photo: James Hunting. A sample for Givenchy (though never used for a garment), where I played with the scale of shisha mirrors. Couture allows you to explore techniques and materials which may not be viable on more commercial and smaller budgets.

the stitch rather than focusing on the outcome. Whilst we work, we should have knowledge of historical context and concentrate on each stitched mark, and then work out what it is that we want our outcomes to be. The challenge lies in trying to find the balance of technical learning, technical exploration and ownership.

I originally trained at Goldsmiths College, London; although it was titled a degree in embroidery, little embroidery was produced. The work that was made had integrity and rigour, which were based on textile traditions. We were encouraged by the tutors, many of whom had learnt in a skill-based curriculum, to remain open-minded in technique and approach. My training at college consisted of a month-long introduction to hand embroidery, working on frames, investigating stitch, exploring the potential once the mechanics had been absorbed and the gestures had become automatic.

I can reproduce hundreds of stitches now, and in discussing this time with a freelance embroiderer colleague who also attended the same course, we agree that our careers have been based on five stitches: stem stitch, couching, the French knot, blanket stitch and the generic stitch of entry and exit of a needle through cloth. I also developed techniques with beading, sequins, and various other materials.

THE COMMISSIONING OF EMBROIDERY

Commissioning designers and clients are not necessarily interested in the techniques you may use, or concerned that you should adhere to a prescribed set of traditional rules. They wish to see how your knowledge can be applied to their work and meet their requirements. In discussion with Jenny Lessin, a bespoke wedding dress designer in London with whom I work on regular basis, we identified specific stages of the embroiderer's role in approaching a job, which I shall now describe.

THE PROFESSIONAL EMBROIDERER?

In her role as designer, Jenny first introduces the idea of embellishment to the client through discussion and the display of a selection of samples, which both Jenny and I have developed. This sampling process is the backbone of the embroidery profession. Unlike the perception of samples held by students (that they are stages towards an outcome), samples for the fashion world are their own outcome.

Twice a year, I prepare a minimum of 20 samples. Jenny and I discuss ideas about the dresses: the fabrics they will be made from, the silhouette and shape they will have, whether they will have trains or veils, and in which films, books, exhibitions, or events we can find examples and illustrations. This knowledge will then be used to create a palette – a selection of fabrics, threads and materials. I will then work with a variety of embroidery techniques, referencing historical periods or different cultures, and produce a collection of samples.

These samples are rarely used as they are. Once the client has agreed to the use of embroidery, I meet with Jenny to discuss the dress, fabric, budgets and deadlines. This enables me to refine samples, discard any that are not relevant to the aesthetic of the dress, and undertake any research or ideas that may have been identified, for example cultural inheritance, physical requirement or client stipulation.

I then meet with the client and Jenny to discuss ideas, which leads to a further specific sample worked on the dress fabric. An agreement to proceed is reached. The importance of the sample can be seen by this process, as the client needs to know what she is going to receive, and the designer needs to know how any embroidery could alter a drape or hang, and when to allocate time for the embroidery – before cutting or after making and construction. The sample acts as a record, together with the budget and deadline, for the embroiderer. The wedding market is one of the remaining areas where the professional embroiderer may work with a budget that will allow a more elaborate and creatively satisfying outcome.

James Hunting
(*left and right*) Samples, 2000; reworked 2010. Photo: James Hunting. I used a cheap background fabric, such as cotton muslin, which was embroidered using silver threads and hand embroidery. It was inspired by India and was later reused as a sample for a client who wanted to draw on her Indian heritage, but with the use of silk satin as the base cloth. Samples are often revisited and reworked.

James Hunting
Samples, 2010. Photo: James Hunting. A collection of samples to fit the following brief: a grey chiffon dress with delicate, flowery, modern embroidery. I explored the three-dimensionality of appliquéd flowers and tested machine-made outlines, handmade outlines and beading. The machine stitch made the flowers too stiff, so the chiffon was washed to make it softer.

Within the more commercial world, the samples play an even more important role. In a similar way, a range of samples is produced for a designer to select those he or she wishes to see developed using their own brief; the ones for use are then selected. At this point, it is always a consideration to produce specific samples on the designer's own fabric, in order to jointly establish the outcomes. I have worked with clients who have counted the sequins within a 50 cm square and then calculated how many of such squares are in a dress, in order to establish the number of sequins that will be sewn on a dress and the cost of such a piece. The dresses have been subjected to spot checks to ensure that they conform. Although this may seem extreme, in a business where the mark-up of individual elements can result in a tenfold increase on the initial cost price of embroidery, it is vital that specifics are imposed on what can be a very vague art. Descriptions such as 'sprinkling', 'sprigging', 'beaded', and 'dotting' need to be quantified to avoid a mismatch of expectations.

Jenny is often approached by embroiderers who wish to work with her. She explains that she wants to see how potential embroiderers are able to 'clue into the aesthetic that I am working within' and show how they can 'bring their own design ideas and knowledge of technique into my style'. She is not overly interested in their technical prowess, or the possible hidden message or statement their work may have or make, or their range of techniques. Jenny, as the commissioning designer, needs people who can say: 'These are the skills I have, this is what I do and this is what I can bring to your work.' It is about the individual's ability to connect with Jenny's sense of design to create work.

There is a developing market for hand-embroiderers who sample for mechanical output. Computer-aided machines can produce most types and techniques of embroidery, and there is a plethora of companies that offer their services. With the virtual world and ease of travel, there is little obstruction to a 24-hour turnaround. What is often lacking within these companies, however, is the specific knowledge, skill and understanding of embroidery that a professional can bring. A technical tambour beader will need a design created by somebody who understands beading, design and working to a brief in order to use their skills well, and those designing for the machines need to be directed by a similar understanding.

It is at this level that the definition of an embroiderer and his or her role becomes more crucial. It is often confusingly used as a cover-all term that can equally be applied to those with a more generic training. I believe that there will always be a need for skill-based knowledge and an understanding of historical precedent, which is not to be mistaken for a backward-looking approach but more of a solid foundation.

In France, the terms are clearer, with a distinction between those artisans who use *la broderie à la main* (hand embroidery), *la broderie de luneville* (tambour work), *plumassier* (feather work) and *la broderie d'art* (art using embroidery). France has a great respect for the traditions, which has resulted in the continuing status of the embroiderer. France does not, however, have a tradition of recognised embroiderers: they have celebrated companies, but not individuals.

THE PROFESSIONAL EMBROIDERER?

James Hunting
The Gardener (formerly *Charlie 3*), 2006. Linen cloth, cotton and rayon thread, hand embroidery. Photo: James Hunting. A hand-embroidered piece worked at a time when I was working in a nursery garden. I was moving away from the fashion world.

It is important to consider the term 'embroiderer'. There is a weight of history within the label, providing a tacit understanding. Were I to use the term 'surface designer' or 'textile adorner', most people might not understand me. If you say you are a textile artist, that can put off potential clients from a fear that you will bring too much of your own message to their work. However, the disappearance of the term 'embroiderer' would be a shame, and the loss of the profession of embroiderer would be inexcusable. So it is important that the teaching of embroidery continues to be of high quality, with an emphasis on skills. Interestingly, it seems to be accepted that printers and weavers learn the technicalities of their specialism, but embroiderers seem to be expected to work it out, leading to an impoverished knowledge and understanding of context. This will in turn affect potential development in the continuum of an embroidery tradition.

As teaching concentrates more and more on self-discovery and self-instruction, without providing the building blocks on which students can underpin their own language and personal development, professional embroidery will be hard to maintain. It is vital that students are offered the skills and knowledge that link the rich past of embroidery to the future, but it is also not a dark outlook. If skills and techniques disappear, they will rediscovered and reworked in the future by the enterprising and enquiring student, drawing on collections and historical artefacts. Embroidery, like everything, will move onwards.

It is encouraging that there is a significant and growing interest in pursuing a career in hand embroidery and away from immediate and disposable fashion. Embroidery will evolve and develop in the hands of the students of today. They will stamp their individuality on it and ensure that their work becomes the innovation of tomorrow.

Making: the voices, memories and echoes

IAN WILSON

The Enduring Trinity of Fingers, Thread and Needle

IN A WOODEN CHEST THAT HAD HELD MY GRANDMOTHER'S vast Edwardian hats when she sailed out with her Irish husband to the then-German colony of Deutsch-Südwestafrika (present-day Namibia), I found – among velvet tablecloths, several ponderous 'Collected Works' of minor Victorian writers and the remnants of a once immense dinner service – three books belonging to my mother, who had died when I was a child.

Two members of this salvaged trio were suede-bound volumes of poetry and the third was an *Encyclopedia of Needlework* (first published c.1890s) by Thérèse de Dillmont, the gilded upper edges of the pages in softly gleaming contrast to the sombre khaki of the covers and spine, which are sparsely decorated with rather elegantly drooping laurel leaves in black outline. Despite having read English literature at university, as well as being wholly unable to thread a needle without the aid of that obliging little metallic device which is so indispensable to the clumsy, it was the manual of sewing that intrigued me far more than did the 'Selections' from Keats and Shelley.

While researching and writing an essay about this handbook which, in the original French, was entitled *Encyclopédie des Ouvrages de Dames*, I asked many people about their reminiscences concerning sewing. Sadly, but possibly predictably, the men who were questioned generally proved a less fruitful source of anecdotes than the women. This was not the case with Matthew Harris, whose constructed cloths are clear evidence of Constance Howard's hand-stitching workshops, which he attended as a first-year student at Goldsmiths College of Art, London. The stories thus collected were far too numerous to include in the article in its original form, but way too enthralling to go unrecorded. This is a small selection from the rich hoard and they serve to introduce not only the de Dillmont book, but also some brief comments on a more contemporary form of instructive literature concerned with needlework.

THE ENDURING TRINITY: FINGERS, THREAD, NEEDLE

The joys and injustices associated with hand-stitching are not emotions of brief duration. Whilst a friend remembers, with great fondness, evenings spent sewing alongside her mother – who was a professional dressmaker – in their television-less, rural Somerset home in the 1950s, the professor who was my tutor at university recalls, with a rancour undiminished by the passage of years, the Order Mark given to her well before the Second World War by the matron at a Nairobi boarding school. This was the penalty for too-quickly completing the Sunday afternoon task of darning her mosquito net.

Eliciting anecdotes of early sewing experiences seems able to unlock great waves of memories. Jilli Blackwood was Scotland's director of costumes for the handover ceremony at the Commonwealth Games in Delhi in October 2010, and designed the outfits for the 346-strong Scottish contingent. However, in primary school she had to hand-turn the seams of the polka-dot cotton dress she was creating. 'It nearly killed me', she confesses, recalling that her suffering was exacerbated by seeing how the edges of the Crimplene fabric that a friend was using posed altogether fewer problems.

The woman sitting beside me at a dinner party described in almost poignant terms the dull thud on the teacher's desk as a bolt of winceyette was turned over, so that lengths of cloth could be cut off to supply each member of the class of aspiring young needlewomen in an English grammar school with the raw material for making a pair of pyjama bottoms. This was a task that had to be completed in Trappist-like quiet. So different from the approach of merry Sister Immaculata, under whose jolly Italian tutelage – in a Khartoum convent – the future costume historian Geraldine Marchand proudly cross-stitched a gaudy bird on a runner for her mother's dressing table. In this desert setting, silence did not reign supreme, for the girls were encouraged to sing as they wielded their needles.

The seeming absurdity of devoting an entire term to fashioning one leg of a pair of knickers (complete with a pocket in which to stow a handkerchief), a project which required an inordinate array of different stitches and techniques, did not quench the pleasure which the textile artist Kerry Littlewood later found in becoming a skilled practitioner with the needle. Quite often it would seem to have been the case that needlework, as a subject, was forced upon unwilling and resentful recipients. The lacklustre comment on a friend's report card from the 1960s reflects the tedium of this situation for both burdened teacher and bored pupil – 'Rachel does her sewing, but is neither industrious nor ambitious.'

An Australian journalist, when attending a secondary modern school in Sydney, dreamed of taking the music and art classes scheduled on the syllabus; instead of which, she was forced to produce a 'throw-over' – a square of muslin used to protect fastidiously laid tea tables or dinner tables from Antipodean dust and flies in the period before the guests actually sat down. Its making required a hand-sewn border involving pinning, tacking, hemming ('Of all the operations we had to master, it was tacking which I loathed most passionately') and, the *pièce de résistance*, an embroidered centrepiece of pink carnations. This fruit of the abhorred

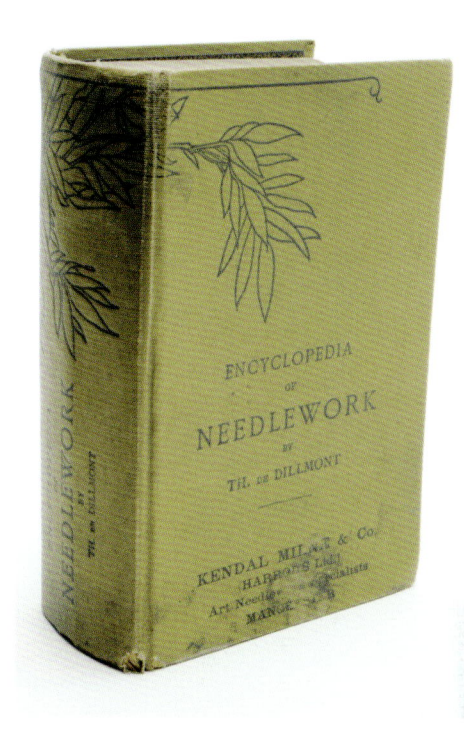

Cover and spine with details of 'the elegantly drooping laurel leaves in black outline', *Encyclopedia of Needlework* by Thérèse de Dillmont (Mulhouse, France: Dollfus-Mieg & Cie, first published c.1890s). 9 x 14.5 x 4.3 cm (3½ x 5¾ x 1⅝ in.). Copy owned by Dr Melanie Miller. Photo: Mary Stark.

needlework class was returned to my friend after her mother's death, and is not only still in use today, but is now regarded with great fondness.

At the school which Kumi Mizumoto – granddaughter of a woman who hand-sewed kimonos – attended in Mie Prefecture, both male and female students attended sewing classes for four years. One cannot help but wonder how many of the boys maintained the accomplishments thus acquired, and whether they would have provided different answers to those slim pickings garnered from my small, but multi-national sample of gentlemen.

One masculine devotee of hand-stitching was the grandfather of the writer and performance artist, Charlotte Rogers. This burly farmer was admitted to a New Zealand hospital for the war-wounded after an agricultural accident in which his leg was caught in a hay-baler. Embroidery was part of the occupational therapy undertaken by Rogers's grandfather and the injured and shell-shocked soldiers.

Suturing has always played a vital role in the operating theatre, and it was Mina Bancheva's surgeon father who taught her to thread a needle and sew a hem when she was a young girl in Sofia, for under Bulgaria's communism, such skills formed no part of the educational curriculum, and traditional embroidery techniques received little encouragement.

Fashion designers Janice Wainwright and Lesley Poole are both graduates of the Royal College of Art, where their first project as students was to cut and sew a shirt. Prior to this, Wainwright had spent six months as an assistant in the tailoring department of the couture house of Ronald Patterson, mastering the problems posed by collars, buttonholes and linings, while a National Diploma in Design familiarised Poole with the workmanship of 'proper English tailoring'. Poole's grandmother, employed on Savile Row, eventually lost her sight after many years of performing such delicate operations as picking up two threads at a time while back-stitching the yokes of shirts. A sad story, but one suspects that she would have been thrilled that it was a dress created by her grandson, a distinguished pattern cutter for Issa, that Kate Middleton wore in the photographs announcing her engagement to Prince William.

A colleague who was born and brought up in Baghdad told me that her English grandmother would post out copies of *Women's Weekly* to the Middle East and recalls with a frisson of rueful resentment how the rag doll she had so painstakingly fashioned from a pattern in that magazine was fought over and damaged by a pair of pregnant teachers at the end-of-year sale of work. Such playthings were rare in Iraq at that time, and the disconsolate 11-year-old toymaker could only stand by and helplessly witness this simultaneously thrilling and appalling spectacle, the uninhibited expression of devotion to their unborn babies by two loving, but somewhat overly covetous and belligerent mothers-to-be.

The penultimate account in this section is the shameful story of the child who, as penance for committing what parental judgement deemed to be misdemeanours, was locked into her room and not allowed out until she had threaded 25 needles, a chastisement bordering on the viciously punitive. The image of the inexpert little fingers painfully attempting, and so frequently failing, to direct the soiled and much-sucked thread through the frustratingly tiny eye of the needle, is a particularly harrowing one. However, by contrast, here is the happy account of Mallika, who dreaded art lessons and for whom the Friday afternoon sewing class in a Bombay school was the joyous climax of the week. She has never forgotten 'the thrill of choosing which colour of thread to use for the endless "practice rows" of various stitches, and then watching the lines of sewing grow under my fingers: it seemed as if time both stood still and rushed past'.

It is with a quotation from *The Craftsman* (2008) by Richard Sennett, the American 'media mandarin', that the focus of this essay now turns upon the compact little volume, the *Encyclopedia of Needlework* by Thérèse de Dillmont (1846–90), which had lain for so many years amongst the muddle within that capacious, widely travelled trunk.

'In cooking on television, Child [Julia Child, doyenne of American cookery writers and television cooks] pioneered the use of the close-up to make sense of the hands moving from one task to the next.'[1] Sennett is discussing the language of instruction – using recipes as an example of the genre – and his words have real pertinence to the subject of this chapter.[2]

De Dillmont's *vade mecum* became a monumental best-seller, which has been translated into several languages and numerous of its readers have stories to tell about their encounters with this book – how they came to know about it or own it, how they have made use of it and whether or not it lived up to the promise in the Preface that 'Careful workers will be able by its use to instruct themselves in every branch of plain and fancy needlework therein described.'

The illustrations are vaunted as one of the glories of the book ('copiously illustrated', 'new engravings introduced', and 'a fresh attraction … in the shape of 13 full-page coloured plates'), and featured frequently in these images is a pair of slender-wristed, long-fingered, seemingly boneless hands emerging from the frilled cuffs edging short lengths of sleeve which are wholly separated from the body. These detached digits aspire, in a floating and disembodied sort of way, to do exactly what the earlier mentioned close-ups of the television cook's hands are intended to achieve – teaching the practices and procedures of the craft. (Incidentally, one also encounters a needle performing, without even the aid of human fingers, such procedures as 'Mode of sewing on the soutache' and 'Six ways of making dots' in the section devoted to 'Embroidery Upon White Materials'.)

The encyclopedia was a promotional tool for the needlework products of the French company DMC (Dollfus-Mieg & Cie, Mulhouse, France). There are many copies offered for sale on the Internet at a wide variety of prices, the majority of them appearing to be more recent than the one I possess, which was a birthday gift to my mother in 1930.[3]

Thérèse de Dillmont moved to the Alsace region of France from Austria in the 1880s and became associated with the DMC embroidery yarn factory at Mulhouse, for whose wares her name and writings became a powerful 'brand' icon. There is an odd little narrative concerning this question of the relationship of her name to the company image:

Title page with angel colophon. *Encyclopedia of Needlework* by Thérèse de Dillmont (Mulhouse, France: Dollfus-Mieg & Cie, first published *c*.1890s). Copy owned by Dr Melanie Miller. Photo: Mary Stark.

Plain sewing. *Encyclopedia of Needlework* by Thérèse de Dillmont (Mulhouse, France: Dollfus-Mieg & Cie, first published c.1890s). Copy owned by Dr Melanie Miller. Photo: Mary Stark.

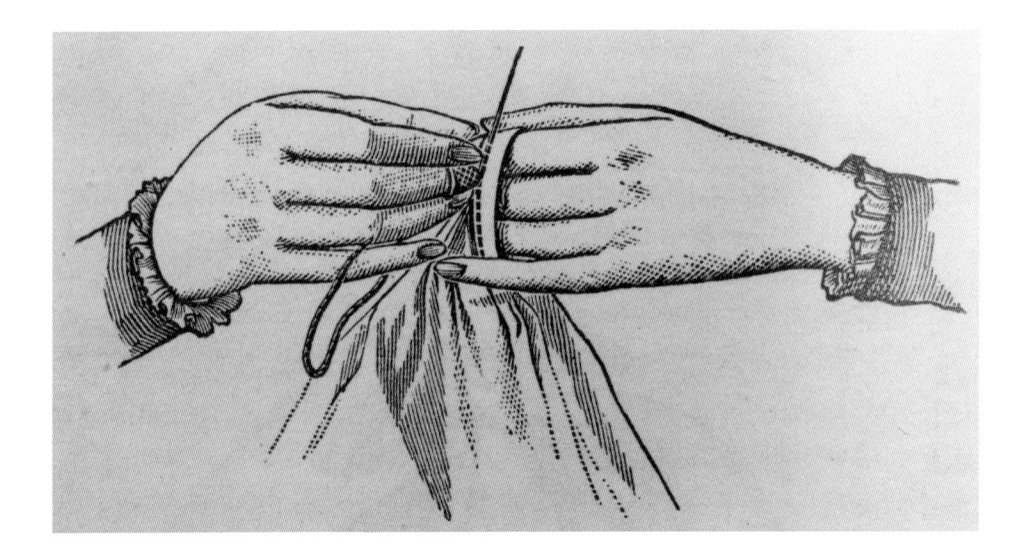

In 1889 Thérèse de Dillmont married Josef Scheuermann. The needlework factory in Mulhouse did not like this at all. One year later, in 1890, Thérèse died. Her niece, with the same name, succeeded her. In her working contract it said that she was not supposed to get married. The reason was that the name de Dillmont could not possibly be changed by marriage because it was so closely related to the factory and to the books.[4]

Opposite the title page there is a statement of the number of copies issued 'until now', but, as none of the dozen or so texts to which I had access gave a publication date, one is left asking the futile, frustrating question 'When was "now"?' Nevertheless, one watches the figures mount with a certain excitement and admiration at the tremendous success achieved by this little tome. Several friends have editions, which give the figure of 620,000 copies produced, while the *Encyclopedia of Needlework* belonging to Dorothy Reglar, who was formerly in charge of all embroidery at the couture house of Bellville Sassoon, quotes 940,000. In my copy there is a statement to the effect that 1,120,000 copies had been issued 'until now', and that belonging to Michael Brennand-Wood, which he bought as a student in 1971, gives the number as 1,650,000. All editions seem to keep the colophon of an angel holding aloft a banner bearing a Latin motto – *Tenui Filo Magnum Texitur Opus* – translated on the DMC website as 'From one fine thread a work of art is born'.

An intriguing question is 'How accessible do contemporary users find this manual to be?' Irene Waller, mother of the textile artist Carole Waller (who is also an owner of this book) and former Head of Woven Textiles at the University of Birmingham, praised the teaching ability of the illustrations and Alice Kettle, well known for her large-scale machine embroideries, consulted it as part of the research undertaken for this present volume. Dorothy Reglar, who did a year's postgraduate training in fashion embroidery at Birmingham College of Art, is another proponent of the instructional usefulness of both the written word and the pictures. Alongside such enthusiasm, however, is the annoyance of a Dutch seamstress who found that the text and illustrations were less explicit than they might be:

THE ENDURING TRINITY: FINGERS, THREAD, NEEDLE

The Encyclopedia does not allow for much fun and easy reading. The text is dense and the black and white illustrations are at first glance not always that much clarifying [sic] … The instructions are very strict and creative variations are not promoted.[5]

This problem might arise from the fact that when it was first published in the last quarter of the nineteenth century, its readership, more likely than not, was accustomed to a much greater exposure to needlework at home and school than is currently the case. Thus, these earlier perusers would feel easier 'reading' both the text and the visual tuition provided by the diagrams. Evaluating the usability or otherwise of this guide, friends possessing varying degrees of sewing skills were asked to follow de Dillmont's instructions for procedures with which they were not familiar. There was a commendably high success rate, and a young student-neighbour who although initially daunted by the 'density' of this instructional prose, was elated when she salvaged a torn but cherished skirt with her first attempt at patching.

Several of my interviewees emphasised that the inclusiveness of the range of material covered in, and the authoritative trustworthiness inspired by, the contents of this encyclopedia mean that it is frequently consulted as a reference tool rather than as a medium of instruction. However, within the rigours of the general approach, there is an occasional cavalier insouciance which unexpectedly manifests itself. Explaining the 'Thirteenth, Fourteenth and Fifteenth openwork patterns on net', in the chapter dedicated to 'Embroidered Laces', one wonders whether the statement that 'The designs are so easy to copy, that no further explanation is necessary' is perhaps a mite too nonchalant to offer comfort to the anxious learner. Conversely, however, this upbeat attitude could well prove encouraging to the beginner struggling to master these 'groundings, powderings and insertions … for subsequent use in the lace patterns that follow'.

What emerged time and again in the course of the conversations and interviews was the immense affection with which the book is regarded, and its solidly comforting and compact size was frequently compared to a hymnal, missal or Bible. This is no slender volume – mine has 811 numbered pages plus a further 60 sides enumerating the various needlework products offered by DMC. For the young Brennand-Wood, these catalogues, which included such alluringly named yarns as 'Locust-bean brown', 'Paroquet green' and 'Scabious violet', each available in six different shades, were like fantastic 'wish lists'.

Studying these 'Tables' induces a satisfying sense of searching for the exactly appropriate material for the job in hand as the information is presented with a great deal of precision, exemplified in the ladder-like diagrams where the increasing breadth of the ascending rungs represents the varying thicknesses of threads. Plenty of dye numbers are supplied, and different strengths of colour are listed, ranging from 'Ultra-dark' to 'Ultra-light'; but in my edition only 'Moss green', 'Indigo blue', 'Tender pink', 'Geranium red' and 'Old red' were available in all seven categories. Nevertheless, one has to admit that the visual colour samples of threads on the DMC Internet site are a more convenient and possibly more accurate guide.

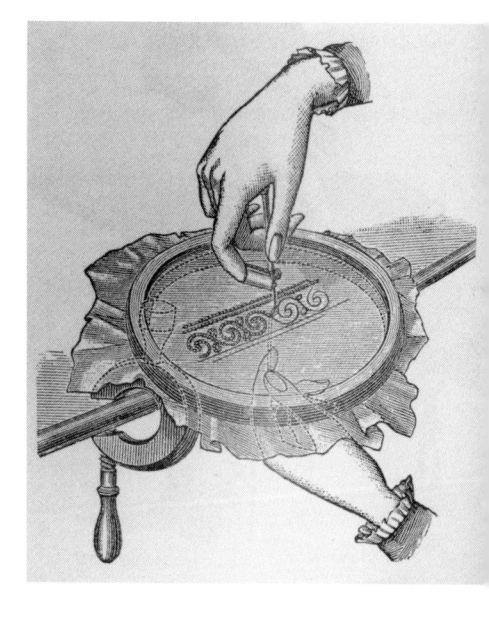

'First position for tambour work' and 'Second position for tambour work'. *Encyclopedia of Needlework* by Thérèse de Dillmont (Mulhouse, France: Dollfus-Mieg & Cie, first published c.1890s). Copy owned by Dr Melanie Miller. Photo: Mary Stark.

(left) Table 'giving numbers and sizes of the cotton articles bearing the DMC trade mark'. *Encyclopedia of Needlework* by Thérèse de Dillmont (Mulhouse, France: Dollfus-Mieg & Cie, first published c.1890s). Copy owned by Dr Melanie Miller. Photo: Mary Stark.

(right) 'Table giving in alphabetical order the names with the numbers of the shades enumerated on the colour card'. *Encyclopedia of Needlework* by Thérèse de Dillmont (Mulhouse, France: Dollfus-Mieg & Cie, first published c.1890s). Copy owned by Dr Melanie Miller. Photo: Mary Stark.

Disconcertingly, there are discrepancies between the various editions. The chapter on 'Knitting' in my book opens with the words: 'Knitting though not one of the kinds of needlework earliest known …' and contrasts with the same lines in the downloadable Internet edition which states: 'Knitting is one of the earliest forms of needlework …'[6] without providing any evidence for this reversal of ideas. A detailed comparison of the various translations and revisions would surely prove illuminating, both on the macro- and micro-levels. This would seem to be the point at which to state that mine was not an academically exacting investigation, but rather an inquisitive and thoroughly enjoyable ramble, with all manner of wholly unsuspected links and discoveries presenting themselves en route.

Inevitably, the encyclopedia contains certain anomalies to current perceptions. One might be wary of adhering too scrupulously to de Dillmont's advice regarding the care of needles, which, evidencing the time when it was written, recommends the toxic-sounding 'powdered stone alum' as a precaution against rust. Neither would one rush to heed the suggestion that 'People with damp hands which make needles sticky in usage' are advised to keep a box of asbestos powder by them 'and dip their fingers occasionally in it'.

However, the appeal of the *Encyclopedia of Needlework* outweighs any qualms concerning the obsolescence of such sporadic hints. Dorothy Reglar was delighted at the immediacy and liveliness of the response of a fashion student who was working in her studio and to whom she introduced the book. The young woman's fascination was a clear fulfilment of the wish that Thérèse de Dillmont modestly expressed over a century ago – 'that this volume will be favourably received by the public to whom it is specially addressed'.

As a coda to this essay, I visited a website entitled Kids' Sewing Projects (www.kids-sewing-projects.com), which enthusiastically encourages teaching young children the pleasures of hand-sewing as a lead-in to machine sewing. In the 'Pre-Beginner Sewing Lessons, Level 1' – clearly the appropriate entry point for one as cack-handed as myself – one meets the heartening reminder to the instructor that 'It may take a lot of practice when learning to thread a needle, be patient and provide encouragement'. (These are lines which one yearns to engrave on the hearts of those parents who inflicted the needle-threading punishment on their poor child.) There are plenty of illustrations of chubby juvenile fingers – so very different from the lissom digits met with in de Dillmont's text – performing various simple operations with a large 'non-sharp needle'. In lesson three there are short videos – 'How to Tie a Knot', for example – where tuition is transmitted via older, more experienced fingers.

More than a hundred years separate de Dillmont's volume and the Kids' Sewing Projects site, but many of the images, whether drawn, photographed or videoed, still have as their focus the abiding trinity of hand-stitching – fingers manipulating thread and needle.

NOTES

[1] Sennett, Richard, *The Craftsman* (London: Allen Lane, The Penguin Press, 2008), p. 185.

[2] An Internet reference gives the date of publication of the original French edition of *Encyclopédie des Ouvrages de Dames* as 1884, under the imprint of 'Librairie Ch. Delagrave, Paris'. Many editions, especially the earlier ones, are listed as 'Sans date' or 'n.d.'. A copy with the handwritten date '1888' on the fly leaf, shares with all later editions I have seen, the absence of any reference to a translator. De Dillmont would seem to have been a prodigiously hard-working person who, in the course of her short life, also wrote *Masterpieces of Irish Crochet Lace, Drawn Threadwork and Assisi Lace* (dates unknown).

[3] None of de Dillmont's books would appear to be available on the official DMC website, www.DMC.com (accessed 16 July 2011).

[4] See www.annatextiles.ch (accessed 12 July 2011).

[5] This quotation was found on www.amazon.com/Complete-Encyclopedia-Needlework-Therese-Dillmont/product-reviews (accessed 14 July 2011).

[6] See www.encyclopediaofneedlework.com (accessed 10 August 2011).

NIGEL HURLSTONE

Speaking up for Silence

WE LIVE IN A NOISY WORLD. The impatient sounds of telephones, computers, televisions, traffic and speaking punctuate our daily lives. Technology continues to spawn ever-increasing ways in which we can participate in a seemingly endless flood of communication. Even the more passive-sounding e-mail is now being superseded by Twitter, which in its very name conjures up a sound analogy to market text-based messaging. Silence can sometimes come as a relief, a refuge in which we can be present without the demanding or intruding noises that prompt us to make rapid and attentive responses without delay – it should not be taken to imply emptiness of thought or idleness. If we look to embroidery, we can see great power in silence and an ongoing tradition that resists and contends the unfettered production of chatter.

I have not always appreciated the ambiguities of silence or the many different ways in which it can be read. As a boy in school, I used to hate noisy classrooms, and the noisiest of them all was certainly the art room. As opposed to the silence imposed by teachers busy explaining the complexities of mathematics or great historical events, it appeared that the prerequisite for the production of art was talk. Freefall conversation somehow came to epitomise the release of imagination and high levels of energy required for the production of drawing or making. Now, as a lecturer in embroidery, I am still influenced by this thinking. I am haunted by silence in the studio and constantly read it as a failure to inspire. For years I have sought to conjure up the cacophony that I always dreaded in the classroom in an effort to convince myself that all is well.

As of late, however, I have begun to welcome silence, and not to fear it. Silence is, after all, part of our own medium of communication and not separate from it. But more often than not, silence is assumed to reflect individual or cultural pathology, and is always deemed in need of treatment. Certainly within the curriculum at school and within the higher education sector, 'silence' is almost exorcised from students, with discourse and discussion being part of the learning, teaching and assessment mantra.

My fascination with silence comes from the subject that I teach, embroidery. With it comes a complex history of those who have sewed in lieu of having a voice, and through their stitching have described the struggles, passions and frustrations of their lives. The French author Colette exemplifies this in her writing. Embroidery is often used as a vehicle to illuminate the femininity of her characters, but also to undermine the social stereotypes that cast women into roles of the subjugated and servile. Interestingly, it is the silence of her daughter that causes her much

A Common Thread, 2005. Film. Sombrero Productions and Mallia Films (a film by Eleonore Faucher). All artwork and distribution by Soda Pictures Ltd. Still image by permission of Soda Pictures Ltd.

consternation. In her novel *Earthly Paradise* (1966), she describes mixed feelings towards the 'sewing habits' of her child, Bel-Gazou:

> *I shall speak the truth: I don't much like my daughter sewing ... If she draws, or colours pictures, a semi-articulate song issues from her, unceasing as the hum of bees around the privet ... but Bel-Gazou is silent when she sews, silent for hours on end ... She is silent, and she – why not write down the word that frightens me – she is thinking.*[1]

Colette's reaction to the silent, hand-stitching Bel-Gazou demonstrates an anxiety about her daughter's behaviour. Bel-Gazou's demeanour, in which her eyes are lowered, head bent and shoulders hunched, exemplifies a position traditionally signifying repression and subjugation, yet her silence and concentration also suggests self-containment and a real sense of autonomy. However, Colette's unease is understandable. As an infamous bisexual and erotic performer with a penchant for challenging societal stereotypes, she may have wished her daughter to exhibit behaviour that was further away from the historical image and narrative of the embroiderer. Historically, the embroiderer was often represented as young and docile, and eager to be subjugated by men. This is especially true in the nineteenth century, and one only has to consider the many portraits of young seamstresses by Millet, Pissaro and Rossetti to find evidence of this association.

In many portraits, the characteristic posture of the embroiderer evokes modesty yet utter submission to a domestic idyll. A young woman is generally pictured seated, her hands occupied with the needlework and her head bowed in silent concentration. We are reminded of the work of the seventeenth-century poet John Taylor, 'In Praise of the Needle', in which he urged women 'to use their tongues less and their needles more'.[2]

HAND STITCH: PERSPECTIVES

Contemporary representations of the embroiderer, however, do not seem to have developed significantly from this historical perspective. In 2005 the French film production company Sombrerc launched *A Common Thread*. The film explores the story of two women and their bond, established through embroidery. The minimal 'talk' and deep concentration of the embroidery process enables a space for thinking and dialogues of mind to develop. Both women work in silence until the end of the film, where muted dialogue reveals the development of a strong yet unarticulated friendship. The revered seamstress Lola teaches the headstrong adolescent Claire how to stitch, and further, how to stitch with perfection. Interestingly, the character of Claire, a fiery redhead, seems tamed through applying herself to stitch. The more she sews, the more she loses of her intractable and wilful manner. In effect, embroidery breaks her obstinate will, leaving her as a more genteel and subservient personality. She becomes the very model of the feminine ideal that centuries-old commentators would have us believe is achieved through talking less and sewing more. In the final frames of the film, Claire is represented as passive: head bent, silent and more or less solitary in her work. She is the contemporary mimesis of John Taylor's 'The Needle's Excellency'.

Not only in the realms of literature and art was the embroiderer a focus of attention throughout the eighteenth, nineteenth and twentieth centuries. In medical discourse, too, men were involved in forming suppositions about the mental and physiological aspects of embroidery in relation to the supposedly troubled state of the female mind. Indeed, their imaginings went so far as to speculate on the particular physical and mental dangers of sewing on the female psyche. Freud saw a connection between sewing and hysteria, believing that 'dispositional hypnoid states could grow out of daydreams to which needlework and similar occupations render women especially prone'.[3]

Given the cultural history of embroidery, it is surprising that any contemporary practitioners would wish to pick up the needle to express themselves. However, it is the very history of the subject itself that has begun to be subverted and called upon to make work that expresses current desires, concerns and comment about popular culture. It is not that the social, economic or medical discourses previously discussed have somehow disappeared, they have merely metamorphosed, and the embroiderer's 'silence', or indeed the lack of it, is everywhere to be found.

In *When This You See ...*, an installation at the project room at MOMA in 1999, Elaine Reichek examined the history of embroidery, knitting and weaving, and wittily revealed much about the relationship between the sexes and the politics of gender that still permeates the business and activity of making art. Reichek presented 31 contemporary versions of traditional samplers that literally spelt out truisms mixed in with decorative patterns and motifs. Quotations were appropriated from art history, literature, science, mythology and popular culture. Her sources were wide-ranging in their scope and included quotes from Mary Queen of Scots to Ad Reinhardt, and from Homer's *Odyssey* to Virginia Woolf's *A Room of One's Own* (1929).

SPEAKING UP FOR SILENCE

Elaine Reichek
Sampler (Dispositional Hypnoid States), 1996. Embroidery on linen. 47.6 x 5¼ cm (18¾ x 20¼ in.). Collection of Melva Bucksbaum. Photo: Adam Reich.

It is through embroidery that Reichek gives these people voice, yet embroidery, conventionally, is hushed in the doing and supposedly requires self-contained focus. In the making of this work, Reichek clearly contends that embroidery is a language, and that language, even or perhaps particularly when silent, is thought. She even quotes a voice we have heard before – Colette – in her archive: 'I don't much like my daughter sewing … she is silent, and she – why not write down the word that frightens me – she is thinking.'

Most of the men and women that Reichek quotes in her samplers have either sewed, knitted, woven or spoken about these activities. For example, Philomela is the character in Ovid's *Metamorphoses* who is violated by her brother-in-law; although imprisoned and silenced (since her tongue is torn out), she manages to tell her story by embroidering it into cloth. Penelope, the wife of Ulysses in *The Odyssey*, holds unwelcome suitors at bay by promising a decision once she has finished making her tapestry. Cunningly, she unpicks her tapestry every night in order to frustrate them all and keep the men guessing. Arachne (who weaves) features too, though unfortunately she takes a rather ill-considered decision to compete with the goddess Athena, who subsequently punishes her by turning her into a spider, the spider of course being nature's own weaver. Madame Defarge, the anti-heroine of Dickens's *A Tale of Two Cities* (1859) is also represented, as she knits a secret score of the aristocrats named for the hit list during the French Revolution.

149

HAND STITCH: PERSPECTIVES

Tamsin Casswell
(*right*) *Work Hard and Thoughts Are Emptied On To Paper Late at Night*, 2006. Hand embroidery on canvas. 30 x 30 cm (12 x 12 in.). Photo: Nigel Hurlstone.

(*below*) *Safe in a Pocket Diary, Thoughts Are Emptied On To Paper Late at Night*, 2006. Back-projected video. Projected size 15 x 11.5 cm (6 x 4¾ in.). (DV transferred to DVD, 30 minutes, colour, sound). Hand embroidery on canvas. 30 x 30 cm (12 x 12 in.). Photo: Nigel Hurlstone.

Defarge, Mary Queen of Scots and Philomela seem linked on the same thread in this history, since all of them use their needles to write messages in a struggle with a persecutor. The theme of *When This You See* then includes silence, secrecy, subjection and, most importantly, fighting back.

The 'chatter' in the silence of embroidery embodied in Reichek's work is also recognisable in the work of Tamsin Casswell. Casswell's work is similarly deeply rooted in both the practice and metaphors of embroidery, and like Reichek, she takes the form of the sampler and develops it into a form of her own. Unlike Reichek, who appropriates and quotes, Casswell is the author of the texts and language brought together in the work. In *Work Hard* and *Pocket Diary* three stitched samplers are laid before the viewer, above which are shown films of her working and talking. They record not only the activity of sewing itself, but her own thoughts and mental meandering as she sews.

Like Colette's Bel-Gazou, Casswell is counting her stitches, fully absorbed in the task, but unlike her predecessor, her mouth does not remain firmly closed. She is thinking, and moreover she does what Colette dreads Bel-Gazou will do – she is writing thoughts down and speaking them directly to us. Here, roles are reversed. Out of the silence of stitch comes a voice that narrates the contents of her head, born out of the self-contained process of embroidery. The monologue 'Anticipated Eleven' is a fragment of what we may hear as we inspect the maker's stitchery.

Anticipated Eleven

First line, second and content, because I have to write this and relieve that I sweat a lot. And part of my brain tells me there is more than there is. And often I am sad about something that hasn't happened, and might never. Now each should be a thread in a soft book and after, change is welcome. So: to realise a document.

So you found me and you find me, tired. I'm calmer today about sewing for money and writing under pressure. There's more clearing to do and thoughts to store. I've learnt that everything is externalised but silence is important. My memories are pen-bound and wouldn't survive a fire unless a written plan saved them.

I've made a manual for life: in my notebook, on my mirror, on the back of my door. There's constant information; the loud things. So important I am anxious, so important I forget. I live life through lists and habits; a constant. If I'm one in four it would be OCD, but if I sew it's silent.

I watched one woman mourn one coffin and wondered if the word is 'shattered'. In one week a unit made up. Ten centimetres to Mary. Millions have died and I have sewn nothing about it.

Casswell's testimonial, however, is more than a self-confessed meander on personal neurosis and living habits. The mental internal dialogue is constantly placed in both visual and textual proximity with the activity of stitch itself. The silence she speaks about is the activity of making itself; an absorption in the craft and skill of literally spelling out the mantra of survival, accomplishment and encouragement needed to work through the day's tasks. The samplers stitched with the phrases 'Work Hard' and 'You are OK' are literally the external manifestation of internal thoughts.

The link between those who stitch and Freud's mapping of hysteria to a specifically feminine condition permeates contemporary discourse about the work and life of Tracey Emin. She is known for her works such as *My Bed* and the collection of stitched blankets, but her drawing work also has affinity to the contortions drawn by Schiele and his models in the period 1909–12 – drawings that map the male artist on to feminine materiality and indeed on to what was understood at the time as the female hysteric.

This association, in regard to Tracey Emin, manifests itself in her autobiographical disclosures, for example the video *Why I Never Became a Dancer*, from 1995, where Emin recalls fleeing from the dancefloor to a chorus of abuse, and in the stitched textile works such as *Mad Tracey from Margate. Everyone's Been There*. Emin, it seems, may have become a contemporary manifestation of nineteenth-century cultural anxieties. The passive, silent, subjugated female has become explicitly critical, accusatory in tone and her body is displayed for all to see as a site of spectacular sexualised ambivalence. More importantly, however, she is sewing.

Domesticity is everywhere to be seen in Emin's oeuvre. There is the infamous unmade bed, a grandmother's chair and home-made blankets, stitched and appliquéd. These objects invoke a kind of failed domesticity – the failure of a house to acquire fully the aspects of a proper home. All this stitching places Emin far away from Edith Wharton's characters in the 1920s novel, *The Age of Innocence* (1920),[4] where the silent industry of the female embroiderer is rewarded in the comfort of marriage and home. But Emin's work is certainly industrious. The large-scale stitched blankets are highly worked by hand, but they are also clumsy in terms of technique and quite deliberately contain misspellings. In part, Emin may be closer to Edith Wharton's character of the young Mrs Newland Archer than we may think: 'She was not a clever needle woman: her large capable hands were made for riding, rowing and open-air activities; but since other wives embroidered cushions for their husbands she did not wish to omit this latest link in her devotion.'[5]

Emin's stitch work may not be proffered as a duty to either entice an admirer or keep a husband, but it is still, in part, a work of devotion, albeit a homage to the self. Keeping to the same tradition as those who have sewn before her, the work does serve to counter feminine stereotypes and challenges the extraordinary power and duplicity of social morality and ideology by confronting its antithesis – female promiscuity and masturbation. And Emin is far from the quiet, subjugated female.

The appliquéd blankets shout loudly in a cacophonous riot of voices. They are accusatory in tone, confessional and confrontational – silence is nowhere to be found. Reichek's work, and to a certain extent that of Casswell, take as their premise that embroidery is a language, and a thoughtful one at that; the resulting work is quiet and reverential. Emin's is still thought – but they are thoughts of sorrow, regret, anger and, to a certain extent, self-affirmation. At last the embroiderer has found a voice that is of its time and is not ashamed to parade human vanity before the needle and fix it defiantly into cloth.

But silence, for some women, has also been a tool of empowerment and self-assertion rather than a manifestation of oppression. Jane Campion's 1993 film, *The Piano*, addresses the communication forms, verbal and otherwise, used by a mute woman living under the veil of patriarchal Victorian society. However, Ada, the pianist heroine of this film, was not born mute. She chooses silence from the age of six, not to escape the oppression of her culture, but rather to defy it. Her voice comes not through her throat, but through the playing of her piano.

It seems generally accepted in our society that power exists for those who name and voice their experiences. Less obvious is the idea that there is equal power in choosing silence. If we look to embroidery, we will find plenty of silence, but also an incredible plethora of voice. However, it is in the gaps of language and sound that much is to be gleaned, especially if we take more time to listen and appreciate the fact that silence may be about presence as well as absence. As Adrienne Rich states, 'Silence can be a plan rigorously executed, the blueprint to a life. It is a presence, it has history, a form. Do not confuse it with any kind of absence.'[6] Add to this that silence may also reflect care as well as neglect, thoughtfulness as well as mindlessness. This in effect is the very essence of embroidery. It is why in the studio I now listen for silence and sound; and why I am more comfortable in the world when both exist side by side.

SPEAKING UP FOR SILENCE

Tracey Emin
Hotel International, 1993. Appliquéd quilt. 257 x 240 cm (101 x 94½ in.).
© Tracey Emin. All rights reserved, DACS 2011. Courtesy of White Cube Gallery. Photo: Stephen White.

NOTES

[1] Colette, *Earthly Paradise* (London: Secker and Warburg, 1966), pp. 214–16.
[2] Taylor, John, 'The Needle's Excellency', quoted in Parker, Rozsika, *The Subversive Stitch: Embroidery and the Making of the Feminine* (Women's Press Ltd., 1984), pp. 86–87.
[3] Breuer, Joseph and Freud, Sigmund, 'Studies on Hysteria' in Strachey, James (ed.), *The Complete Works of Sigmund Freud*, Vol. 2 (London: The Hogarth Press, 1956), p. 12.
[4] Wharton, Edith, *The Age of Innocence* (London: Penguin Books, 1974), Chapter 5.
[5] Ibid.
[6] Rich, Adrienne, quoted in Carter, Rodney G., 'Of Things Said and Unsaid: Power, Archival Silences and Power in Silence', in *Association of Canadian Archivists*, Issue 61, North America (September 2006).

LESLEY MITCHISON

'Out of the Ordinary'

'OUT OF THE ORDINARY' IS THE TITLE OF A COLLECTION OF WORKS by the American fibre artist, Anne Wilson. It is the overarching title from a collection created under the auspice of 'topographies'. Anne is a prolific artist and educator, involved in projects that range from hand stitch to video works and performance art installation. In this chapter, I will be focusing on the 'Hair Work' project undertaken in the 1990s, as this has formed the basis for much of Anne's recent work and includes departures into the area of weave and lace deconstruction.

I will also be discussing the works of Tabitha Kyoko Moses, a British-based artist whose approach to practice engages both community and installation aspects in terms of context. Tabitha chooses to use the familiar skills of hand stitch to create intricate, linear stories on the surfaces of her artefacts, often in response to collections of objects that fascinate because of their links with past histories and events. It is the commonality in process and sometimes methodology that brings the work of these artists together.

'The Pioneer of Modern Craft' and 'Making Clothes for Children' series of works from my own collection will also be discussed alongside the works of Anne and Tabitha, as the histories explored and the use of hand-work techniques and approaches to materials create several parallels of enquiry worthy of discussion.

Anne creates beautifully considered hand-stitched pieces that evoke a huge range of emotions and responses. The 'Hair Work' series of pieces are in their physicality white, crisp and clean, adorned with black thread and hair stitching. The stitching subverts the idea of mending, as it often accentuates holes that are already present in the cloth, so in effect the stitching makes more of the histories of the cloths she chooses to work on. The viewer is drawn into the fabric's structure and the element of contemplation begins. Anne refers to her work as 'a "subversive" mending project, because rather than repairing, the holes are "disrepaired", accentuated to display a contrary experience and sensibility'.[1]

It is this subverting of the mending that begins to draw a parallel with some of the research behind my own work. *Have Nothing* refers to the quotation by William Morris: 'Have nothing in your houses that you do not know to be useful or believe to be beautiful'.[2] This embroidered piece of work is made up of reworked woven fragments that are appliquéd on to an antique linen napkin. The choice of mending and joining yarns is traditional, whereas Anne adds another dimension to her historical references by utilising strands of hair as the thread of repair. The associations and the layering of metaphorical meaning magnify because 'hair' makes us consider bodily functions, as Anne states: 'These stitched textiles are physical

Lesley Mitchison
Have Nothing, 2006. Antique linen napkin, woven and stitched appliqué, silk, linen and cotton yarns. 40 x 36 cm (15¾ x 14¼ in.). Collection of the Whitworth Art Gallery Manchester; 'Artist Handling Boxes'. Photo: Lesley Mitchison

'OUT OF THE ORDINARY'

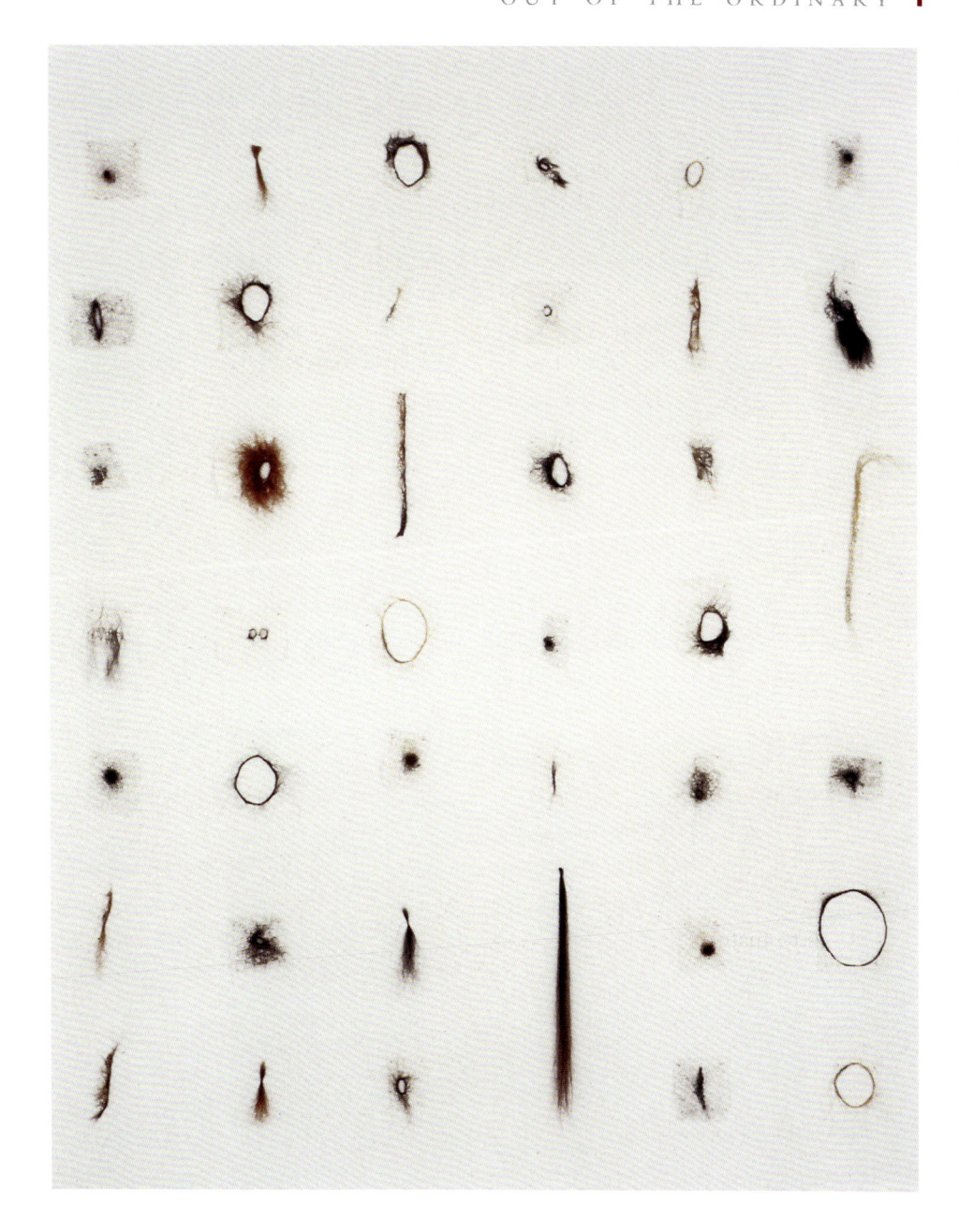

Anne Wilson
Hair Work, 1991–93. Hair, thread, cloth.
161 x 140 x 9 cm (63½ x 55½ x 3½ in.).
Collection of Museum of Contemporary
Art, Chicago. Photo: Stephen Pitken.

drawings referencing wounds, burns, orifices, signs of decay and microscopic, specimen-like images.'³

We are repelled and fascinated at the same time as the sophisticated handling of this repairing thread takes on the role of embroidered details often found in historical and commemorative fabrics. In *Grafts* (No. 2), 1993, the intensity of stitch is centred around the holes; one would think that these holes may have evolved over time as the cloth has been used, or folded over and over again, so that the crease lines of the fabric begin to show the signs of wear. The use of hair adds the final dimension in its ability to intrigue and rebuke at the same time. It is the occasional wandering hair that disconcerts me more, the trace element.

155

Worn fragments of table cloths and pillowcases are disrepaired with stitches and mattings of hair, creating abstract, tangible 'drawings' which ironically juxtapose the refinement and formality of delicate cloth with the more animal aspects of the human body. All of Wilson's works reveal an understanding of and a fascination with the physical gesture and its trace – the evidence of our daily ritual, both private and public.[4]

It is in *Hair Work a+b* where Anne uses a culmination of hair and thread fibres to stitch around the hole central to the fabric's dimension. One considers whether the hole was always that big or was it the continual stitching around the edge that gradually increased its size to deliberately make more of the 'wearing away' element. By unpicking the fabric's structure in this manner, the dark edge of the hole now starts to indicate other possibilities and take on other associations. The loose hair strands soften the harder edge of the shape and suggest orifices and plugholes, places to clean and remove the trace.

In *Mendings*, Anne often refers to the origins of her fabrics in a personal context; fabrics donated and passed down from family members: 'It was a "presentation" textile, meant to be kept bleached clean, white and starched. The origin of this cloth is from my own family; it is among the many household linens, some from two generations back, which were passed down to me.'[5]

Anne Wilson
Mourning Cloth (drape), 1992–93. Hair, thread, reconstructed cloth. 183 x 81 x 5 cm (72 x 32 x 2 in.). Photo: Stephen Pitken.

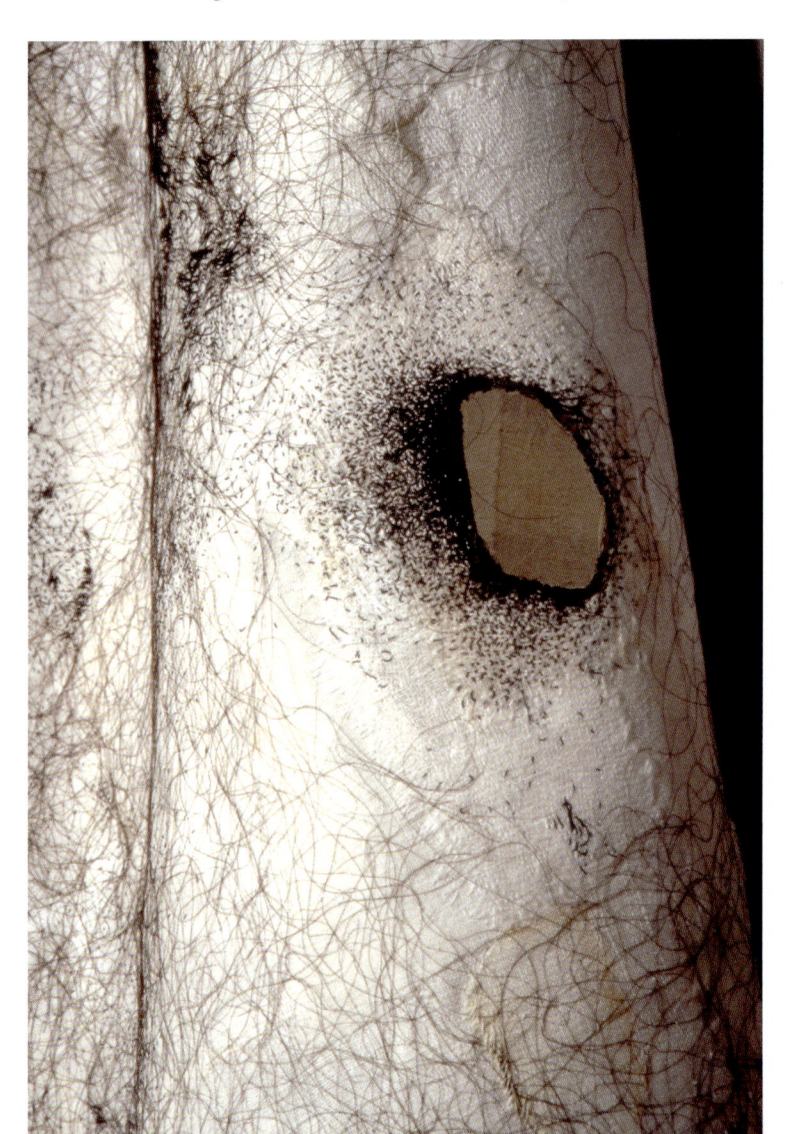

'OUT OF THE ORDINARY'

Lesley Mitchison
Ethel, Pioneer of Modern Craft (detail), 2006. Woven utilising a 'pick-up' technique; hand-stitched cotton and silk yarns. 168 x 50 cm (66 x 20 in.). Collection of the artist. Photo: David Brodie.

So does this give the fabrics more resonance as Anne unpicks her own histories? In this piece it is the recreation of the beautifully embroidered stemmed fern's head that we are drawn into; the image has disappeared, either through time or deconstruction, and has been replaced with a darkly stitched edge that serves only to emphasise the loss of what should have been. There is a great sense of familiarity in the fabrics Anne uses – the antique, embroidered fabrics of our own heritage and histories – and we can instantly draw parallels of meaning on both a personal and social level. These precious cloths and tableware were often the occupant of the bottom drawer, cleaned, starched and folded away for that special occasion. In the taking away of the embroidered image in *Mendings*, we are left with a void, another hole of contemplation.

In 'The Pioneer of Modern Craft' series of works, I have been preoccupied with the importance of skill-based history, which has fallen out of favour with much contemporary craft criticism and the fundamental values of craft work and its processes. In the making of this piece of work and the inclusion of hand stitch on the woven surface, there are fundamental values that I am trying to enforce with regards to skills in the translation of ideas. I add scraps of antique materials to the weaving, which have inspired me to create a new approach to 'historical referencing'.

The comparison here would be to say that Anne is enforcing her own history and at the same time jolting our memory of the past and encouraging us to reflect on this work in many ways. Anne's work is multi-layered, like the fabrics in the bottom drawer – stacked up, crisp and complex in texture and origin.

The titles of these works are almost chronological in terms of the processes that are employed as Anne grafts, mends and makes cloths of ceremony, such as the *Mourning Cloths* and in the creation of *Feast*. The mourning cloth pieces are suggestive of our past histories and what we have forgotten. We carefully put away and store our precious and best linens only to bring them out again on a special occasion or in the event of a death. It is often only then that we remember what we have forgotten, and each and every couched-down hair on these cloths serves as a reminder of all that we have lost in the process of remembering.

HAND STITCH: PERSPECTIVES

Lesley Mitchison
Making Clothes for Children 1, 1998. Woven, stitched and heat-transfer-printed cotton, polyester, paper and silk yarns. 36 x 32 cm (92 x 81 in.). Collection of Nottingham Castle Contemporary Textiles. Photo: Mark Watson.

It is the particular choice of materials that serves to emphasise the ideas behind the work in *Making Clothes for Children*. The choice of paper, as a yarn to weave and stitch with, was used to highlight the importance of being resilient and resourceful during times of extreme crisis such as the Second World War. The unpicking of the woven surface and the re-stitching of the garment shape back together at the hemline, using a traditional faggoting stitch, enforces the importance of the passing down of such skills and practices to our children.

Feast was an installation project for the Museum of Contemporary Art, Chicago, within the exhibition entitled 'Anne Wilson, Anatomy of Wear', in 2000.

'OUT OF THE ORDINARY'

On a white-painted table measuring 22 ft long x 5½ ft wide and 2½ ft high, hundreds of holes forming the wear in table linen are held to the tabletop with small brads and pins. The table is positioned diagonally to fill the gallery space, and can be viewed intimately at the table's edge, or seen overhead from the open stairway moving up to the next floor.[6]

This huge dining table implies a social space, the interaction of diners, and different histories of use. The holes and linear tears pinned to the table are fragments from found dining linen, stitched open with human hair and fine thread. They can be seen as remnants from dining, or from the long-term use of the table linen, removed from its original context. In contrast to Wilson's framed works, these holes have a connection to their origin through their horizontal presentation on the table surface. The varied colours of hair and the many shapes and sizes of the holes and tears form a topography of absence and memory, suggesting a mapping of the internal body and landscape beyond physical body.[7]

As the title suggests, *Feast* evokes an array of emotions and a plethora of meaning, from the singular lost hair that adorns the table, meticulously stitched on to its surface, to those that become part of a bulbous mound. The frayed and fragmented sliver of cloth represents the stains of many dinners and the presence of many diners, which could never be washed away. There is indeed a feast of information on this large and onerous installation and it should be viewed as the culmination of a decade's work.

Of the bringing together of the 'Hair Works' series and the careful extraction of appropriate elements to create a landscape of life past and present, Anne states:

This is an abstract topography suggesting mapping and navigation, both internal and external to the body: pools, clusters, craters, mounds; fractals, particles; cellular-like; self-organised systems, blips and parts meandering as in a natural organism; displaced, interrupted, paired and split.[8]

This ability to disconcert and to make uncomfortable, as well as intrigue and fascinate, is also evident in the work of Tabitha Kyoko Moses. The selection and sourcing of the appropriate materials to work with and on to is crucial in both the work of Anne and Tabitha. Inherent differences are in the artist's own physical link with those chosen surfaces. Anne often refers to the history of the fabric in a personal context: 'The cloth is generally old (turn of the century to 1940), from family or gifts, mostly laces.'[9] Whereas in Tabitha's case, the history is often in response to a story that has been recently archived. 'Tabitha Kyoko Moses is a collector, a rag and bone archivist of the peripheral. Her studio, in the aptly Victorianesque-sounding Bridewell area of Liverpool, is full of faded ephemera and unwanted residual fragments of material existence.'[10]

As described by Alex Michon in 'The Lost and the Found' interview, Tabitha is an 'art archaeologist' and what is uncovered is poignant not just in terms of content but in terms of quality. Discoveries are often imbued with 'melancholia and misdemeanour'.[11] These have become recurring themes in much of Tabitha's work. It is often the use of unusual or unexpected materials that make the viewer

Anne Wilson
Feast, 2000. Hair, thread, cloth, insect pins, wood table. 80 x 168 x 671 cm (31½ x 66 x 264 in.). Collection of the Museum of Contemporary Art Chicago. Photo: James Isberner.

HAND STITCH: PERSPECTIVES

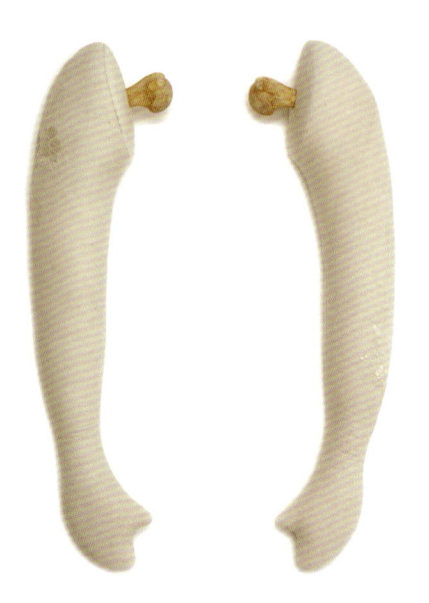

Tabitha Kyoko Moses
(*left*) *Untitled* ('Arms'), 2006. Cotton fabric, sawdust, human humerus bone, various threads. Human sized. Photo: Ben Blackall.

(*right*) *Untitled* ('Arms'), (detail), 2006. Cotton fabric, sawdust, human humerus bone, various threads. Human sized. Photo: Ben Blackall.

take a second glance at the work, but it is equally hard to believe that the attention to detail in the embroidered cotton fabric in 'Arms' is not that of a historical one, such is the intricacy of the stitch work. But the second-take factor is certainly evident when the viewer investigates the bone embedded into the central cavity of the arm form to discover that it is indeed a human one.

It is this 'melancholia and misdemeanour' in Tabitha's work which could also be seen to draw a parallel with some of the research in my own practice. Research often unearths nuances and stories that make one think more deeply or broaden out our thinking in a manner not entirely expected. When embarking upon the 'Making Clothes for Children' series of works, I was at that time undertaking a residency in Australia at the Canberra School of Art, and had an opportunity to visit the Conservation Centre at the Australian War Memorial Museum in Canberra (which houses the main collection of wartime memorabilia in Australia). It was there that I was shown a collection of paper garments and, more significantly, the Changi quilts. These items evoked a sense of transient memory, the passing of time, fragility and vulnerability, all of which derived from the particular circumstances and time of their making. The impact of this find on my work was immense and has proved to be an integral part of much of the research I have undertaken since that period of time.

The Changi story goes a bit like this. Women and children were interned in Changi prison in Singapore during the Second World War. The quilts were made by the female prisoners as an attempt to communicate their existence and survival to the men interned in the male prison. There was to be a quilt for each nationality – British, Australian and Japanese. When complete, they were to be given to the commandant in each prison as a gift, with the hope that the male prisoners would be able to see the quilt and maybe recognise a signature, message or some form of communication from the women in the female prison. The important function of the quilts was to identify the women who were alive.

'OUT OF THE ORDINARY'

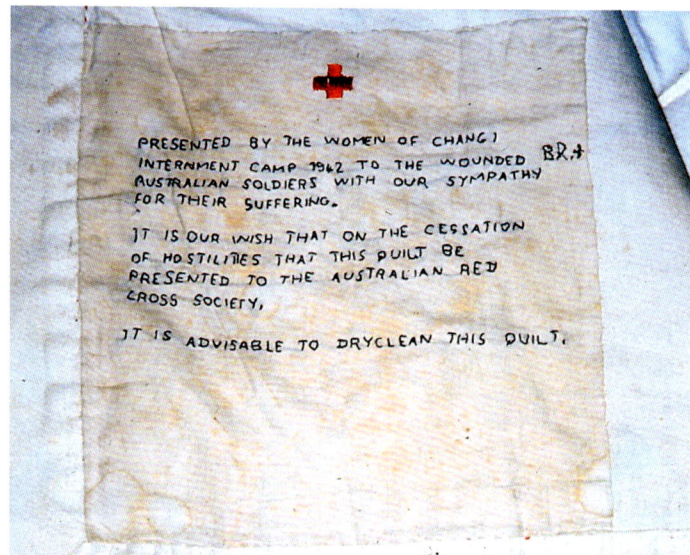

Each woman was given a 6-inch square from a rice sack and asked to put her name and something of herself into the square. When sewn together the final three quilts demonstrate the women's astute political awareness. They knew they had to act in an even-handed and conciliatory manner to achieve their aims and the dedication on each quilt expresses an impartial sympathy for the suffering of British, Australian and Japanese soldiers.[12]

This story became fundamental to the basis of further research in my work, particularly in relation to the importance of the passing on of knowledge through skill and how that sense of skill can inform on many levels.

In both Tabitha's and Anne's work it seems to me that there is a great (if not always evident) importance placed on the level of skill in the translation of ideas and in the retelling of their stories and narratives. They weave and wind their narrative threads exquisitely into their objects and artefacts.

In Tabitha's work, the preoccupation and association with narratives is much more evident and can be literal in conception, but subtle in translation as the materials provide the basis for the questions we as viewers may ask. The stories Tabitha surrounds herself with do create an air of intrigue and melancholia, this prose often passed down by word of mouth, or in many cases the narrative comes directly from the lost and found objects she so creatively selects.

The way that Tabitha tells her stories draws parallels with the work of Anne by material association alone. Tabitha makes similar choices to Anne in the qualities of fabrics she works upon, as in the piece *Three Knots*. She selects an old, not particularly special but never the less aged style of hanky, beautifully embroidering on to its surface in hair the words of this story:

I remember one of the McAllisters in Tobermory, there was an old woman, a relation, and when he was going to fish she would give him a three-knotted handkerchief. You opened the first knot if there was no wind and the second if there was not enough, but no way would you open the third! Heaven would fall down.[13]

Elizabeth Burnham
(left) *Hope Springs Eternal*, made between 8 March 1942 and September 1942, Changi prison. Photo: Mr Michael Archer. Photo reproduced by kind permission of Dr Bernice Archer. A quilt made for the British Red Cross and housed at the British Red Cross Museum in London. Elizabeth Burnham was a British nursing sister who was interned in Changi prison during the Second World War. The date '8/3/42', in the bottom left-hand corner, refers to the date when the women were marched to the prison. The 'E. Burnham' in the right-hand corner is her name, and the word 'Penang' underneath refers to where she lived with her husband before the war.

(right) Maker unknown. Australian Changi quilt, made between 8 March 1942 and September 1942 at Changi prison. Collection of Australian War Memorial in Canberra, Far Eastern War section. Photo: Mr Michael Archer. Photo reproduced by kind permission of Dr Bernice Archer. For further information on the women interned in the Far East during the Second World War, see Bernice Archer, *The Internment of Western Civilians Under the Japanese 1941–45: A Patchwork of Internment* (London: Routledge Curzon, 2004 [hardback] and Hong Kong University Press, 2008 [softback]).

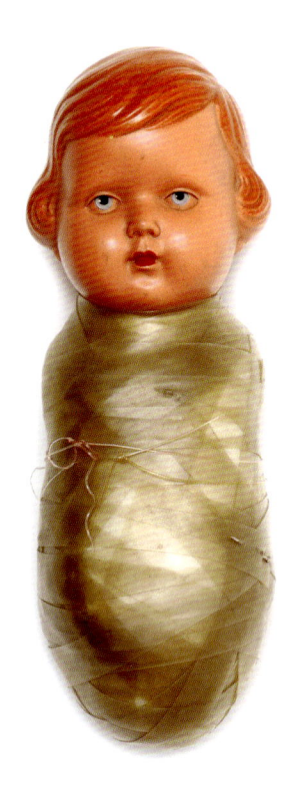

Tabitha Kyoko Moses
The Dolls, 2004. Dolls, fabric, plastic, thread, human hair, bits and bobs. 25 cm (10 in.) high. Photo: Ben Blackall.

HAND STITCH: PERSPECTIVES

The thin wisps of hair that randomly fall across the surface of the fabric suggest an energetic and gestural quality, as if upon a piece of paper with a quill pen. The attention to detail and the level of craftsmanship evident in the stitching are paramount to the credibility of this piece of work. A particular feature of Tabitha's work is her ability to recreate a sense of history through the accuracy and understanding of the materials she works with.

In 'The Lost and the Found' exhibition (2007), the doll was central to much of the work featured, inspired originally by a mummified girl encountered during a residency at Bolton Museum. Tabitha began to explore the humanity and deathliness of the doll, and although an avid collector of assorted doll objects, she states: 'I wasn't interested in a particular genre of doll, or in creating a collection or a history. But I suddenly discovered I had a lot of them. It was almost as if they found me.'[14]

Kate Davies, writing about Tabitha, begins by retelling a chilling story about a doll: 'Several hundred feet beneath the streets of Edinburgh's Old Town, a doll sits in a cold, dark room. The tattered plaid she wears is showing signs of age. Her limbs are dirty and her hair is white with dust. Gathered around her are hundreds of companions.'[15] The story goes on to recall an event: 'In 1992 a Japanese psychic, Aiko Gibo, visited Edinburgh's rediscovered city-beneath-the-city and reportedly felt the tugging hands of a girl left there to die in a plague year.' The psychic comforted the ghost by leaving her a tartan doll. Since then, numerous visitors to what is now known as Annie's room have done the same. Davies asks the question, 'What are we to make of this shrine, this spontaneous doll-memorial to the ghost of a girl no one remembers? Are we to be moved or repelled by Annie's room?'[16]

Stories such as these create an atmosphere of intrigue and sadness as one wonders about the sad, lonely child who once was there; maybe a doll would have brought great comfort. Whether you believe the story or not becomes almost immaterial, because what the story suggests is almost enough: the sense of neglect and despair. In observing the collection of dolls made by Tabitha (maybe in response to such stories as this), it appears that those dolls are some of the saddest and most lost, part-assembled, with missing limbs, full of melancholy but beautifully stitched and embroidered upon. In 'Arms' it is in the dismembering of the doll that brings to mind 'murderous curiosity, internal anguish, guilt and fascination. For who, in moments of dark childhood fantasy, has not killed their dolls?'[17]

The opportunity to study the works of Anne and Tabitha has enabled me to appreciate the subtleties of their work and to analyse this work alongside my own. The complexities of Anne's pieces are counterbalanced by the minimalist approach she adopts in the presentation: 'She does after all belong, in terms of loyalty and education, to the current long moment of post-minimalism. In this moment hierarchies that had organised and driven both art history and popular culture for over a century have come unhinged.'[18]

There are also associations, in Anne's work, with the work of Eva Hesse and Claes Oldenburg, artists of the Art Fabric movement. In the work of Hesse, it is the use of textile materials that serve to depict 'soft and fugitive' qualities that tend toward an 'often trivialised nostalgia, a profound sadness'.[19]

This 'sadness' is evident also in Tabitha's works. There is an air of contemplation and reflection that we experience when viewing, studying and analysing these works. This is not to find it depressing and sad, but rather reflectively sad. Considerations of the past are not to be forgotten but are something to be celebrated and cherished. In Tabitha's narratives we are reminded of stories and events from the past. Superstitions that no longer form part of our modern-day life were once integral to the foundations of dealing with the raw elements of a 'life at sea' and the 'unknown', as in the *Three Knots*. This may seem to be a light-hearted anecdote, but is it really?

The sadness in my own work is again more of a reflective sadness, a loss of something we once had, as in *Making Clothes for Children*. The commentary here is about what we don't do any more and is also a reference to particular aspects of our past social history.

Parallels of obsessive making, remaking, construction and deconstruction are elements in all of the works I have discussed in this chapter. Anne responds to the already frayed edges and surfaces that depict the qualities of wear and age. Tabitha finds or creates the sense of age and makes more of it through the clever references she skilfully embroiders back into the cloth, to give it back its history. My obsessive attention to detail is evident in the weaving of the cloth itself, often in layers (triple and quadruple cloths), deconstructing it back into separate pieces to emphasise the memories trapped within garments that we wear, keep or pass on.

NOTES

[1] Anne Wilson, interview with the author, 2011.
[2] Coatts, Margot, *A Weaver's Life: Ethel Mairet 1872–1952*, (London: Crafts Council, 1983).
[3] Anne Wilson, interview with the author, 2011.
[4] Tina Yapelli, curator of exhibitions (from Introduction in catalogue to 'Anne Wilson: Body into Culture', Madison Museum of Contemporary Art, Wisconsin, 1993).
[5] Anne Wilson, interview with the author, 2011.
[6] Ibid.
[7] From wall label, 'Anne Wilson, Anatomy of Wear', Museum of Contemporary Art, Chicago, 2000.
[8] Anne Wilson, interview with the author, 2011.
[9] Ibid.
[10] Interview with Alex Michon, writer and co-director of the Transition gallery in East London.
[11] Ibid.
[12] Archer, Bernice, 'A Patchwork Perspective of Internment: Quilts from Changi Prison', *Quilters' Review* (21), Summer 1996.
[13] *Three Knots* by Tabitha Kyoko Moses
[14] Davies, Kate, 'Goodbye Dolly', interview between Kate Davies and Tabitha Moses.
[15] Ibid.
[16] Ibid.
[17] Ibid.
[18] Sherk, Bonnie, *High Performance* magazine, 1980 (extract: Anne Wilson, Portfolio Collection series, Brighton: Telos Art Publishing).
[19] Ibid.

The Past to the Present

ANN FRENCH

But what can the Museum do to Encourage Embroidery? Museums, collectors and embroidery

INTRODUCTION

THE QUESTION 'BUT WHAT CAN THE MUSEUM DO to encourage embroidery?' was posed by A. F. Kendrick, the first official curator in charge of textiles at the South Kensington Museum (now the Victoria and Albert Museum, London), in the *Museums Journal* of 1909, in an article titled 'Why Should a Provincial Museum Collect Embroideries?'[1] In this short piece, he outlined an idealised relationship between an embroiderer and museum collections. A museum collection should 'stimulate originality', 'provide instruction' and in return an embroiderer can 'work a diagram of useful stitches' to be 'hung in some accessible corner of the local museum'. Kendrick assumed that a symbiotic relationship between historic pieces of art and contemporary work lay behind the formation of many museum collections, and the scope of this essay is to explore specific embroidery collections to interrogate this assumption.

Making such a connection between hand-stitch embroidery and the resource provided by museum collections emerged from researching the archaeologists R. M. Dawkins and A. J. B. Wace, who collected historic Greek domestic embroideries while based at the British School of Archaeology at Athens (BSA) in the early twentieth century. These collections of Greek embroidery were later donated to the Victoria and Albert Museum (V&A) or bought by Liverpool Museums, and those of other BSA members are in the Fitzwilliam, the Ashmolean and the Whitworth Art Gallery, providing English museums with some of the best collections of such embroidery outside Greece. Dawkins' and Wace's relationships with the above museums and with the embroiderer and teacher, Louisa Pesel, exemplify Kendrick's assumption regarding the origin and application of museum embroidery collections. The nature, status, purpose and craft of hand stitch are constantly evolving, as this book reveals, so this essay aims to provide an alternative but historical perspective, and a reminder of the resources still available within museum collections for contemporary workers in stitch.

Before embarking on such a specific story, two influential factors need outlining: the emergence of embroidery as a declared art form during the late nineteenth century and the early formation of museum collections, especially that of the South Kensington Museum. Dawkins, Wace and Pesel were not unique, but they are exemplars of the many others who helped build, and used, the museum collections of historic embroidery now available in the UK.

ATTITUDES TO EMBROIDERY

Embroidery was, of course, not a new skill in the early nineteenth century, but the advent of industrial cotton printing had brought patterned materials within almost everyone's reach, removing the need to embroider decorative curtains and hangings, while the Reformation had meant that the impetus to create vestments for the Church had been removed for several centuries. Catholic Emancipation of 1829 and the redistribution of population through industrialisation into new and concentrated areas had, however, resulted in a prolific church-building programme for both Catholic and Anglican communities.

Crucially for design and for hand embroidery, the new churches were built and furnished to Tractarian and Gothic Revival ideals that emphasised furnishings to provide warmth, light, colour and splendour. For both Anglicans and Catholics to express their commitment, newly designed vestments and church furnishings were therefore created. Until the 1830s, these furnishings were imported from the Continent or were made by suppliers to the military or court, but from the 1840s, the wives and sisters of architects such as G. E. Street, and woman of local parishes, increasingly formed embroidery societies to undertake the work.[2] In 1854, the Misses Street and Agnes Blencowe formed the Ladies' Ecclesiastical Embroidery Society, which made copies of medieval embroidery as well as working new designs for Street and other architects. Agnes Blencowe contributed the drawings to *Ecclesiastical Embroidery* (1848), one of many publications produced to assist the production of embroidery and church furnishings, which began the assault on 'Berlin wool work'.

'Berlin wool work' was the most popular form of domestic amateur embroidery in the middle decades of the nineteenth century, benefiting from a new approach to providing embroidery designs through colour-printed designs on squared paper, which could be copied square by square and stitch by stitch. Little or no skill was required; the predominant technique was tent stitch on canvas, and elaborate designs could be reproduced with patient counting.[3] The resulting products were applied to a wide variety of household items, from slippers to footstools. Both product and technique, while making for highly successful supply businesses, contradicted the alternative ideologies of Pugin, Ruskin and Morris. Their followers condemned Berlin wool work as 'fancywork … all uselessness and ugliness', and urged a reappraisal demanding action. 'Examine the work being sold in the fancy-work shops, illustrated in ladies' newspapers or embroidered in the drawing rooms of to-day, and consider in what respect it differs from the old work such as that exhibited in the South Kensington Museum.'[4]

Morris, Marshall, Faulkner & Co. itself produced embroidery, displayed first by the firm at the 'International Exhibition' at South Kensington in 1862.[5] Morris's embroidery designs used motifs and formats found in historic fabrics, especially from Turkey and Persia,[6] and employed techniques different from canvas and raised work: darning, running stitch, long and short stitch, satin and stem stitches being favoured as they accentuate the lines of designs more effectively. The products also differed, even when produced domestically from 'kits'. Large hangings and items of use were typical, rather than fancy-work knick-knacks.

In 1885, Morris's daughter May took over the embroidery section of Morris & Co. In 1893 she wrote three essays: 'Of Embroidery', 'Of Materials' and 'Colour' for *Arts and Craft Essays*, edited by her father, and a book, *Decorative Needlework* (1893). This last is very practical, clearly written by a practitioner, and is infused with her father's ideals, thereby acting as a short summary of 'Art Embroidery'. She covers historical examples,[7] stitches which are 'technicalities to master' and 'best learnt from a piece in a museum or even better in your own hands', patchwork and quilting, working techniques (frame or no frame), design and colour.

To raise needlework to the rank of art, 'Art Needlework', certain principles were cited: intelligence, adaptation to the materials used, and use and beauty. New designs were encouraged, different techniques urged and the study of historic and other embroideries considered essential.

Formal art and design teaching was available to women from the 1840s, encouraging embroidery to be included in the subjects taught. The Royal School of Needlework was founded in 1872 by Helen Welby and Lady Alford. The school was philanthropic in its aims – to teach and to provide employment for distressed gentlewomen. These objectives were far from innovative, but its commitment to execute 'ornamental needlework for secular purposes only' was original.[8] The school maintained close links with the South Kensington Museum and worked many pieces designed by leading artists, including William Morris, Edward Burne Jones, G. F. Bodley and Walter Crane, thereby reinforcing the connections to the leading lights of the Arts and Crafts Movement.

This revived interest and market for such a variety of hand-stitch embroidery is reflected in the wealth of books on the subject published after 1840[9]: historical surveys, reference books, and books on design and colour reflecting the changing face of embroidery. They trace the antiquarian roots surrounding the interest in medieval embroidery in particular, encompass global and historical surveys, and apply classic typology to the grouping and naming of stitches. The Royal School of Needlework itself produced a *Handbook of Embroidery* in 1880 that exemplifies the field.[10]

THE ROLE OF THE SOUTH KENSINGTON MUSEUM

The South Kensington Museum provided a reference point for all these activities, and acted as an exemplar for regional foundations such as the Whitworth Art Gallery and others. Established in 1852,[11] the museum formed, from its inception, an integral part of national art education, with the mission to reform art and design training in England, to improve English goods from an artistic perspective, and to enable the country to compete more favourably in foreign markets. The result was a museum and associated teaching programme that combined commercial aims with a broader educational purpose, with a given audience of artisans and designers, all reflected in the collections thus acquired.[12] By 1900, an ordering system based on materials was established, with four main divisions of classification – ceramics and glass, metalwork, textiles, and furniture and woodwork.

The textile collection began with the contemporary woven and printed textiles acquired from the Great Exhibition of 1851 and the Paris Exhibitions of 1855 and 1867, and initially the emphasis was on acquiring pre-nineteenth-century material, especially medieval textiles, many in the form of vestments. Loans and loan exhibitions performed a crucial role in promoting and extending the range of displays and objects,[13] with a permanent 'loan court' established for the purpose. In 1873, a 'Special Loan Exhibition of Decorative Art Needlework Made Before 1800' was initiated by Princess Christian, HRH the Duchess of Teck, Lady Marion Alford (Viscountess Cust) and Victoria Welby. The scope of the exhibition was 'Needlework made before 1800 noted for its artistic, archaeological and historic merits', but it excluded lace and tapestry, and noted that 'The ancient Art of Needlework or Embroidery has formed a section in the artistic development of all civilised countries'. A catalogue followed this exhibition, and from 1871 to 1900, a further five catalogues were written on the textiles collections at South Kensington; the first by Mrs Bury Palliser and four by Alan Summerly Cole. All

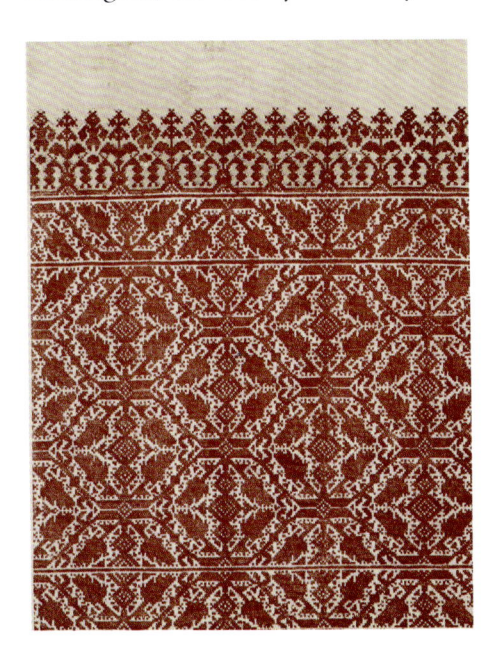

From 1881, the South Kensington Museum published high-quality lithographic plates taken from its collections, especially textiles, entitled the *Portfolios of Industrial Art*. These were intended as educative material for designers and manufacturers, and included portfolios of Oriental, Persian, Saracenic, Indian, Egyptian and Chinese art. Within the plates for Oriental art, there are two plates titled 'Petticoat: Turco-Greek or Turco-Syrian, 18th century S.K.M. 2063-76', which is the Cretan embroidery purchased from Thomas Sandwith in 1876. Acc. no. T.2063-1876. Library Whitworth Art Gallery, University of Manchester. Photo: Michael Pollard.

stressed the antiquity of needlework carried out 'since man has been known to exist', but 'Yet with the needle in its modern perfection, the bulk of embroidery produced at the present day is on the whole devoid of that particular quality, which monastic devotion and skill secured for needlework of the Middle Ages'. The remedy for this malaise was to study historic examples, especially those in the South Kensington Museum and their publication from 1881 of (see illustration on previous page) *Portfolios of Industrial Art*.

The earliest major acquisitions of historic Greek embroidery for the South Kensington Museum were from Thomas Sandwith, the British consul on Crete (then part of the Ottoman Empire). In 1876, the museum acquired 160 pieces at the recommendation of Mrs Bury Palliser, one of the South Kensington's 'art referees'. The role of art referee was to advise as to whether objects were genuine and good of their kind, whether the price was reasonable, and to make suggestions as to other objects that might be acquired. During the late nineteenth century, referees included Frederick Leighton, G. F. Bodley, Sir A. H. Layard, L. Alma Tadema, William Morris and Walter Crane, and their role was highly influential.

Mrs Bury Palliser recommended the Cretan pieces for their brilliant colours and the demonstration of new stitches for the practical worker (being particularly suited for schools of art needlework and museums) but deemed them to be of no marketable value. Two pieces were to feature in the *Portfolios of Industrial Art* (1881) and this collection may well lie behind the work called Ruskin or Greek lace.[14] A few items probably worked their way into the personal collection of William Morris.[15]

Morris was not the only artist/designer to create a personal collection, and many of these collections contained Greek pieces. Frederick Leighton lent the 1873 South Kensington exhibition some Greek pieces, delightfully but inaccurately described as curtains or cushions from galleys serving the Knights of

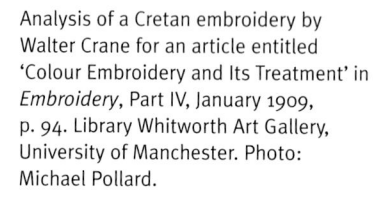

Analysis of a Cretan embroidery by Walter Crane for an article entitled 'Colour Embroidery and Its Treatment' in *Embroidery*, Part IV, January 1909, p. 94. Library Whitworth Art Gallery, University of Manchester. Photo: Michael Pollard.

Rhodes. The collection of Lewis Foreman Day and his wife was displayed at Platt Hall, Manchester in 1930, and of 330 pieces listed in the catalogue, 22 pieces were Greek. The small catalogue states the hope that the embroideries might encourage others to follow the example of former days and of other countries, not to copy the past slavishly, but, by studying what was good in the past, to produce beautiful needlework expressive of their own age. Day's collection is now scattered across various collections including those of the V&A, Manchester City Art Galleries, and the Rachel Kay-Shuttleworth Collection at Gawthorpe Hall.

THE COLLECTORS

R. M. Dawkins and A. J. B. Wace[16] collected over 1,200 pieces of Greek embroidery, of which Dawkins bequeathed his entire collection to the Victoria and Albert Museum.[17] They seem to have started collecting embroideries almost immediately upon their arrival in Athens in 1902. Dawkins's unpublished autobiography recalls a Rhodian pedlar who brought items to the school for members to purchase, and they used a number of antique dealers in Athens, but then took to acquiring embroideries on their travels around Greece. Crucially, however, they catalogued and photographed their pieces, recording provenance, measurements, loom widths, colours, pattern and stitch, together with a photograph number, a methodology that relates directly to their archaeological work.

Coincidently and critically, in Athens at the same time was Louisa Pesel, working as director of the Royal Hellenic School of Embroidery and Laces.[18] She left Athens in 1907, returning to Bradford, and involved herself in teaching and philanthropic causes, including founding the West Riding Needlecraft Association in 1912 'to improve modern craftsmanship through the systematic study of the Designs, Colours and Stitches found in old Embroideries'. She was an early member of the Society of Certificated Embroideresses, founded in 1907, which became the Embroiderers' Guild in 1920, with Pesel herself as president.

Louisa Pesel also collected embroideries, which are now in the collection of the University of Leeds.[19] Pesel, like Dawkins and Wace, used a very structured approach to the analysis of historic embroideries. For her personal use, she had cards printed with headings to note provenance, group, type, influence, description, use, measurements, materials, colours, stitches, owner, number, where bought, cross-references, remarks and further comparisons. Her cards are not so much a personal catalogue, like Dawkins's and Wace's, but a reference collection of embroideries. As she herself explained: 'It will be found useful to tabulate all particulars relating to such embroideries after the manner shown for the coloured plate ... Embroideresses should aim at having three definitions applied to their work. By study and comparison of styles their work must earn the term of a science, by their skill and patience their craft must earn the designation of an art, and lastly, by its conception and beauty of colour, it must be worthy of being classed as an inspiration.'[20]

Dawkins, Pesel and Wace disseminated their interest in Greek embroidery. In 1906 they put on a small exhibition at the Fitzwilliam Museum, Cambridge,

Photograph of an embroidered jacket found in a photographic album in the Louisa Pesel Collection, University of Leeds International Textiles Archive, using designs taken from prehistoric Mycenaean motifs, possibly sourced from the library of the British School at Athens. The Louisa Pesel Collection, University of Leeds International Textiles Archive.

HAND STITCH: PERSPECTIVES

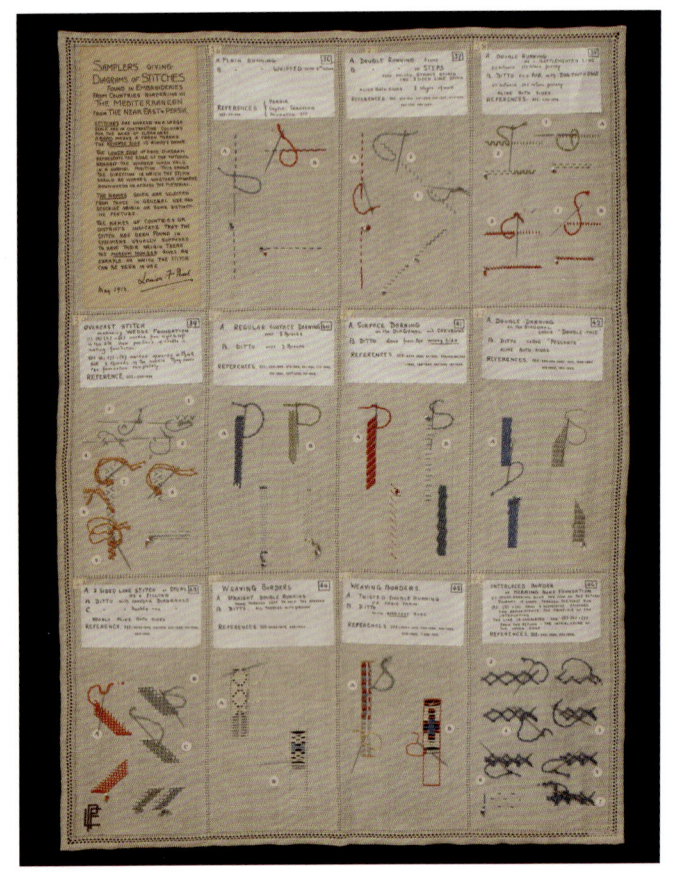

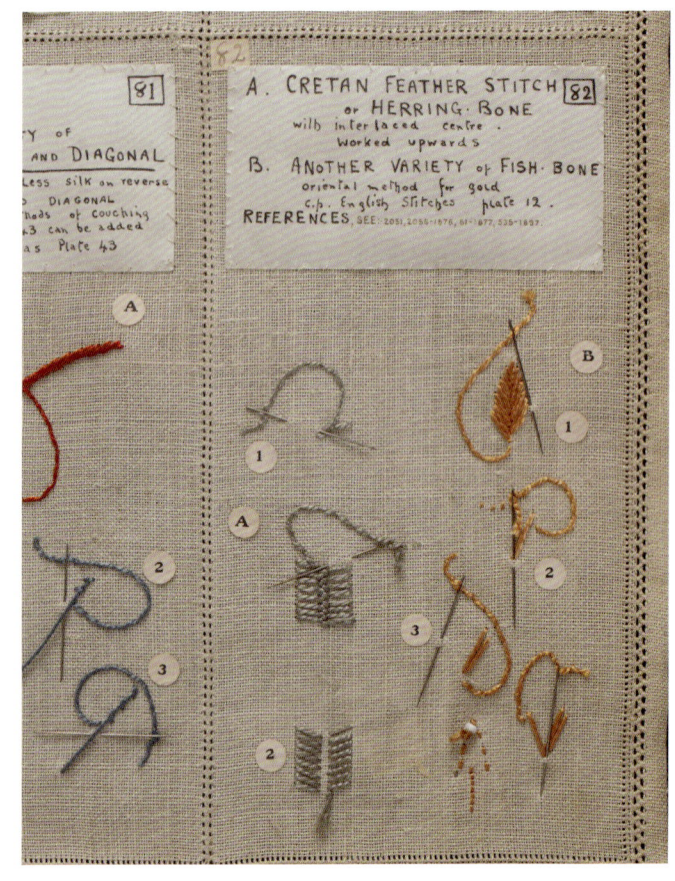

(*above left*) Louisa Pesel's stitch sampler, displayed in the Textile Study Rooms of the Victoria and Albert Museum, London until January 2010, which formed the basis for Pesel's *Stitches from Eastern Embroideries*, 1913. Acc. no. T.271.1913. © Victoria and Albert Museum, London.

(*above right*) Detail from Louisa Pesel's stitch sampler, No. 82 Cretan Feather Stitch or Herringbone, published in *Stitches from Eastern Embroideries*, 1913. Acc. no. T.275.1913. © Victoria and Albert Museum, London.

(*right*) Coloured plate, analysis and stitch schema details from Louisa Pesel's *Stitches from Eastern Embroideries*, 1913. Photo: Michael Pollard.

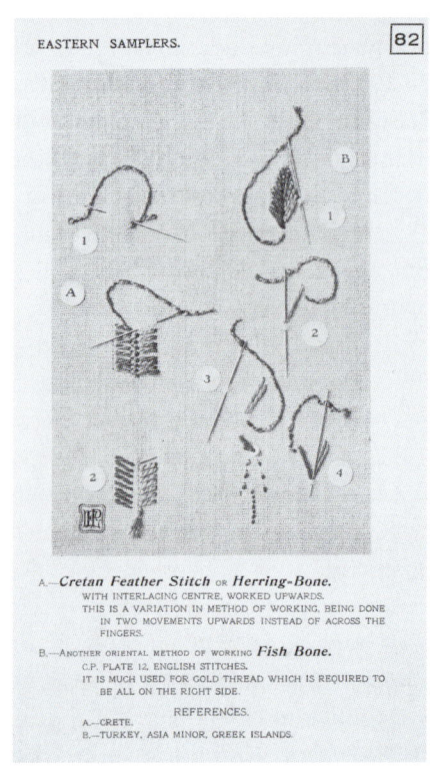

compiling a small but unillustrated catalogue. Louisa Pesel attended the annual conference of the British Association for the Advancement of Science in York in the same year, gave a lecture entitled 'Greek Embroideries', and wrote articles for *The Burlington Magazine*.[21]

This work came to the attention of A. F. Kendrick at the Victoria and Albert Museum, and a mutually cooperative relationship was established. The V&A gained access to the local knowledge acquired by Dawkins and Wace in their travels around Greece, Louisa Pesel provided the V&A with her stitch samplers, and the V&A supplied all with photographs of its own collection for reference.

These samplers[22] formed the material basis for Louisa Pesel's stitch portfolios: *Stitches from Old English Embroideries, Stitches from Eastern Embroideries and Stitches from Western Embroideries*. These combined highly practical stitch schema (from face and reverse), a typology for the stitches (including alternative names), a guide to where they were used and a completed analysis form.

Dawkins and Wace lent the V&A embroideries to display in its Loan Court from 1914 to 1925, and these embroideries were almost certainly those used for the exhibition held at the Burlington Fine Arts Club in the winter of 1914–15: 'Old Embroideries from the Greek Islands and Turkey', only the second exhibition of embroidery the club had initiated. Wace complied a catalogue, and Dawkins and Wace wrote two more ethnographic articles.[23] Kendrick, despite the outbreak of war, had the whole exhibition photographed in a series of 42 installation shots, providing a unique glimpse into methods of display and interpretative methods of the time.

Although Dawkins and Wace were the primary lenders to the exhibition, other lenders reflect the network of interest in such embroideries. They include other members of the British School (of Archaeology) at Athens (R. C. Bosanquet, Guy Dickins), two museums (Royal Scottish Museum and the Whitworth Institute), Lady Egerton, Professor Percy Newberry and A. M. Daniel. Essie Newberry and Marjorie Daniel were great friends of Louisa Pesel and were themselves embroiderers;

(*left*) Case G at the exhibition 'Old Embroideries of the Greek Islands and Turkey' (1914) – containing 18 pieces from the collections of Dawkins, Wace and Daniel largely from the Island of Skyros, which Dawkins visited in 1905 to observe a Lenten carnival. Reproduced courtesy of the British School at Athens.

(*right*) Case I at the exhibition 'Old Embroideries of the Greek Islands and Turkey' (1914) – containing seven pieces from Crete (mostly skirt borders of the kind first acquired by the South Kensington Museum in 1876) and analysed by Walter Crane (see p. 168). Reproduced courtesy of the British School at Athens.

HAND STITCH: PERSPECTIVES

(*right*) The fragment belonged to Marjorie Daniel, who gave it to Rachel Kay-Shuttleworth, who noted it as 'Janina (Epirus) ? part of a table cloth or curtain. Surface darned, it is the 5th thread that is picked up. Then the diagonals are all even. Blue, green, red which is dominant & yellow (see illus. in Pesel's *Stitches from Eastern Embroideries*). The design probably adapted from a brocade. Note the bold voided patterns in the patches of work. There is a neat border of floral type. Donor: Lady Daniel'. Acc. no. RKBS 25028. By permission of the Trustees of the Rachel B. Kay-Shuttleworth Collection, Gawthorpe Hall, Padiham. Photo: Ann French.

(*far right*) The curtain is labelled by Rachel Kay-Shuttleworth: 'Greece 20th C. worked by refugees in Athens from a Janina design in double darning on the diagonal, satin & stem stitch. 3 rich shades of rose silk – very thick floss being used on local material. The whole effect being exceedingly handsome. The school for these refugees was organised by Lady Egerton wife of the British Ambassador, and supervised by Miss Lousia F. Pesel, whose books on stitches are classics, and who worked the samplers shown in these for the Victoria and Albert Museum – Pesel 41. Donor: Lady Daniel'. Acc. no. RKBS 25025. By permission of the Trustees of the Rachel B. Kay-Shuttleworth Collection, Gawthorpe Hall, Padiham. Photo: Ann French.

Marjorie Daniel had been a student at the British School of Archaeology in Athens in 1903–4. The Newberry embroideries were eventually donated to the Whitworth Art Gallery, and the Daniel embroideries to the Fitzwilliam Museum and to Rachel Kay-Shuttleworth at Gawthorpe Hall. Newberry, Pesel and Kendrick were to compile *A Book of Old Embroidery* in 1925, a geographical and historical survey, illustrated with pieces from public and private collections, including those of the V&A, Pesel, Newberry and Wace.

Books, articles and catalogues remain easily accessible as the literary results of research into historic embroidery, but other tangible results in the form of designs and embroidery itself can be found scattered across collections and archives.[24] These reveal the extraordinary output of those (mostly women) who studied, taught and stitched embroidery, forming the basis of much twentieth-century work, professional and amateur.[25]

The fragment (see illustration above left), now at Gawthorpe, similar to that referenced in Pesel's *Stitches from Eastern Embroidery* (1913), is part of a tablecloth or curtain. A rare example of the work produced under the aegis of Louisa Pesel is the curtain (above right). This pair of embroideries, when seen side by side, show that while the historic piece provided design and technical inspiration, direct imitation was not a requirement. The new piece is designed for a contemporary function, employs more stitches and uses a fashionable colour scheme.

Designs were taken directly from historic pieces. Wace bought the Cretan cushion (see illustration page 173) in Athens in the 1920s, but among the many needlework designs left to Rachel Kay-Shuttleworth at Gawthorpe is a watercolour on tracing paper of the piece, drawn by Dr Sybil Welsh, Marjorie Daniel's sister. It is a copy of the historic embroidery and could have been the basis for a transfer drawing.

BUT WHAT CAN THE MUSEUM DO...?

Wace lent Pesel at least one embroidery for an exhibition organised by the West Riding Needlecraft Association in 1914, at which she delivered a lecture, 'The Antiquity of Embroidery: How, When, and Where to Teach It'. One of these was a Rhodian cushion. He bought this cushion in a village on Rhodes called Seroni, on 13 July 1908, his notebook recording that traditional dress was still being worn there – but with 'bad embroidery'. Among Pesel's archives is a stitch analysis by E. Arnold of the pattern found on the cushion (below).

Amongst the many stitch analyses and design drawings by Pesel herself is one of another Wace embroidery, whose current whereabouts is unknown. An example of how she adapted these analyses to her own work is the altar frontal worked by

(*left*) The Cretan cushion bought by Wace in Athens in the 1920s. Liverpool Museums. Acc. no. 56.210.358. Courtesy of Liverpool Museums. Photo: Ann French.

(*right*) Detail. The Cretan cushion was copied by Sibyl Welsh in a watercolour on tracing paper, for use as an embroidery design. Acc. no. RKBS 3232. By permission of the Trustees of the Rachel B. Kay-Shuttleworth Collection, Gawthorpe Hall, Padiham. Photo: Ann French.

(*far left*) Detail of a Rhodian cushion bought by Wace on 13 July 1908 in Seroni, a village on Rhodes where traditional dress was still worn. It was lent to the West Riding Needlecraft Association in 1914. Liverpool Museums. Acc. no. 56.210.333. Courtesy of Liverpool Museums. Photo: Ann French.

(*left*) Among Pesel's archives is a stitch analysis, by E. Arnold, of the pattern found on the cushion, where it is described as 'Pillowcase joined with feather stitch joining in green. Tassels made of all the colours joined. Openings closed by cords with tiny tassels and a small cross-stitch pattern.' Courtesy of the Louisa Pesel Collection, University of Leeds International Textiles Archive.

173

HAND STITCH: PERSPECTIVES

the handicraft section of the Khaki Club, an association for shell-shocked soldiers, which she supervised during the First World War. It is now part of the collections of Bradford Cathedral and is labelled on the reverse: 'This frontlet was worked by shell-shocked soldiers in the autumn of 1918 at Bradford Khaki Handicrafts Club for use at their services at the Abram Peel Hospital. It was lengthened and the frontal added by their teachers in 1919 and was accepted in memory of them for the Bolling Chapel in 1920.'

Sample pieces reflecting historic pieces were another method of recording and evolving embroidery patterns. Pesel worked many sample pieces many clearly Greek in inspiration, all now in the University of Leeds International Textile Archive (see illustrations below).

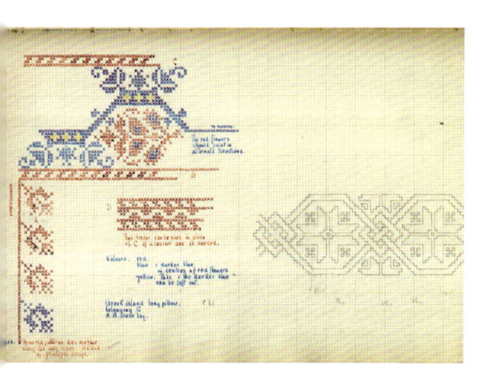

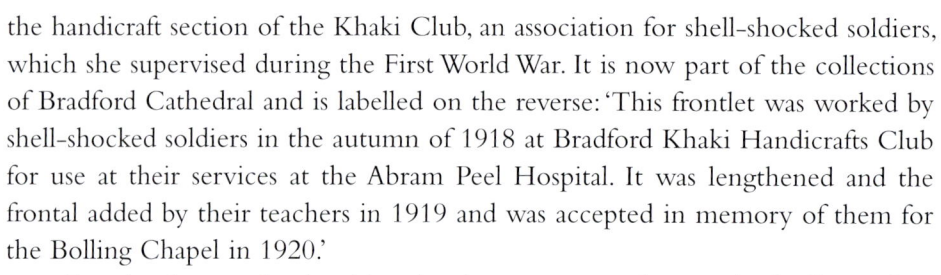

CONCLUSION

The evolution of hand stitch in the twentieth century in its form, function and purpose can be traced to its roots in attitudes to art in the late nineteenth century, especially those of the Arts and Crafts Movement. Collections (public and personal) of historic embroidery provided both technical typology and design inspiration for a wide variety of practitioners. These historic connections can still resonate both for modern practitioners and for understanding the typological nature of many museum collections. The collections, work and application of Dawkins, Wace and Pesel regarding Greek embroideries are one illustration of the ongoing relationship that can exist between museum collections and the hand-embroiderer.

Stitch analysis and design drawing by Louisa Pesel from a Wace embroidery whose current whereabouts is unknown, but called a Greek Island long cushion. Courtesy of the Louisa Pesel Collection, University of Leeds International Textiles Archive.

Detail from altar frontal, worked by shell-shocked soldiers at Bradford Khaki Handicrafts Club during the First World War and now in the collection of Bradford Cathedral. Courtesy of Bradford Cathedral. Photo: Ann French.

(*left*) Cushion from Rhodes bought by Wace from the pedlar who visited the British School at Athens and lent by Wace to the West Riding Needlecraft Association in 1914. Liverpool Museums. Acc. no. 56.210.328. Courtesy of Liverpool Museums. Photo: Ann French.

(*right*) Textile sample stitched by Lousia Pesel showing inspiration and adaptation of designs from Greek embroideries. Archive. Acc. no. 1183. Courtesy of the Louisa Pesel Collection, University of Leeds International Textiles.

NOTES

1. Kendrick, A. F. 'Why Should a Provincial Museum Collect Embroideries?' in *The Museums Journal*, 14 (1909).
2. Schoeser, Mary, *The Watts Book of Embroidery: English Church Embroidery 1833–1953* (London: Watts, 1998).
3. Morris, Barbara, *Victorian Embroidery* (London: Barrie Jenkins, 1970).
4. Lockwood, M. S. and E. Glaister, *Art Embroidery: A Treatise on the Revived Practice of Decorative Needlework* (London: Marcus Ward, 1878; facsimile edition 1978).
5. Parry, Linda (ed.), *William Morris* (London: Philip Wilson in association with the Victoria and Albert Museum, 1996).
6. Parry, Linda, *William Morris Textiles* (London: Weidenfeld & Nicholson, 1983).
7. The only illustration in the book is that of the Syon Cope (T.83-1864) in the V&A collections, about which May Morris was to write a further article in *The Burlington Magazine for Connoisseurs*, Vol. 6, No. 22 (Jan 1905).
8. Hulse, Lynn, 'Introductory Essay', in Letitia Higgin and Lady Marion Alford (eds), *Handbook of Embroidery* (London: Royal School of Needlework, 2010).
9. Edwards, Joan, 'A Survey of English Literature of Embroidery 1840–1940', in *Bulletin of the Needle and Bobbin Club*, 59 (1976).
10. Higgin, Letitia and Alford, Lady Marion, *Handbook of Embroidery* (London: Royal School of Needlework, 1880).
11. See www.vam.ac.uk/vastatic/microsites/1159_grand_design/essay-museum-collections-histories_new.htm/(accessed 26 August 2011).
12. Now the Victoria and Albert Museum, based at South Kensington from 1857. See www.vam.ac.uk/vastatic/microsites/1159_grand_design/essay-the-idealist-enterprise_new.html/(accessed 26 August 2011).
13. Eatwell, Ann, 'Borrowing from Collectors: The Role of the Loan in the Formation of the Victoria and Albert Museum and its Collection (1852–1932)', in *The Journal of the Decorative Arts Society*, 24 (2000).
14. Greensted, Mary, *The Arts and Crafts Movement: Exchanges between Greece and Britain (1876–1930)* (University of Birmingham, 2010); Haslam, Sara E., *John Ruskin and the Lakeland Arts Revival, 1880–1920* (Cardiff: Merton Priory Press, 2004).
15. For example, now V&A T.121-1939. From Pholegandros, bequeathed to the V&A by his daughter, May, in 1939.
16. Both classicists, they came to Athens and Greece with an ethnographical approach to archaeology encouraged by their mentor Professor William Ridgeway, Disney Professor of Archaeology at Cambridge (1892–1926), and by Professor John Linton Myres, Wykeham Professor in Ancient History at Oxford (1910–38). Both were themselves to become leading Oxbridge academics, Dawkins as Sotheby and Bywater Professor of Modern and Byzantine Greek at Oxford (1919–39) and Wace as Laurence Professor of Classical Archaeology at Cambridge (1934–44).
17. Dawkins's entire collection is in the Victoria and Albert Museum and Wace's collection is divided amongst the V&A, the Textile Museum, Washington DC and Liverpool Museums. See Further Reading.
18. This had been established in Athens in 1897 by the wife of the British minister (or ambassador), Lady Egerton, to enable refugee peasant women to earn a living and to revive a craft tradition using supplied historic and classic designs. In 1902 she employed Louisa Pesel at the recommendation of Lewis Foreman Day. Louisa Pesel was educated at Bradford Girls' Grammar School but moved to London in 1887 to train and work under Lewis Foreman Day.
19. See http://ulita.leeds.ac.uk/wiki/mediawiki-1.10.1/index.php/Collections#Louisa_Pesel_Collection/(accessed 26 August 2011).
20. Pesel, Louisa, *Stitches from Eastern Embroideries* (Portfolio II) (London: Percy Lund, Humphreys & Co., 1913).
21. Pesel, Louisa F., 'The Embroideries of the Aegean', in *The Burlington Magazine*, X (XLVI) (1907); Pesel, Louisa F., 'The So-Called "Janina" Embroideries', in *The Burlington Magazine*, XI (XLIX) (1907).
22. Four Pesel's samplers were on display in the Textile Study Rooms of the V&A until January 2011.
23. Wace, A. J. B. and R. M. Dawkins, 'Greek Embroideries – I: Ethnography', in *The Burlington Magazine*, 26 (140) (1914), pp. 49–50; and 'Greek Embroideries – II: The Towns and Houses of the Archipelago', in *The Burlington Magazine*, 26 (141) (1914).
24. See list of institutions below.
25. Marsh, Gail, *Early 20th Century Embroidery Techniques* (Lewes: Guild of Master Craftsmen, 2011).

TRACY GILL

Research and the Imprint of Stitch

I have a vision of a place of meeting where neighbours will come for many reasons to seek stimulating thought by meeting other active minds, to find refreshment and inspiration and a joy in beauty.

— Rachel B. Kay-Shuttleworth, 1912[1]

MY ROLE AT GAWTHORPE HALL IS TO BUILD on Rachel Kay-Shuttleworth's vision for her textile collection (RBKS Collection) and to develop new pathways for access to the collection as an educational tool. One of my intentions has been to understand the value of stitch in the modern world.

This has opened up many avenues in my own practice. I wanted to develop creative and enjoyable teaching methods to enrich the experience of learning textile craft by exploring the social value of learning commonplace sewing skills. If teaching is to help to integrate craft skills into the curriculum, it is important to unravel the beneficial and therapeutic factors in order to optimise the experience for teachers and learners.

Professor Anne Morrell inspired my initial research study visit to the RBKS Collection, leading me to discover the value of precious archive materials. I was captivated by the wealth of embroidery and literary treasures, and my affinity with Rachel Kay-Shuttleworth's vision of making and stitch has become an important influence.

As my eyes scanned the items in the archive, I began to trace the pathway of a collector. The use of logging, both numerically and alphabetically, has become an accepted classification process. Couture fashion pieces were carefully conserved alongside vast categories of embroideries and textiles, which invited the question of why we cherish and store objects. My practice previously explored how moral values impact upon daily activities. In today's society it appears that we are on a consumer treadmill, keeping up with the latest trends, and we often forget the importance and value of possessions. Craft skill can offer an individual maker a sense of achievement and self-worth, and helps teach numeracy, literacy and cognitive skills. It can act as a leveller, calming you down and taking you away from the hustle and bustle of daily life. A basic knowledge of stitch, both functional and decorative, can provide enrichment to life, which cannot be bought.

Our reliance on technology has become demanding, and this raises questions about teaching stitch and its lack of importance in the current curriculum. Stitch is no longer seen as a core requirement within the household, as it is cheaper and quicker to discard a garment than to repair or alter it. Domestic science was once a key part of the curriculum, but abandoning the teaching of the subject, alongside material changes to lifestyles, has had an impact on the value that society places on this practical task. Stitch has served to communicate, to be functional and to have status in contemporary art forms and fashion. Hidden within the depths of our museums are archived collections that can inspire us all.

THE QUIET AMBASSADOR FOR STITCH AND TEXTILES

The RBKS Collection is an impressive and varied array of textiles initially collated by the Hon. Rachel Beatrice Kay-Shuttleworth MBE, who died in 1967. Her lasting legacy is a treasure trove. Its range encompasses embroidery, printed and woven cloth, patchwork and quilting, costume, lace and many other related textile craft techniques from all over the world, dating from the seventeenth to twentieth century. It continues to be added to today. The RBKS Collection has over 30,000 items and is housed in Gawthorpe Hall, a National Trust property near Burnley in Lancashire, where a significant number of items are on public display in dedicated galleries. Over the years, RBKS trustees have been working to develop access for students, teachers and enthusiasts to study the beauty and diversity of the collection. The trustees and in-house team endeavour to honour Rachel's original aims, through the dissemination of knowledge of traditional and creative textile workshops and study visits.

This collection can tell great stories. Rachel's aim was to pass on her knowledge and wisdom to as many people as she could through teaching and lecturing on the value of crafts, in particular embroidery and lace-making. The pieces she collected are the unique foundation of what is now a truly remarkable educational resource. Her enthusiasm and organisational skills can been seen from over 60 years' work in cataloguing the items she collected, including many donations from friends and contemporary craft practitioners. The collection represents the whole of the twentieth century, illustrating the changing face and use of stitch and its relationship with the evolution and accessibility of textiles.

The intriguing aspect of the collection is that it ranges from the exquisite to the practical techniques and processes used every day in the home. Rachel had the ability to transcend the class system and this is what makes this collection, her life's work, so captivating. She has been described as an eccentric but quiet individual, whose passion for stitch left you fascinated yet wiser through the stories she told about pieces she had collected. Being a notable craftsperson herself, she was totally absorbed in life-long learning and the sharing of information. She found her own way to be in touch with the local community through teaching women needlework skills at a time when the economic and social climate was depressed. I would describe her as the quiet ambassador for stitch and textiles.

Photo of Rachel Kay-Shuttleworth taken at Gawthorpe Hall, 1960. 30 x 24.5 cm (12 x 9½ in.). Courtesy of the RBKS Collection Reference Library. Reproduction of photo: Mary Stark.

THE VALUE OF CREATIVE HERITAGE

Reflecting on my time of study at Gawthorpe Hall, I recall a feeling of excitement before I opened the boxes, sensing a kind of magic, which took me back to childhood. However old we are, play is therapeutic and an integral part of our nature. From an early age, children enjoy playing with blocks, ordering things and making patterns. The design and build process is part of our human make-up and evolves as we grow. Children's samplers of the nineteenth century are a social document, showing skill, craft, technique and in some cases, individual creativity.

Samplers show how stitches are formed and were used as a way to learn both the alphabet and numbers. As sewing was once passed down from generation to generation, so too was a level of primary social skills. By watching the parent sew, the child gained a sense of the value of learning actions and attitudes from them. As sewing has diminished from family life and also from within the educational system, there is a need to champion the skill.

My research data suggests that the important factors in maintaining the heritage of stitch and its teaching are multi-dimensional. Knowing the historical value of stitch can benefit society now and in the future. The gap in knowledge across generations since domestic science/home economics was removed from the curriculum will be difficult to bridge. Knowledge is a process of evolving and just like the lifecycle of a butterfly, the gaining of knowledge can bring about a metamorphosis. Revitalising long-forgotten skills is an illuminating process, providing a thread to breathe new life into the tradition of stitch.

CONNECTING WITH RACHEL'S COLLECTION

Gail Marsh, the curator at the RBKS Collection, had selected items for my study visit, so I was unaware of exactly what I was going to see. Through this, I experienced Bruner's[2] theory of playful discovery activity, which encouraged me to foster problem-solving and thinking skills. Box 142, labelled 'Teaching Aids', contained over 30 pieces of unfinished samples from Miss Isabel Walton.[3] All were beautifully stitched, labelled and numbered, but left many unanswered questions for the viewer. These fragments drew me in to seek a closer look. I felt the desire to explore both the tag description and the type of stitches used. The quality of the stitch made the samples feel and look seductive. No one could explain what their true purpose was now, so it would have to be left up to individual interpretation. Baudrillard[4] argues that seduction is challenge, not desire. One can choose not to respond to desire, but with challenge, we feel we need to. The hush of the room was a calming reminder of the peace and tranquillity that one feels when stitching. Yet the joy of seeing the eloquent stitches gave me a new thirst to stitch again. All the samples were protected and enclosed in a conservation material. I wanted to feel the samples, but couldn't. I related to Crary's[5] indication of the loss of touch as a conceptual component of vision. This meant the release of the eye from the hand, thus allowing the eye to judge without influence from another sense. As the stitch process involves hand and eye coordination, this was an interesting twist. Seduction

RESEARCH AND THE IMPRINT OF STITCH

by a piece of textile can come in many hidden forms. Usually, as a creative person, the initial reaction is to touch and feel the texture and make-up of the fabric. Yet we can see and learn so much more from looking and investigating historical or mythical stories of data that are recorded in museum collections.

My affinity to Rachel grew from recognising the value that she placed on her personal collection and the time she dedicated to researching and recording these pieces. Through her storytelling about the pieces in the collection, she has left a timeless legacy. The collection continues to grow and whilst some donations have a personal recorded history, others are based on historical facts, with their stories left open to interpretation.

STORYTELLING THROUGH STITCH

Rachel was inspirational and generous with her knowledge; she carefully recorded information on all the items she collected, whilst pursuing many adventures in both the sourcing and researching process. Students studying the collections benefit from the care she took in these processes. One piece of work cherished by the collection is the 'Colifichet', a framed embroidery depicting St Aloysius Gonzaga, the patron saint of students. Both sides of the embroidery are identical, a tremendous technical feat. Rachel purchased it for a few lire from a shop on the Oltr'arno, Florence, shortly before the First World War. She recorded how it was so full of dust that only the central figure, on both sides, was visible. Throughout the train journey home, she lovingly cleaned it with a feather from her hat, gently inserting it between the glass and the embroidery. On her return, she took it to the V&A, where the embroidery department dated it at around 1708. The piece is worked on parchment paper and the outline was probably pricked before stitching. The exquisite shading is worked with great skill in coloured silk and metal threads.

Unrecorded maker
Silk threads on linen, 1930s. 10 x 7.5 cm (4 x 3 in.). Courtesy of the RBKS Collection. Acc. no. 28014. Photo: Mary Stark. Experimental stitching sample from a collection of teaching aids from Miss Isobel Walton, Blackburn College of Art. She encouraged her students to use a lot of colour and texture in their samples.

Unknown maker
'Colifichet', 1708. 21 x 17 cm (8¼ x 6¾ in.). Courtesy of the RBKS Collection. Acc. no. 950. Photo: Mary Stark. A colifichet is a knick-knack. This embroidered picture is worked through a pricked design on parchment, so that the design is shown on both sides. This rare embroidery shows St Aloysius of Gonzala in a garden. It is worked in coloured floss silk with some metal threads defining whorls and swirls. The technique was taught in convents, explaining the devotional subjects.

179

Unknown maker
Hair embroidery picture stitched on ivory silk backed with hessian and linen, 1790–1810. 20.5 x 29 cm (8 1/16 x 11 1/2 in.). Courtesy of the RBKS Collection. Acc. no. 4009. Photo: Mary Stark. Landscape of a derelict temple with fallen stone and pillars with bushes growing out of the top. Reeds and trees surround the arch on the left. In the background, ships sail on the water. There are some cloud formations with sunrays in delicate stitching.

I found further inspiration in an early eighteenth-century embroidery stitched with hair. This exquisite image is of a historic landscape and has a contemporary feel. The sophisticated use of hair on silk fabric, stitched in the style of an etching, pushed the boundaries of embroidery beyond the ordinary. Embroidering on paper and with human hair may be up to the minute, but visitors to the collection can observe that it was all happening over two hundred years ago.

The RBKS Collection offers a study programme for individual or group visits to Gawthorpe Hall. Following an introduction to the collection, visitors closely study the items and gain advice. The team run textile and craft workshops using specific collection items as inspiration, whilst teaching traditional and contemporary techniques.

My personal passion for developing ideas and concepts has led to 'RESOURCE', a service where themed items from the collection are taken out to educational institutions. The initiative links into curriculum projects or subjects to develop visual awareness, breadth of research, specialist and historical knowledge, whilst also inspiring individual creativity and valuing cultural heritage, and has provided fuel for students, practitioners and enthusiasts.

My work campaigns to conserve historical stitch values, and to build on and contribute to the collection. Participants are actively encouraged to create a piece of work that is inspired by an item from the collection. Inviting people to create a twenty-first-century piece of textile craft will allow the cycle for study to be continued. Visits to guilds, schools, colleges and universities engage and educate people of all ages to appreciate historical textiles, thus bringing treasured pieces back to life and setting people on a mission to develop new ideas from the original sources. The pieces created are archived as part of the collection, with some placed on public display. Rabia Sharif, a degree student, took part in the 2010 campaign and her work is on display in the Hall with that of 30 other embroiderers.

RESEARCH AND THE IMPRINT OF STITCH

Rabia created an uplifting piece of hand-stitched work, which tells a story of its own. Rabia's artwork is a contemporary link to culture and social life today. The fact that she has seven children, studies full time and manages to find time to stitch is in itself inspiring. Her embroidery is about unity and love. It is a combination of a verse from her religion and a gentle hand inspired by a Rachel George[6] embroidery, *Woman with Flowers*. Rabia's work represents the idea of religion uniting people, which in turn generates love. 'If there is a love for people, then it creates a love for society', says Rabia.[7] She worked the piece by hand to demonstrate her love for stitch. She felt that the time and effort that are put into a handmade piece hold a place in the heart of the receiver. Education has allowed her to see the world through different eyes, awakening her senses in new ways. Looking at, researching, being inspired by and valuing historical embroidery has given Rabia a new outlook.

Rabia recalled a weekly visit to her uncle's house where she saw a vase and commented on its beauty. Her uncle responded that it had been there for a long time. Rabia acknowledged that her newly acquired skills allowed her to appreciate the colour and pattern, connecting them to stitch techniques and increasing her confidence. Rabia has a love for working with a needle and she

Rabia Sharif
Untitled, 2010. Lace, silk and cotton threads on silk. 25.4 x 25.4 cm (10 x 10 in.). Courtesy of the RBKS Collection. Acc. no. 67. Photo: Mary Stark. Embroidery panel hand-stitched with a quote taken from the Qur'an (18:109): 'If all the sea were ink for my sustainer's words, the sea would indeed be exhausted 'ere my sustainers words are exhausted'. The hand and flower petals were inspired by the *The Lady with Flowers* embroidery piece by Rachel George. Donated to the RBKS Collection as part of a collaboration project with Burnley Uclan, 2010.

HAND STITCH: PERSPECTIVES

Rachel George
The Lady with Flowers, 1920–30. 37 x 30 cm (14½ x 12 in.). Courtesy of the RBKS Collection. Acc. no. 11466. Photo: Mary Stark. The appliquéd embroidery is worked in satin stitch and couching on purple linen.

says, 'When you get into a rhythm you don't want to stop.' Before embarking on her college course, she could not make the time to stitch in the way that she does now. Stitching in an educational environment is different to hobby stitching. At home it is for personal satisfaction; however, in the company of other students, it is for a much wider audience. Rabia comments that the presentation of her work relates to her handwriting: 'I want to make it as neat and tidy as possible, so I master it until I feel happy. I can feel the difference in my stitch when I get it right. It is all about respect for the past, for the stitch and where it came from; [of] learning a technique and finding a way of using it for the future and moving it on.'

182

PERSONAL SYMBOLIC REFERENCING

It may be a significant experience in life or simply an opportune moment that makes a person start to learn or restart something creative. Stitch has the unique ability to slow people down, to get them to sit quietly, to think and engage with the fabric. It is a therapeutic process, which is universal to all cultures. Stitch utilises all the five senses, but has an emphasis on its incredibly tactile dimension.

Communication is the key to teaching, learning and development. As part of my work with children, I have created signs and symbols to represent individual stitches. By analysing the name and shape of individual stitches, I transformed them into characters. I felt that this was a fun way to connect people with stitch.

Stitch has its own style of communication and personal form of calligraphy, much like handwriting. Some people are neat and tidy, whilst others are freer. Stitch is like a recipe: the more you learn about ingredients and method, the more your skills develop. The migration of stitches and the practice of stitch as a movement is a theory compiled by Anne Morrell.[8] She states: 'Understanding the use of stitch by changes in movement reveals creative use of stitch.'

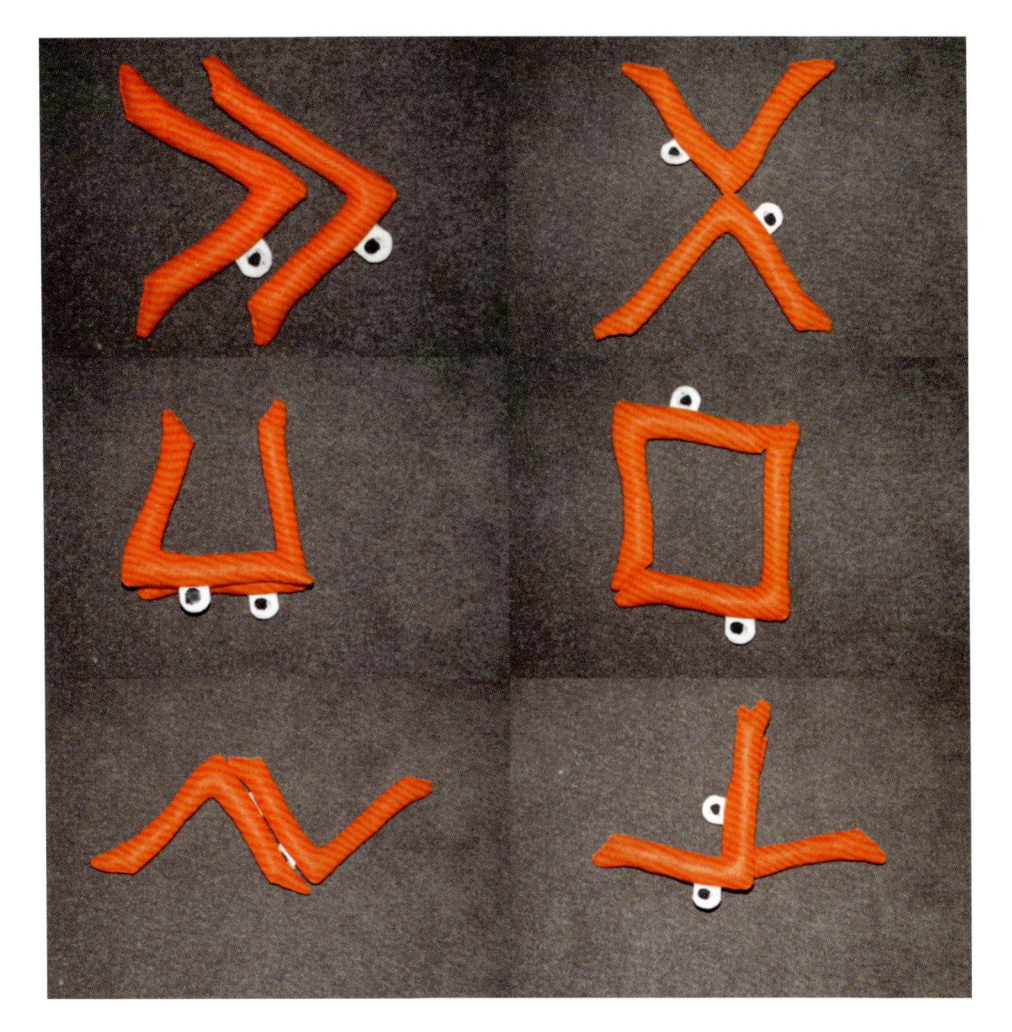

Tracy Gill
3D Stitches, 2009. 25 x 20 cm (10 x 8 in.). Photo: Tracy Gill. A series of photographs showing play with stitch marks using 3D felt stitches. Concepts developed by Tracy Gill during master's degree programme at Manchester Metropolitan University, 2009.

During a visit to my local flea market, I found a book called *Handwork in Early Education*, by Laura Plaisted (1913). She was a lecturer in education and hand work at Bingley Training College in Yorkshire. I was so excited when I opened it, as it contained many theories and processes that I had been researching. I even read it whilst I was walking back to the car. As soon as I got home, I began playing and making stitch characters from clay. I found that the three-dimensional shape offers a new way of looking at stitch, as it allows the hand and eye to explore the stitch without a needle and thread. Laura captured the value of this activity, declaring: 'For the purposes of self-expression the mobile clay offers a medium by which [the learner] can embody in concrete form his own vague conceptions, and in many cases convert them into sound and workable knowledge.'[9]

The possibilities with this activity are endless: the stitch shape and size can vary; there can be repetition of one stitch; play can commence by placing stitches in different directions. This fun process demonstrates the versatility of stitch without the initial learning of complex techniques. Its aim is to actively engage, encourage the creation of pattern and stimulate observation. A sampler can easily be created without the use of a needle and thread. Even very young children can experience tactile stitches.

To capture the art of life so beautifully is what stitch is all about – to leave your imprint and mark in the fabric of society. Stitch need not be prescriptive. Often, people want to be able to make things, but lack the patience or the skills to do so. To make sure that a skill is sustained, it needs to be taught at a basic level and offer progression. Parents, guardians and teachers hold the key to a child's development. My work at the RBKS Collection attempts to start communicating a belief in the importance of practical skills. A two-pronged approach – home and school – is needed to bring the skill of functional and decorative stitching into everyday life. To encourage the use of the collection by children, I have taken steps to link it into the school curriculum, combined with practical workshops for local children and their guardians, and liaison with community groups such as the Brownies, where a workshop helped them prepare for their toy-making badge. There are many ways to revive knowledge and encourage participation in stitch.

I have been surprised by the extent to which this historical collection has captured my attention and I will continue to learn more and develop my newfound knowledge. I will advocate, with passion and enthusiasm, the value of both objects and their surrounding data conserved in museums. Collaborative work with the RBKS Collection is just one of the avenues to disseminate this data and I sense that a shift is emerging, which values the purpose and future of stitch. My journey has demonstrated that stitch is multi-dimensional, with its roots firmly embedded in its historical, social and therapeutic links to society. An important message for the twenty-first century must be to ensure that the feet of the next generation are firmly rooted into promoting the craft of stitching.

RESEARCH AND THE IMPRINT OF STITCH

Tracy Gill
Sculpting sampler, 2009. 90 x 90 cm (35½ x 35½ in.). Photo: Tracy Gill. Experimental sampler showing a collection of clay stitches placed to create a lively display of stitch shapes. Concept developed by Tracy Gill during master's degree programme, 2009.

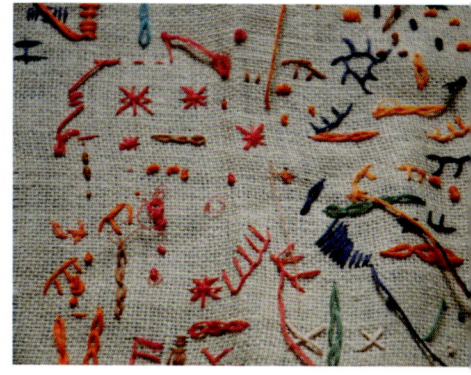

Tracy Gill
Experimental teaching stitch sampler, 2005. 25 x 25 cm (10 x 10 in.). Photo: Tracy Gill. Sampler showing a style of handwriting through stitch.

NOTES

[1] Quote from Rachel Kay-Shuttleworth, Gawthorpe Hall.

[2] Bruner, J. S., *Towards a Theory of Instruction* (Cambridge, MA: Harvard University Press, 1966). Boocock, S. S and E. O. Schild, *Simulation Games in Learning* (Beverly Hills, CA: Sage, 1968).

[3] Isabel Walton was a good friend of Rachel Kay-Shuttleworth and shared an interest in embroidery. She taught creative stitching and weaving at Blackburn College of Art.

[4] Baudrillard, J., *The Ecstasy of Communication* (New York: Semiotext(e), 1988).

[5] Crary, J., *Techniques of the Observer: On Vision and Modernity in the Nineteenth Century* (London: MIT Press, 1998).

[6] Rachel George was a pupil of Ann Macbeth at the Glasgow School of Art. Rachel went on to teach at Accrington School of Art, Lancashire. She was an embroiderer and friend of Rachel Kay-Shuttleworth.

[7] Rabia Sharif, degree student at the University of Central Lancashire. Interview with the author, July 2011.

[8] Morrell, A., *The Migration of Stitches & the Practice of Stitch as Movement* (Ahmedabad, India: Calico Museum of Textiles, 2007).

[9] Plaisted, L. L., *Handwork in Early Education* (London: Oxford University Press, 1913), p. 257.

SUE PRESTBURY

The Staircase Stitchers: re-stitching the past

Looking at a house that has been decorated and furnished by its residents, is like reading an open book depicting the daily lives of the occupants within. Colour schemes and decor speak volumes about contemporary style and personal taste. The integral quality of the furniture, its materials and workmanship could be said to demonstrate the family's wealth and social standing. Appliances and technology define the intricacies of their routines and aspirations. Pictures and keepsakes store memories and information pertinent to the household and its place in history.

Situated in the heart of Stockport's historic marketplace, Staircase House is a Grade 2 listed building, a medieval townhouse dating back to *c.*1460 and recognised as Stockport's oldest house. The Shallcross[1] family owned the house from 1605 to 1730 and was responsible for installing the now rare Jacobean staircase, which gives the house its name.[2] The series of rooms that make up the house have been imaginatively restored, and it is the attention to historical detail in the furnishings that help to bring the house to life for visitors.

In trying to convey a wider understanding of daily life in a seventeenth-century merchant's house, Staircase House has recruited help from the community. This chapter is about the project that brought together a group of people with the common interest of finding pleasure in hand stitch, whilst using traditional skills and techniques to equip Staircase House with a range of opulent furnishings relevant to the seventeenth century. They were to become known as the Staircase Stitchers.

HISTORICAL BACKGROUND

The Shallcross family owned the house during a turbulent period in English history, with the outbreak of the English Civil War between Royalists and Parliament, the execution of Charles I, and Cromwell's rule as Lord Protector finally giving way to the Restoration of Charles II. Textiles were produced in increasing quantities to provide comfortable and colourful furnishings. Embroidered clothes, book covers, wall hangings, bed hangings, linens, carpets and soft furnishings were highly prized by the rich and the aristocracy. King Charles I, renowned as one of the greatest art collectors and patrons of the seventeenth century, employed both foreign and home-grown artists, including the professional embroiderer Edmund Harrison. Following an eight-year apprenticeship, professional embroiderers created embroidered items

THE STAIRCASE STITCHERS

to commission, often leading a workshop of stitchers to produce commissions in much the same way as the Staircase project would be directed.

Whilst Harrison and his workers may usually have been employed on heraldic work for royal thrones, hangings, tents and carpets, he also produced pictorial embroideries such as *The Life of the Virgin Mary*, a series of six images dated 1637, allegedly for Sir William Howard. It was during the 1630s that pictorial embroidery for its own sake, rather than as part of domestic furnishings, developed. In her opening essay as assistant curator to the 'Exhibition of Seventeenth-Century Pictorial Needlework', Ann Sumner tells us that embroiderers copied popular images of the dead king after Charles I's execution in 1649.[3] She also describes 'one of the most charming raised-work pictures in the exhibition', produced *c*.1665, celebrating the Restoration of King Charles II. Silk and metal thread raised-work embroidery was applied to domestic items such as caskets and mirror frames. Symbolic and biblical figures were often depicted. Sumner relates that many embroiderers were thought to have had Royalist sympathies, detected in the recurring lion, stag and leopard motifs, supporters of the royal arms.[4] Sumner goes on to explain the symbolisation of Charles I as the familiar caterpillar, with the butterfly representing Charles II and his hopes for Restoration.

Even during the period of great austerity when England was ruled by Cromwell, in 1653–58, and furnishings of daily life were simple and functional, embroidery was still being used to decorate houses. Anne reports that: 'Oliver

Dressed bed with six curtains, coverlet, four monochrome cushions and a linen sheet.

HAND STITCH: PERSPECTIVES

Cromwell's wife reputedly employed several clergymen's daughters to do the needlework for her.'[5] Crewel-work bed hangings were a popular form of English domestic furnishing during the seventeenth and early eighteenth centuries. A bed was a most prized possession, a symbol of wealth and rank that had the most sumptuous furnishings the owner could afford. A set of hangings comprised two curtains at either side of the bed and another two at the foot of the bed, ensuring warmth and seclusion when drawn at night and colourful decoration against an otherwise austere interior. Merchants, traders and other middle-class ranks, unable to afford expensive imported fabrics, furnished their beds with embroidered hangings.

Whilst professional embroiderers were available to the rich, middle-class ladies would often embroider their own furnishings, spending hours working intricate and lavish designs. Often the entire household would be employed in the stitching, a fact that can sometimes be detected when looking at surviving pieces. This was to be a tradition followed by the Staircase Stitchers in working the bed hangings, the chemise and the linen bed sheet in particular.[6]

Although many gentlewomen were skilled embroiderers, not all of them could draw the detailed patterns which were so fashionable. Local artists or pattern draughtsmen were employed to draw the required designs on silk, although it is believed that some patterns could be purchased already drawn or stamped on to fabric. This would explain the frequency with which designs were repeated from one object to the next.

WISH LIST

Drawing on what is known about the Shallcross family, an early planning meeting identified a number of specific items for the original 'wish list' required to furnish a variety of period rooms throughout the house. The Bedchamber was the main focus, requiring six bed curtains and a bedcover, long pillows, a casket and a raised-work mirror frame. Some motifs would be taken from the carvings of lilies and marigolds on the bed head, with embroidery techniques covering canvas work, canvas slips, crewel work and raised work. Two cushions and a table carpet for the top of the chest were required in the Dowry Room. The motifs would be taken from the designs carved on the chairs and the strapwork design from the staircase. They would be worked as canvas slips and strapwork appliqué.

The Dining Room, furnished as it would have been in 1732, required embroidered pictures of classical landscapes or figures in long and short stitch in silk thread on silk cloth. The Regency Parlour was to have cushions and pictures, again using long and short stitch, but also embroidery using more unusual materials, for example shells, hair, feathers and wire. Finally, the Wartime Bedroom was to reflect the 'Make-do and mend' approach, featuring a bedjacket, a *Radio Times* cover, a nightdress case and an embroidered felt hat; with embroidery techniques ranging from smocking to appliqué, and canvas work to cut work.

Flower motif with leaves on Cheshire chair. 30 x 40 cm (12 x 15¾ in.) section. Photo: Sarah Cotton.

GETTING STARTED

Sarah Cotton was Stockport Council's Collections Access Officer in 2003, when the idea for the project first came to life. She remembers: 'We wanted [the visitors] to feel as though they had stepped back in time into someone's house.'

In trying to create a lived-in feel, visitors would be encouraged to sit on, try on and generally handle the greater part of the exhibits. Original seventeenth-century textiles would have been difficult to source, making it inevitable that replicas would be needed, a decision which brought its own set of problems, as Sarah explains: 'We weren't quite sure how we would afford to commission replica textile furnishings … the time taken to make them would have been prohibitively costly and we couldn't [wait for the length of] time it would have taken to have them made.'

Sarah visited similar houses displaying replica textiles and furnishings. She was particularly impressed with volunteer textile projects by the Ancient High House in Stafford and the Ford Green Threaders of Ford Green Hall, Stoke-on-Trent, coordinated by specialist historical embroiderer Jane Dew.

Jane was commissioned to coordinate local volunteers to produce a set of six crewel-work bed hangings for the replica carved tester bed purchased by Stockport Heritage Trust for display within the house, and to ensure that other Staircase projects were authentic to the seventeenth century. Jane had previously worked with the Globe Theatre, London, on reproduction stage costumes. Her specialist skills and knowledge in this field were also employed to create historical costumes for display in the house.[7]

Quilted coverlet (detail). Satin, chain and fill stitches on silk fabric with four-strand silk. 200 x 200 cm (78¾ x 78¾ in.). Photo: Mary Stark.

Forty volunteer stitchers were recruited, ranging from absolute beginners to experienced teachers. The biggest pull for the volunteers was undoubtedly the historical aspect of the work. When asked about their attraction to joining the group, many responses were along the lines of: 'I wanted to learn a new skill with a historical theme'; 'Being able to pursue local history'; 'To learn about the history of the house and of the stitching once there'.[8]

EARLY DAYS

The restoration work complete, Staircase House opened its doors to the public in 2005 and the Stitchers set to work in October of that year. Being able to stitch was not essential, but an enthusiasm for learning and taking part was paramount. During this time, the group continued to be so popular that new volunteers had to be turned away. Sarah remembers: 'We had 40 or so women (and two men!) coming religiously every month; we were forced to start a waiting list. I'm sure they would have come more regularly if we had [had] the resources.' A satellite group was installed at Bramall Hall to accommodate Stitchers working on the bed coverlet. 'Five or six women started meeting fortnightly on their own, chatting quietly around the frames [unlike] the frenzy of the monthly meetings.'

Considerable thought had to be given to the logistics of the project. It took at least a year to instigate a workable structure, with support for the Stitchers, in the project. As Jane explained, 'Projects of this size and complexity, where an important element is the historical accuracy, take a little time to get going.'

Jane provided access to a wealth of books and other visual resources to ensure authenticity of materials, designs, techniques and construction; a 'sharing of knowledge'. Comparing herself to 'a plate-spinner', part of Jane's role was to keep the Stitchers moving along with their own strengths and abilities. Her frequent reminder of 'This is how they would have done it!' steered them to confidently recreate each piece to increasingly high standards.

The designs, patterns, motifs and techniques used by the Stitchers were all based on existing examples of historical embroidery or design. As a practical introduction to seventeenth-century embroidery, the Stitchers were each encouraged to select an image from Richard Shorleyker's pattern book of 1632.[9] This book contains line drawings of flowers, fruit, leaves, insects, birds, fish and various animals, with some examples of fill designs, hatching and patterning. It contains a square grid with directions for increasing or decreasing the size of the design and it would have been an invaluable resource for embroiderers in its time. In Britain, the output of pattern books was very small, with only four titles having been recorded. More skilful embroiderers could move between lace and embroidery pattern books to others designed for calligraphers or bookbinders, or to herbals or books of emblems.[10]

Originally, patterns were transferred to fabric using a technique called 'pricking and pouncing'. This was done by using a pin to prick out the outline of a design through the paper it was drawn on. The paper was then laid on the fabric

THE STAIRCASE STITCHERS

(*left*) Evening Stitchers' group at Staircase House, working the second curtain on the frame. 'Renaissance-dyed' wools and linen twill. Photo: Sarah Cotton.

(*right*) Bed curtain crewel work. Wools and linen twill. 175 x 140 cm (70 x 55 in.). Photo: Mary Stark.

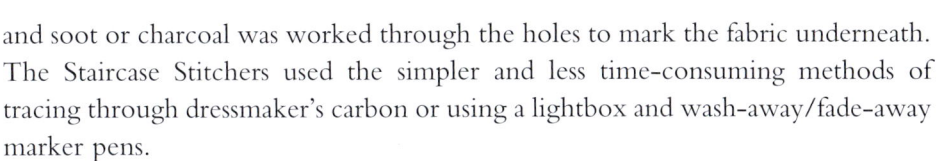

and soot or charcoal was worked through the holes to mark the fabric underneath. The Staircase Stitchers used the simpler and less time-consuming methods of tracing through dressmaker's carbon or using a lightbox and wash-away/fade-away marker pens.

After transferring their designs to fabric, the Stitchers tacked the work to a fine cotton cloth, which was then hooped ready for stitching. Some designs were worked as simple monochrome outlines of running stitch, stem stitch or chain stitch; others were worked with satin stitch, French knots or fill stitches. Thread varied from the crewel wool used on curtain fabric, to four-strand silk used on lightweight silk habotai and linen. Every Stitcher completed an embroidered sample, which she finished into a needlecase for her own use; a personal reminder of their own skills.

STEADY PROGRESS

The Staircase bed hangings are based on those created at Ford Green, with similar trailing Tree of Life designs, hummocks,[11] large figurative leaves and exotic flowers, interspersed with oversized bugs and creepy-crawlies! Jane took direction and inspiration from earlier research, identifying several original sets of hangings in existence up and down the country.[12]

The word 'crewel' refers to the type of thread used, rather than the type of stitches: usually two strands of wool twisted together to make one strand, worked on a linen ground – in this case a linen twill from Scotland, the same as that used nearly 400 years ago. The threads were produced as authentically as possible, with

HAND STITCH: PERSPECTIVES

(*above*) Monochrome coif. Stem stitch and seeding with four-ply stranded silk on fine white linen. 30 x 46 cm (12 x 18¼ in.). Photo: Sarah Cotton.

(*right*) Monochrome cushions. Four-ply stranded silk on linen fabric. Various sizes from 30 x 45 cm (12 x 17¾ in.) to 45 x 60 cm (17¾ x 23⅝ in.). Photo: Mary Stark.

woollen yarns dyed using historically accurate methods. Natural plants and minerals were used to achieve the vibrant colour range that would have existed then and also traditional techniques for fixing them. The four-stranded silk threads used on some of the other pieces could be well matched in colour to the authentically dyed yarn, even though they were chemically dyed. As Sarah herself comments, 'The other great benefit of having replicas was that visitors could see the colour and how the furnishings would have looked originally – rather than the ancient examples we see in low light in museum cases.' The Stitchers themselves could hardly believe the vibrancy of the colours used.

The hangings were worked by multiple Stitchers on large frames that could only accommodate four or five people at once. Early in the project, individual canvas slips were worked by most Stitchers, which were later trimmed, invisibly tacked to the framed hangings and couched into place.

Slow progress over the first three years finally saw the completion of the first bed hanging in 2008. With increasing skills and efficiency, a number of slips were ready to be applied to the second and third bed hangings, and the group was now able to forge ahead independently. Jane's attendance was reduced to meeting with the stitchers on a bi-monthly basis, being gradually diminished to quarterly visits until the end of the project.

The success of the project thus far could be measured by the quality of the work produced, the new skills acquired by the Stitchers, and the continued confidence and enthusiasm demonstrated by the group. Two of the completed bed hangings were displayed alongside various other items including the bed cover, a tapestry cushion and four long pillows.[13] By the end of the Stitchers' fifth year, the third curtain and another tapestry work cushion had also been completed. Having completed the bed cover, the Bramall Hall group set to work the fourth

THE STAIRCASE STITCHERS

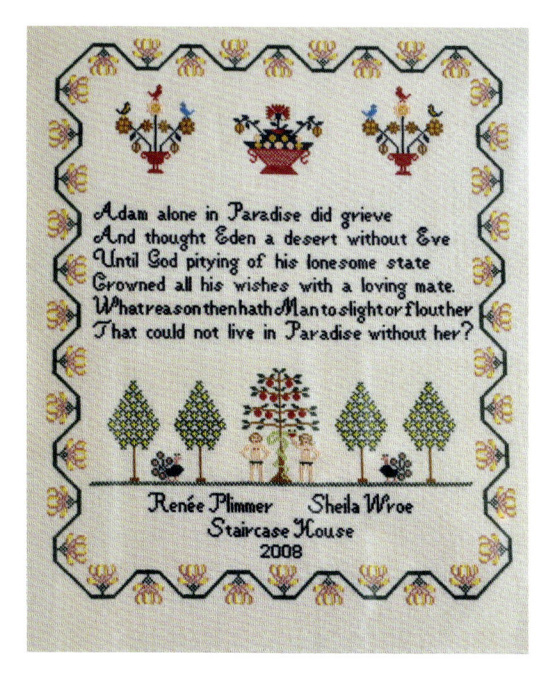

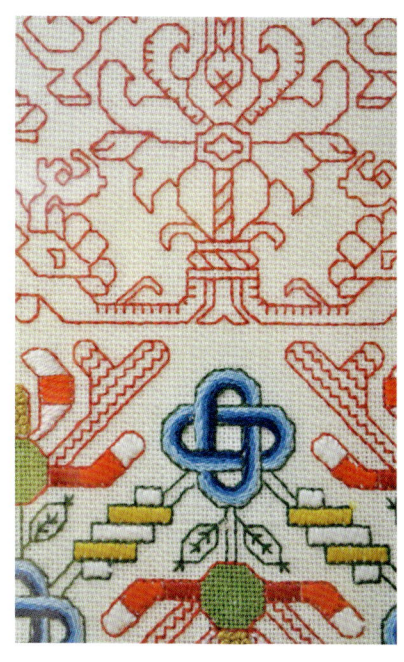

(*far left*) Sampler. Cross-stitch, four-ply stranded silk on linen fabric. 40 x 32 cm (15 x 12½ in.). Photo: Mary Stark.

(*left*) Sampler. Cross-stitch, chain stitch and satin stitch with four-ply stranded silk on linen fabric. 94 x 30 cm (37 x 12 in.). Photo: Mary Stark.

curtain, with the last two smaller curtains progressing well at Staircase House.[14] The nineteenth-century sampler was framed to go on display in the Parlour,[15] whilst the seventeenth-century widow's costume was soon to be on display in the Bedchamber.[16] Whilst maintaining the importance of not interrupting the integrity of original pieces, the seventeenth-century sampler for the Dowry Room was redesigned to include a representation of Staircase House.[17]

WORKS IN PROGRESS

Other projects being individually worked progressed steadily at their own pace – the monochrome coif, the petit-point coffer carpet and the raised-work mirror frame. Worked in black silk thread on fine white linen, the monochrome coif is the work of Angela Conway. The design is typical for the period, with interlacing motifs repeated across the sections. Whilst involved in a number of the other projects, the coif was Angela's favourite: 'I have improved as I have gone along', she says of it.

A mammoth undertaking was Jacqueline Lacey's work on the cupboard carpet for the chest in the Dowry Room, measuring 1 m (39½ in.) long and 30 cm (12 in.) wide. Worked under tension on a standing frame, Jacqueline's carefully planned design was stitched using a mixture of wool and silk threads on canvas, with 18 stitches to one inch, totalling approximately 150,000 stitches in all. From pattern books, Jacqueline found a number of cross-stitch designs incorporating the letter 'S', which she used in one of her border designs in reference to the Shallcross family name. The initials 'MS' appear in the middle of the border to represent Mary Shallcross herself. A fill design closely resembles the Arabic-influenced designs which were very popular around 1640. Jacqueline was also influenced by the

HAND STITCH: PERSPECTIVES

beautiful geometric patterns in the stone minaret of the Damghan Great Mosque in Iran, converting one of the designs into a cross-stitch motif for the border. The Shallcross coat of arms and family motto were painstakingly converted into a workable design to feature at the centre of the piece.[18] The inner designs of the carpet were taken from the designs of the strapwork to be seen on the staircase in the house.

Work on the mirror frame is ongoing. Divided into three sections, the top illustrates a popular castle-like building, flanked by trees on top of a hummock. The sections either side of the mirror show the biblical story of Esther and Ahaseurus, the accepted interpretation of which symbolises the plight of the Royalists during the Commonwealth.[19] The lower section has a fountain with metalwork serpents and fantastical fish. Each corner of the frame has a roundel with birds and beasts (the lion and leopard previously mentioned) meticulously worked in beads.

Staircase House can now take its place amongst a handful of attractions that possess excellent historical replica furnishings, inimitably demonstrating the important role of textiles in Stockport's past. As a visitor attraction, it has been designed to make people feel at home, so they can interact freely with the exhibits.

Although the project was slow, its success is attributable to various factors, but for Sarah, 'It was as much about the process as the product at the end of it. It was really inspiring to see this work going on in the house: it made it feel [alive] and it made it seem like a really valuable resource to the local community – there was obviously a need for it.'

Talking to the Stitchers towards the end of the project, it was evident that most of them had initially expected to be shown exactly how to work the embroideries, and they were surprised to have been left to their own devices. Over time, they had come to realise that they had been allowed to demonstrate their own skills, develop at their own pace and help each other to learn and improve, indicative of the way that embroidery groups would have been organised historically. The work has also been a great healing tool for the Stitchers, therapeutically helping with bereavement, illness and other traumas along the way because of the camaraderie and support of the group. All the Stitchers' names are recorded on the work they have completed, forming part of the historical archive of the project.

Kathleen says: 'A sense of achievement, to remember with pleasure that I was involved with it.' Sarah agrees: 'Of all I did at Staircase that was the project I felt most proud of … I was so thrilled the day I came back and saw the two finished curtains.'

Visitors to the Bedchamber in Staircase House.

NOTES

[1] The Shallcross family name is sometimes referred to as Shawcross.

[2] Funding by Stockport Council, supplemented by grant aid from the Heritage Lottery Fund, English Heritage and Northwest Regional Development Agency.

[3] Sumner, Ann, *Men, Birds, Beasts & Flowers: An Exhibition of Seventeenth-Century Pictorial Needlework* (Bath: Holburne Museum, 1987), p. 6. Exhibition held at Holburne Museum and Crafts Study Centre, Bath.

[4] Ibid.

[5] Ibid.

[6] The design is a continuous scrolling pattern worked in chain stitch in a red Madeira silk thread.

[7] Garments that would have been worn by the reasonably wealthy Widow Shallcross: a chemise, a Payre of Bodys, a farthingale, a fore-skirt, an overskirt with cartridge pleats, a jerkin and an over-gown.

[8] Reviews were taken throughout the venture to gauge the Staircase Stitchers' engagement with, and enjoyment of, the work.

[9] The original book was published in 1632 by Richard Shorleyker, and is currently available as a facsimile under the title *A Schole-House for the Needle*.

[10] Books with a collection of descriptions, classifications and illustrations of plants, which flourished throughout Western Europe during the 15th and 17th centuries.

[11] Elaborately worked hillocks and mounds, either traditionally or exotically coloured.

[12] Worked by the majority of the group at some stage and based on existing sets at the Potteries Museum and Art Gallery Collection, Stoke-on-Trent; Whitworth Art Gallery Collection, Manchester; Blickling Hall Collection, Norfolk; Traquair House, Innerleathen, Scotland; Museum of Fine Art, Boston; Lady Lever Art Gallery, Port Sunlight and the Victoria and Albert Museum, Kensington.

[13] Monochrome long pillows worked by Joyce Oldham, Jeanne Grundy, Joan Izard and Maureen Lytwyniw, with design sources as follows: Thomas Trevelyan's *M/S Miscellany*, 1608; Hardwick Hall collection, Inv. T/290; Santina Levey's *Elizabethan Treasures* (London: The National Trust and New York: Harry N. Abrams, 1998), pp. 45–46; V&A Museum's collection, acc. no. T32. 1936, in *The Victoria and Albert Museum's Textile Collection: Embroidery in Britain from 1200 to 1750*; V&A Museum's collection, acc. no. T115-118. 1928, in Nevinson, John, *The Catalogue of English Domestic Embroidery* (London: Victoria and Albert Museum, 1938).

[14] The crewel-work bed coverlet worked by Patricia Daniels, Pauline D'Souza, Rosemary Harrison, Shirley Andrews and Joan Bullock was based on an existing design in the V&A's collection: acc. no. T.63-1993. See Nevison, John, *The Catalogue of English Domestic Embroidery* (London: Victoria and Albert Museum, 1938) and Endpapers in Beck, Thomasina, *Gardening with Silk and Gold* (Newton Abbott: David & Charles, 1997).

[15] A 19th-century 'Adam and Eve' sampler (original dated 1830) reworked by Renee Plimmer and Sheila Wroe. Sheila sadly died whilst still a member of the Stitchers.

[16] Monochrome ruffles, collar and cuffs for a linen chemise with animal, fruit, vegetable, insect and flower motifs worked by Jane Dew and Angela Conway. Sources taken from: Shorlyeker, Richard, *A Schole-House for the Needle* (1632) and a portrait of Elizabeth Talbot, Hardwick Hall.

[17] The original, as part of the V&A's collection, dated 1660, was worked by Margaret Mason.

[18] Jacqueline's avid research into the Shallcross coat of arms uncovered religious symbolism and a connection to the Crusades.

[19] That is, the persecution of a minority.

ALICE KETTLE AND JANE MCKEATING

Contemporary Practices: where are we now?

THE RICHNESS OF HAND STITCH IS EVIDENT through the variety of methods that contemporary makers and artists exploit. Mainstream art practice has embraced hand stitch to some extent, so it occupies a varied platform, from one-off conceptual artworks to highly specialised functional textiles. Many makers use a recognised vocabulary of stitches and the familiar materials of thread and cloth, whilst others utilise a variety of invented forms and a backcloth that could be anything from stone to film, with intentions that are similarly varied, from design to high art. The labour-intensive nature of hand stitch accentuates the economic challenge of its use in the design industries. It remains a bespoke item within fashion and design, as it competes with the productive manufacturing processes.

Arranged thematically, the selection below is a small snapshot of the breadth of contemporary hand-stitch practice.

SHADOW AND LINE

The Japanese artist Kazuhito Takadoi takes inspiration from nature to make stitched works, which substitute grasses, leaves and twigs for thread. The grasses are partially dried, ensuring that they retain enough flexibility with which to work. His delicate, tensioned works balance the sense of the interior and exterior. Arranged in geometric compositions, the colours will slowly and subtly change over time as with the seasons. Some works are made to go outdoors: transitory and impermanent, they slowly decay and are reclaimed by the earth. Kazuhito's work evokes a fragile landscape where light and shadows add a vital dimension.

Roanna Wells's stitching also explores a shadowed space. Her fabric is often transparent, with the thread glimpsed through, over and under the surface, capturing light between connecting lines. The sketchy spontaneity of the line springs out of the cloth, which appears as a delicate internal skin. The thread makes calligraphic and repeated gestural marks, which form a subtle exploration of the drawn line as a three-dimensional filament pulled loosely through fabric.

Elizabeth Brimelow similarly explores the surfaces of the landscape through the marks and patterns of stitch. Translating man's interventions with the land, 'ploughing, planting, harvesting, mining and building', *Feltwell Furrows* is a double-sided quilted piece inspired by a drawing of the Fens in East Anglia. Layers of transparent cloths give an ethereal quality to the patterns of the furrows in the centre of the piece. Layers are trapped using couching, feather stitch and tying,

CONTEMPORARY PRACTICES

Kazuhito Takadoi
Happa (Leaves), 2003. Stitch, twigs and grass on washi paper. 110 x 76 cm (43 x 30 in.). Photo: Kazuhito Takadoi.

Roanna Wells
Eclipse, 2010. Hand stitch on silk. 80 x 80 cm (31½ x 31½ in.). Photo: India Hobson.

HAND STITCH: PERSPECTIVES

Elizabeth Brimelow
Feltwell Furrows, 2011. Double-sided transparent silk quilt. 147.5 x 154.7 cm (58 x 61 in.). Photo: Michael Wicks.

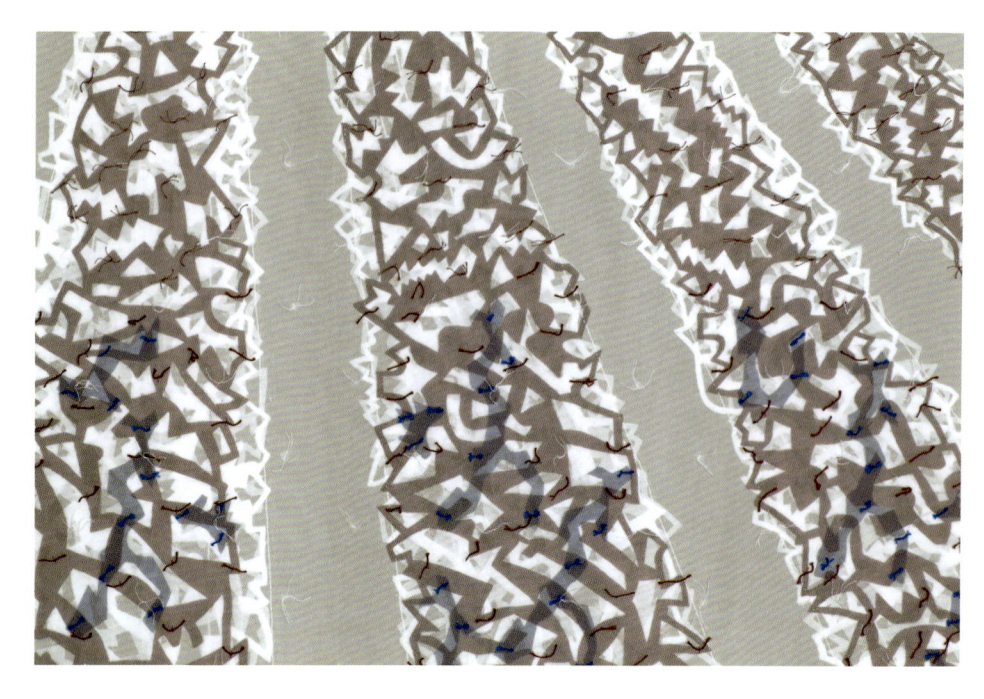

Debbie Smyth
Fly Away Home (detail), 2011. Pin and thread installation. Steel pins, cotton thread and acetate. 8 x 3 m (315 x 118 in.). Created as part of the 'Wordplay' exhibition, Stroud International Textile Festival. Photo: Zac Mead.

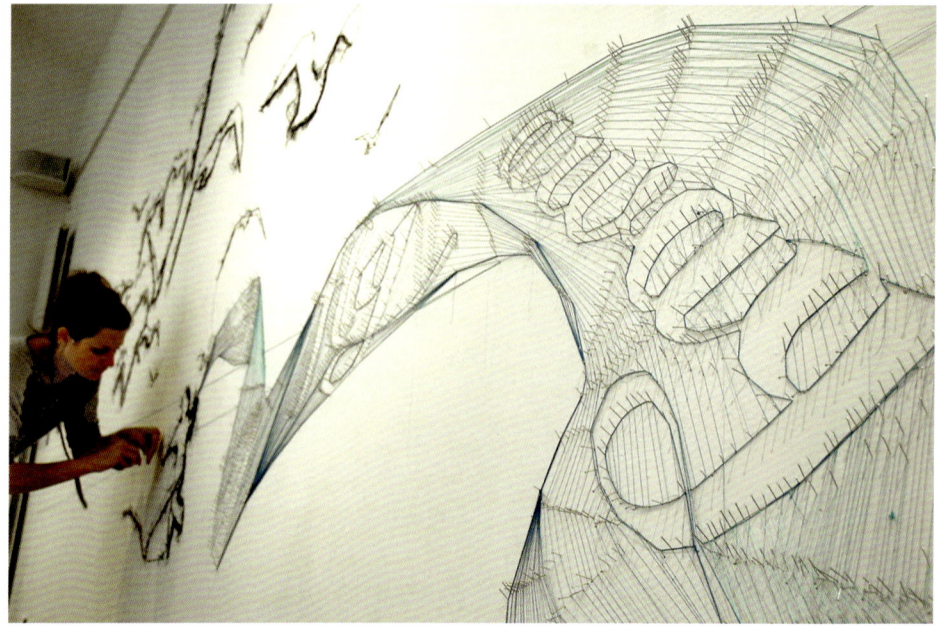

'an inversion of the usual process of quilt-making, which puts patterning on the outside and hides the middle'.

Debbie Smyth's network of threads has no link with fabric: it uses the wall as the base, with lines weaving between and around plotted pins. These complex pin and thread drawings are often temporary installations of floating linear structures and shadow, which extend around corners and from walls to floors and ceilings. The works echo a graffiti-like impermanence as temporary markers and interventions. Debbie's message is not political or socially disgruntled, yet she forces

CONTEMPORARY PRACTICES

Kai Chan
Two Islands in the River, 2010. Hand stitch with silk thread. 248 x 210 x 6 cm (97⅝ x 82¾ x 2½ in.). Photo: Cheryl O'Brien.

us to question established cultural territories with her delicate webs, which neither deface nor vandalise.

Kai Chan uses thread to interpret and negotiate his cultural identity as a Chinese Canadian. The thread is utilised to explore a place that is rooted in the traditions of making art and craft as well as in a 'new realm that is enigmatic and ambiguous'. His works spring from his immediate surroundings, the simple and the everyday, and is a response to light, atmosphere, earth and water. He explores tensions, tautness and soft corners by twisting the threads into a pictorial, web-like curtain, which he describes as 'a way of holding shapes together' and as a metaphor for an inner personal strength.

Mary Stark combines film and stitch to transgress the boundaries between the digital, the analogue, the material and the virtual. Her work negotiates the parallel worlds of illusion and material reality. She weaves and stitches celluloid objects from strips of film to create photographic prints, or works with film and video which is cut, copied, layered and edited, and then projected. Thus she has two states of being within her work: the static and still stitched photographic image, and the moving and transitory, which is film-based. She examines the shared common language and terminology of stitch and film-making, and the transformation as one is applied to the other. Mary's work examines the temporal nature of stitch and the place where the mediums of stitch and film become synonymous.

Mary Stark
3.5 Seconds of Charlie's Big Fight, 2011. Digital image from a photographic print created by enlarging woven standard 8 mm film in a black and white darkroom. 50 x 50 cm (20 x 20 in.). Photo: Mary Stark.

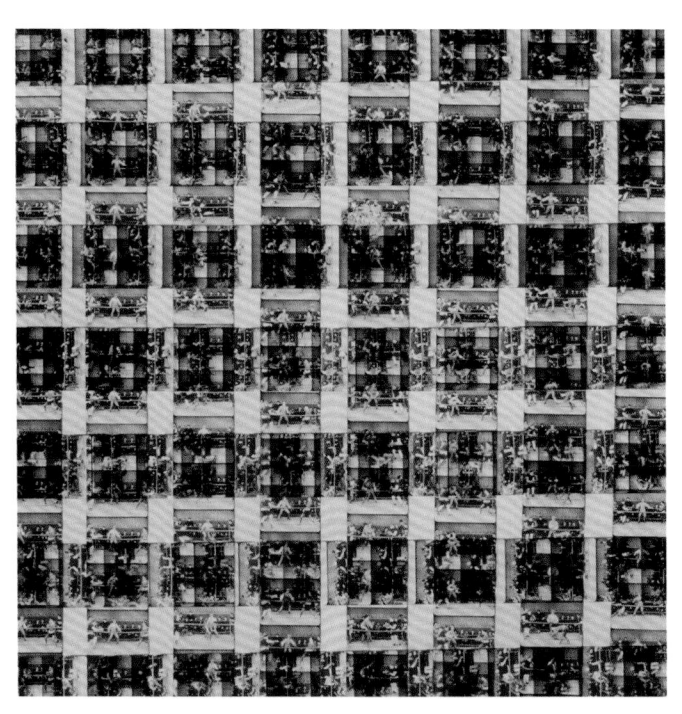

HAND STITCH: PERSPECTIVES

Jilli Blackwood
Tilda, 2010. Embroidery and weave. Silks, wool, linen and leather. 10 x 135 x 52 cm (4 x 53 x 20½ in.). Collection of The National Museums Scotland. Photo: Ken Mellin.

RICH CLOTH LANDSCAPE

Jilli Blackwood expresses her Scottish roots in the colour and form of her embroidery. *Tilda* is the traditional wraparound Scottish kilt, which spins around like a danced 'reel' in a wheel of colour. Blackwood describes her technique as 'slash and show' – a building up of layers of hand-dyed fabrics which are stitched and hand-pleated to reform into a new, rich cloth. The stitches and fabrics are cut away and joined back to make patterned surfaces where stitches lie beneath and through fabrics, emerging and disappearing between the layers and folds. She wants us to think of fabric 'differently', where the stitch is firmly embedded into cloth and part of a mix of colours that are those of the Scottish colourist painters – intense, bright and resonant.

Clyde Olliver literally stitches the rock and stone from his Cumbrian landscape. His use of hard materials is less a gendered response to hand stitch and embroidery than a desire to evoke the locality by working with slate and agricultural twines, which convey the structures that punctuate and mark the landscape – drystone walls, barns, gateposts, standing stones and stony paths. 'In Cumbria the gateposts (called locally "stoups") are huge slate uprights with large holes cut through them. Various twines are threaded through these holes by farmers to enable gates to be tied shut, and sheep's wool often clings to the stone.' Clyde uses stitch to mark the stone, sometimes embedded or laid and couched in cut channels and grooves. The works variously echo textile motifs as he connects fragments together in stone quilts and stitched sculptures.

CONTEMPORARY PRACTICES

Clyde Olliver
Welsh Quilt, 2010. Stitched slate.
116 x 94 x 7 cm (45⅝ x 37 x 2¾ in.).
Photo: Lucy Barden.

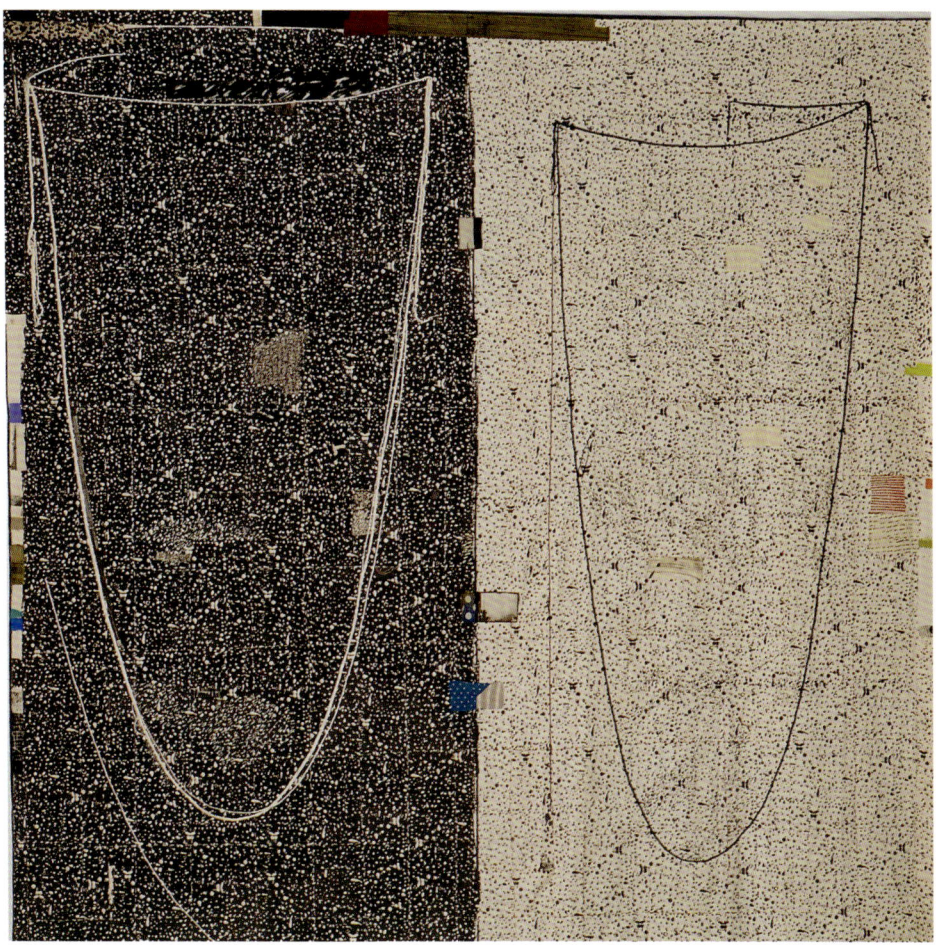

Dorothy Caldwell
How Do We Know When It's Night?, 2010. Wax resist discharge printing on cotton with stitching and appliqué. 304.8 x 589.5 cm (120 x 232 in.). Photo: David Ramsey.

HAND STITCH: PERSPECTIVES

Eleri Mills
Tirlun barddol II (Bardic Landscape II), 2010. Paint, hand stitching and appliqué on cloth. 67 x 90 cm (26½ x 35½ in.). Photo: Dewi Tannatt Lloyd.

Dorothy Caldwell looks to her immediate Canadian landscape to characterise the marks in her vast cloth drawings. She describes the natural phenomena of lakes, hills and sweeps of land in the Ontario Kawartha Lakes region by utilising the traditions of stitched mending and darning from the samplers and quilts that were part of the domestic landscape of the pioneers. The works can be huge and contemplative in their scale. She cites the influence of Rothko's paintings, with their stained coloured grounds, which invoke a sense of spirituality. Caldwell's dyed and marked background cloths are expansive, and the stitch tracks through the cloth and makes channels and discrete passages of clustered hand stitch.

Eleri Mills's images come from the Wales she grew up in, passed down through the generations. It is a land steeped in stories, and she makes rich cultural connections that provide a constant, ever-changing source of imagery. The work contains embroidery, rather than being embroidery. Eleri moves from paint to thread seamlessly, each finding its function in the expression of an idea. Developing marks on the base first, through a painted surface, the stitched marks add a depth, creating the atmosphere that is so evocative of the landscape. No attempt is made to cover up the paint; the stitch simply introduces something new.

PORTRAITS

Louise Bourgeois uses fabric and stitch for their intense symbolism in the reparation of the psyche. The presence of textiles was fundamental in her life; she collected and hoarded clothes and household linen, which were later cut up and stitched back together as artwork. Bourgeois grew up in a tapestry restoration studio run by her parents, and the recurring themes of complex family hierarchies, of relationships, sexuality, childhood, female identity and trauma, are all played out in her textile

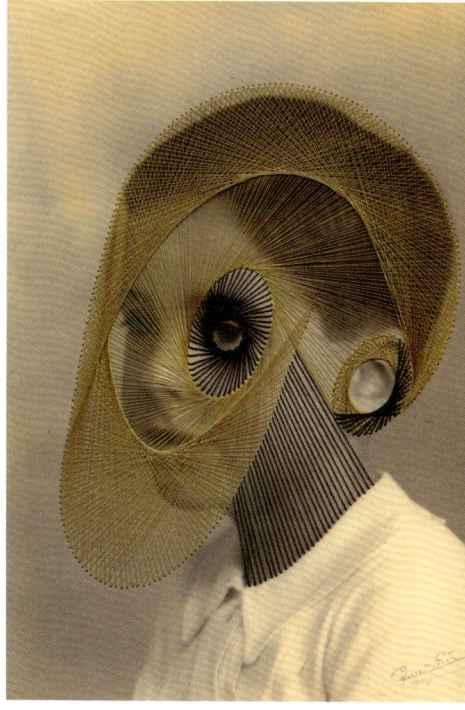

CONTEMPORARY PRACTICES

Louise Bourgeois
(*left*) *Untitled*, 2002. Fabric and aluminium. 30.5 x 30.5 x 30.5 cm (12 x 12 x 12 in.). Photo: Christopher Burke. © Louise Bourgeois Trust/DACS, London/VAGA, New York 2011.

Maurizio Anzeri
(*above*) *Angelo*, 2010. Embroidery on photo. 24 x 18 cm (9½ x 7 in.). Private collection. Courtesy of the artist. Photo: Frederico Gallo.

work through the restorative nature of stitch. The series of sculptural head artworks are like life-sized ancient busts, trapped with their innermost pain and doubts in 'cell-like' cases. The stitch in Louise Bourgeois's work is a suture and agent of transformation, which she utilises to represent the construction and deconstruction of the body and the inner self. An extraordinarily radical and influential artist, she used textile throughout her life, with her stitched fabric drawings becoming a key focus in later years. She recalled: 'When I was growing up, all the women in my house were using needles. I have always had a fascination with the needle, the magic power of the needle. The needle is used to repair the damage. It's a claim to forgiveness.'

Maurizio Anzeri studied at the Slade School of Art in London. His work appropriates photos from the 1930s and 1940s, with stitch interventions that are both beautiful and disturbing insights into the psyche. 'With embroidery and sewing, I use all forms of threads as a way to capture images. It is my way of recording experiences. Writers do it by using written lines of words. They create stories, characters, situations. I do the same with thread. I "write" my own possible worlds, with their characters and scenarios. Thread, embroidery is my current way of mark-making, of visualising stories.'[3]

HAND STITCH: PERSPECTIVES

Primmy Chorley
These Precious Last Days Together, 2011. One of a pair from 'Mrs Whippet's Story' series. Stem stitch and French knots on flannel with appliquéd wools, velvets, silk and knitting, held on with buttonhole stitches in wools and stranded cotton. 30 x 45 cm (12 x 17¾ in.). Photo: Shaun Russell.

CONTEMPORARY PRACTICES

Tilleke Schwarz
Free Recovery, 2010. Hand embroidery with different threads on linen. 68 x 66 cm (26¾ x 26 in.). Photo: Rob Mostert.

'In the UK I often saw signs along the road, stating: "Free recovery, await rescue". I like them a lot as they are so optimistic and full of trust. This work contains more memories of our trip to the UK. For instance: Mr Tom Bola's messages we received each morning to kindly inform us about the precise time (exactly) we were invited to enjoy our breakfast in his cosy Oxford B&B. The breakfast room was too small to accommodate all guests at the same time and he made a new schedule every day. His last name was Bola, I am not certain about the first name but liked this combination best.'

Primmy Chorley makes work directly from life: her home in Snowdonia, her family and animals. Using stitch to record happenings, memories and events, she describes them as like 'our wallpaper'. She makes them amidst daily life, not separate from it. The work is strongly imbued with a sense of the world she lives in as a participator, not an observer. The pieces are carefully and lovingly made, inspired by the way that quilts and possessions were once made and passed down in families or between friends. The pieces are things to be lived with, rather than seen as artworks.

Tilleke Schwarz's thread is a line of a story, which meanders and unravels in a playful map diary of events and thoughts. The works are a juxtaposition of impressions, graphic triggers, ideas and images, which collide in a random stream of consciousness. The subjects are daily life, mass media, her cats, the intimate and the everyday, and they blur one into another in a stitched graffiti of social comment. Tilleke uses hand stitch for its slowness and texture; she describes how she 'likes to hold my work in my hands while making something'.[4] The works are striking in colour and an intricate stitchwork of visual poetry and humorous commentary.

Bernie Leahy's portraits are mainly black and white graphic stitched drawings. Her images emerge from the canvas cloth with stitches of cross-hatching and tone, which is reminiscent of ink drawings. They are positioned off the edges of fabric, as though the lines have gently settled on to the surface in an accomplished scattering of thread-drawing.

Bernie Leahy
(*above*) *Ma'a Ma: Matilda Ripton*, 2010. Stitching on unbleached canvas. 44 x 59 cm (17⅜ x 23¼ in.). Photo: Rebecca Peters.

205

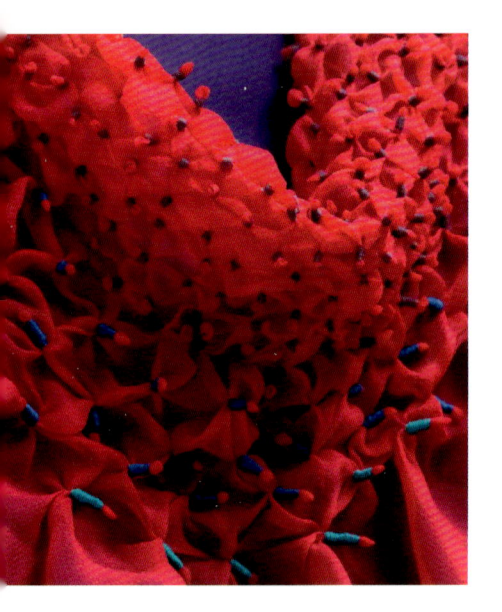

HAND STITCH: PERSPECTIVES

LINE AND PATTERN

Tanvi Kant makes wearable jewellery from reclaimed textiles. She uses unwanted saris, scarves and dressmaking offcuts, which she binds with threads, knots and stitches to make sculptural reconstructed forms to adorn the body.

Alison Willoughby uses a simple skirt form as her background for stitch. Her signature shape has provided the canvas for experimentation with stitch in a rich variety of processes. She rips strips of fabric, gathers it, makes ruffles, scores lines and circles, screen-prints with paper stencils, and uses foils, tailor tacks and cords to make works that are wearable, sculpted wall pieces. The skirt gives a three-dimensional plane on which to draw delicate stitched marks and abundant additions of embroidered motifs and fabric form.

Betty Pepper reuses found objects and discarded memories, stitching them into new objects. The stitch as an agent for mending, darning and reworking echoes a tradition of oral storytelling, where words are passed on and retold over and over again. Betty's work recycles the 'savings' and leftovers of fabric and the decayed and cast-off ephemera, which she pieces back into new composite forms using tiny pictorial stitched drawings.

Richard McVetis describes his practice as deeply rooted in hand stitch because of 'the repetition, the methodical, the meticulous, the obsessiveness, the continuity of the line, hidden beyond the limits of fabric surface'. 'His work shows repeated shapes, and architectural references and playful juxtaposition of scale with repeated stitch motifs of embroidered dots and crosses.'[5]

Lauren Steeper became interested in utilising the time-consuming nature and controlled quality of embroidery techniques to make something uncontrolled and random. From a starting point of words cut from a dictionary and collected in a jar, weekly lottery numbers became the method to select the word, font style and colours of the pieces produced. Using cross-stitch, she describes it as the 'perfect medium', due to the repetitive action involved in the stitching. The resulting works

Tanvi Kant
Pink Bandhani, 2010. Hand-bound and hand-stitched on remnant of sari fabric. Necklace size. Photo: Tas Kyprianou.

Betty Pepper
(*right*) Rita Necklace, 2011. Textile/silver wire hand-stitched necklace. 16 cm (6¼ in.) in diameter (approx.). Photo: Betty Pepper.

Alison Willoughby
(*far right*) Circles of Running Stitch, 2010. Thread, dyed cotton. Photo: Alison Willoughby.

CONTEMPORARY PRACTICES

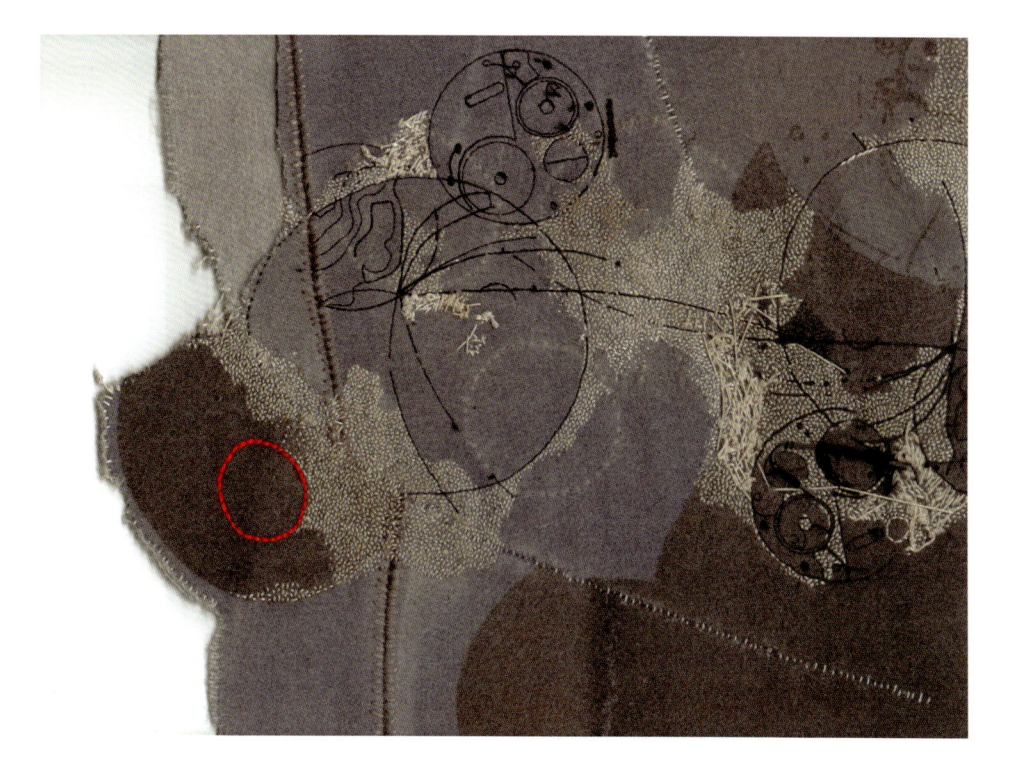

showcase words presented out of context, selected by chance. Juxtaposed as a group, these images use hand stitch to challenge the viewer to make meaning from the apparently meaningless.

Janet Haigh works with personal references and visual symbols – amulets and talismans. She stitches messages, as though they were charms, onto cloth to record her most frightening and memorable dreams. 'I am now concerned with making worthwhile things for people to use – comforters, bolsters, security blankets and safety curtains.'[6] The slow and repetitive making of stitch reveals the ideas. She describes this process in hand stitch as 'a signifier of value'.

Richard McVetis
(*left*) *Processed*, 2008. Wool flannel, seeding stitch, seaming (insertion stitch), blanket stitch, running stitch, couching; screen-printed, transfer printed, heat-pressed. 44 x 44 cm (17⅜ x 17⅜ in.). Photo: Richard McVetis.

Lauren Steeper
(*above*) *Lottery Words – Cellulitus*, 2010. Cross-stitch with cotton thread on cotton with pulled thread edging. 24 x 26 cm (9½ x 10¼ in.). Photo: Lauren Steeper.

Janet Haigh
(*below*) *And Then I Woke Up*, 2010. Embroidered cotton on vintage linen pillowcase. 70 x 70 cm (27½ x 27½ in.). Photo: Janet Haigh.

NOTES

[1] McKeith, Eimear, 'Louise Bourgeois: *Stitches in Time* at the Irish Museum of Modern Art, November 2003–February 2004', *Circa Contemporary Art in Ireland*. See http://www.recirca.com/reviews/louisebourgeois/index.shtml (accessed 4 August 2011).
[2] Quoted by Cristin Leech, 'Art Getting to the Point' in the *Sunday Times*, 21 December 2003. See http://www.recirca.com/reviews/louisebourgeois/index.shtml (accessed 4 September 2011).
[3] Interview with Alice Kettle, August 2011.
[4] Ibid.
[5] Ibid.
[6] Ibid.

JANE MCKEATING

Glossary of Stitches

INVENTIONS STITCH GLOSSARY

There is invention in making stitches, and the examples shown here illustrate an exploration of their form. The stitches are not rigidly classified, but presented here as a visual story of how some artists, designers and students have utilised particular stitches in interesting ways. The materials and components used for making each stitch are a key part of their impact. The same stitch can look completely different when the 'stuff', scale or context changes.

Students at Manchester Metropolitan University, supported by Coats Threads UK, undertook a week-long project to explore hand stitch, and many of the featured examples come from the work made during the project. Others come from a variety of sources, giving breadth to this glimpse of what stitches can be.

Piercing

The surface of the fabric is pierced as though for a stitch, so the idea of stitching influences the making process.

Running stitch

Running stitch is the simplest of stitches, but one of the most versatile. Here it is represented by a mixture of straight and interlaced running stitches, demonstrating a breadth of usage. As a seeding stitch, the dense build-up creates a mass on the surface.

Ashlee Grant
(*right*) Piercing. The start of a stitch without a thread, 2011. Hand-stitched coque feathers, razor blades and nails, with foil, flocking and screen-printing. From the series 'Beauty, Disgust and the Disturbing'. 16 x 30 cm (6¼ x 12 in.). Photo: Mary Stark.

Jane McKeating
(*far right*) Running stitch, 2011. No. 6 from the 'Regular Haircut' series. 19 x 19 cm (7½ x 7½ in.). The stitch, made with a floss thread, is worked over digitally printed layers of organza, both holding them together and creating a surface. Photo: Jane McKeating.

GLOSSARY OF STITCHES

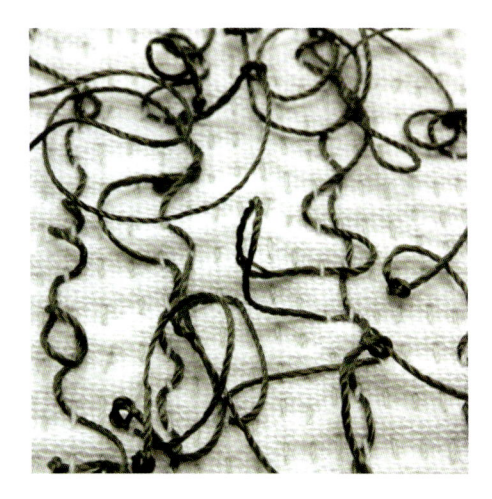

Hannah Leighton Boyce
Laced running stitch, 2011. Linen thread on linen. 22 x 20 cm (9 x 8 in.). MMU–Coats hand-stitch project. Stitched loosely without pulling the thread fully through, creating an informal surface that hardly looks stitched. Photo: Mary Stark.

Ali Neilly
Seeding stitch, 2011. Cotton thread on muslin 9 x 9 cm (3½ x 3½ in.). MMU–Coats hand-stitch project. A thick rainbow thread on fine muslin, in a dense mass, builds up a shape. Photo: Mary Stark.

Chain stitch

Here shown in a variety of forms, chains make the simplest of lines and the most complex surfaces. The chain emphasises the three-dimensionality of thread and connects stitch to lace-making and crochet.

Kit Li
Rosette chain stitch, 2011. Cotton yarn with cotton perle on calico, using thread changes to create a stripe. 7 x 8 cm (2¾ x 3¼ in.). MMU–Coats hand-stitch project. Photo: Mary Stark.

Kit Li
Rosette chain stitch, 2011. Cotton perle and silk thread on black silk net, letting holes in the cloth mix visually with the surface of the stitch. 7 x 13 cm (2¾ x 5¼ in.). MMU–Coats hand-stitch project. Photo: Mary Stark.

Anne Laycock
Cable chain stitch, 2011. Clay. 180 x 5–9 cm (71 x 2–3½ in.) (width varies). From the 'Chain' collection. Lengths of extruded clay cut at various lengths and formed with or without a twist, and then linked whilst the clay was in its 'plastic' state. Photo: Anne Laycock.

209

Couching

Because the top thread never needs to penetrate the surface, couching can be used to connect different substances to cloth.

Laura Faithfull
Couching, 2011. Variegated cotton yarn on open-weave cotton. 9 x 5 cm (3½ x 2 in.). MMU–Coats hand-stitch project. Photo: Mary Stark.

Mixed hand techniques in the style of Rebecca Crompton, date unknown. 74 x 54 cm (29 x 21¼ in.). Special Collections at Manchester Metropolitan University. Photo: Mary Stark.

Alice Colson
Jacobean couching, 2011. Rubber, cardboard, staples. 29 x 18 cm (11½ x 7 in.). MMU–Coats hand-stitch project. Inspired by the rubber bands that the postman discards, stapled on to a used cardboard package. Photo: Mary Stark.

Student practice piece, c.1930–33. Ecclesiastical needlework. Mounted on linen, possibly samples towards a book cover. Floss silk threads with silver and gold couching; calyx padded. 23 x 16 cm (9 x 6¼ in.). Rachel Kay-Shuttleworth Collection. Acc. no. RBKS1096. Photo: Mary Stark.

GLOSSARY OF STITCHES

Buttonhole stitches

The name 'buttonhole stitch' describes a use, but the versatility of this stitch makes it useful for constructing, edging and decorating.

Jennifer Wilson
Buttonhole stitch, 2011. Mixed cotton thread in buttonhole wheels on a cotton base. 10 x 8 cm (4 x 3¼ in.). MMU–Coats hand-stitch project. Photo: Mary Stark.

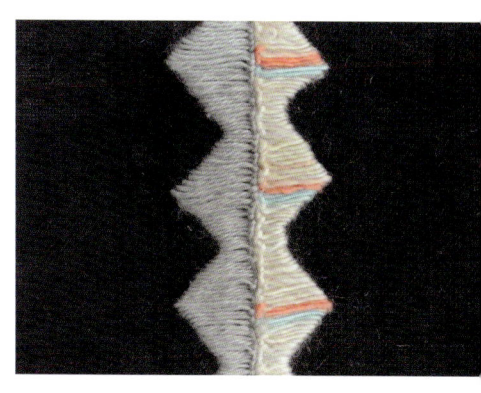

Jennifer Wilson
Buttonhole stitch, 2011. Mixed wool and cotton thread on a black cotton base. 6 x 9 cm (2½ x 3½ in.). MMU–Coats hand-stitch project. Photo: Mary Stark.

Anne Jones
Buttonhole insertion stitch, 2011. Space-dyed machine thread on layer of sheer over white cotton organdie. 18 x 18 cm (7 x 7 in.). MMU–Coats hand-stitch project. Photo: Mary Stark.

Anne Jones
Buttonhole insertion stitch, 2011. Cotton perle, black glacé thread on bark and Holland linen. 19 x 21 cm (7½ x 8¼ in.). MMU–Coats hand-stitch project. Photo: Mary Stark.

Lisa Salama
Detached buttonhole stitch, 2011. Waxed thread, sequins and acrylic charms on wool crêpe with chiffon. 29.7 x 42 cm (11¾ x 16½ in.). From the 'Pseudo/Science' collection. Photo: Mary Stark.

Anne Jones
Buttonhole insertion stitch, 2011. Glacé thread, organdie, leather and knitted wire, layered. 8 x 8 cm (3¼ x 3¼ in.). MMU–Coats hand-stitch project. Photo: Mary Stark.

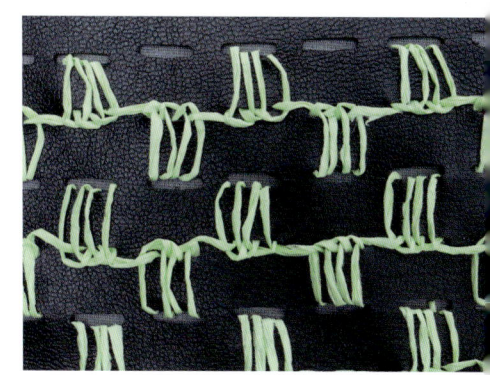

Anne Jones
Buttonhole insertion stitch, 2011. Paper string on hole-punched leatherette. 16 x 16 cm (6¼ x 6¼ in.). MMU–Coats hand-stitch project. Photo: Mary Stark.

HAND STITCH: PERSPECTIVES

Cross-stitch

Perhaps the most widely used and recognised stitch, cross-stitch here is explored in materials other than thread.

Mark Beecroft
Cross-stitch, 2006. Tent poles on grass. 120 x 120 cm (47¼ x 47¼ in.). Photo: Mark Beecroft.

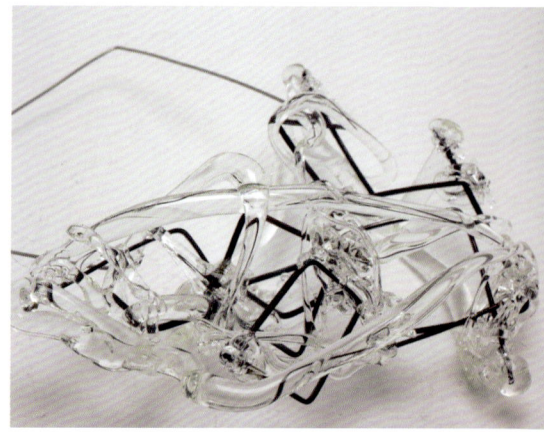

Kirsty Pearson
Cross-stitch, 2011. Cluster necklaces made from borosilicate glass and stainless steel. 150 x 90 cm (59 x 35½ in.). Photo: Mary Stark.

Front and back

The form of the stitch is of interest from both the front and the back: the way that stitches are made creates a different quality on the underside, which is often seen as equally interesting.

Laura-Jane Atkinson
Portuguese border stitch, 2011. Cotton thread on stiff paper. 29.7 x 42 cm (11¾ x 16½ in.). MMU–Coats hand-stitch project. The stitch size and thread density were varied to investigate the effect on colour mixing. Photo: Mary Stark.

Janice Egerton
Cross-stitch. Bowl, 1982. Paper and raffia. 20 x 39 cm (8 x 15½ in.). The front and the back of the stitch are visible, and integral to the design of the bowl. Photo: Steve Yates.

GLOSSARY OF STITCHES

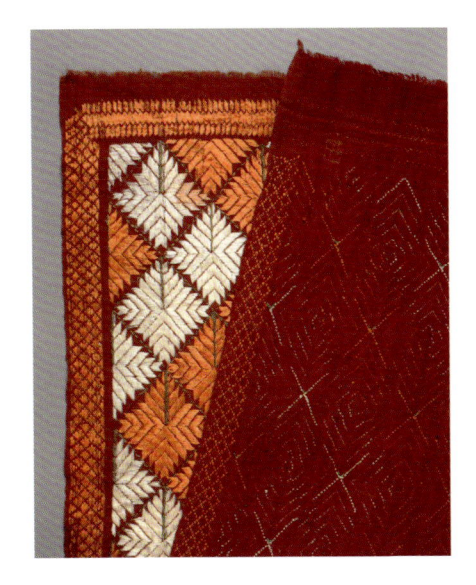

Darning stitch, Phulkari, India, mid-20th century. Cotton fabric, silk floss (*heer*) thread. Detail showing both sides; the stitch is worked with the reverse (right of the image) facing the worker – there is no right side and wrong side. Collection of Anne Morrell. Photo: Michael Pollard.

Ruth Hadwin
(*left and right*) Satin stitch, 2011. Cotton perle and soft cotton threads on vinyl. 330 x 210 cm (130 x 82¾ in.). Traditional floral subject matter used to contrast with a material usually used for flooring. Photo: Mary Stark.

Ayasha Wood
Blanket stitch, 2011. Mixed cotton threads on black cotton giving a drawn effect that works equally well where it is less controlled on the reverse. 12 x 12 cm (4¾ x 4¾ in.). MMU–Coats hand-stitch project. Photo: Mary Stark.

Sophie Brown
Sheaf (filling stitch), 2011. Black cotton thread on Velcro, which holds its form and emphasises both sides of the surface. 60 x 3 cm (23⅝ x 1¼ in.). MMU–Coats hand-stitch project. Photo: Mary Stark.

Sarah Burgess
Chevron stitch, 2011. Glacé cotton thread on linen, 29 x 10 cm (11½ x 4 in.). MMU–Coats hand-stitch project. The thread is used to manipulate white open-weave linen, showing the shadow effect of the right and wrong sides of the stitch and the three-dimensional quality of the stitch construction. Photo: Mary Stark.

213

Assorted possibilities

A small selection of named hand stitches captures a snapshot of the breadth and diversity of approach taken with a stitch.

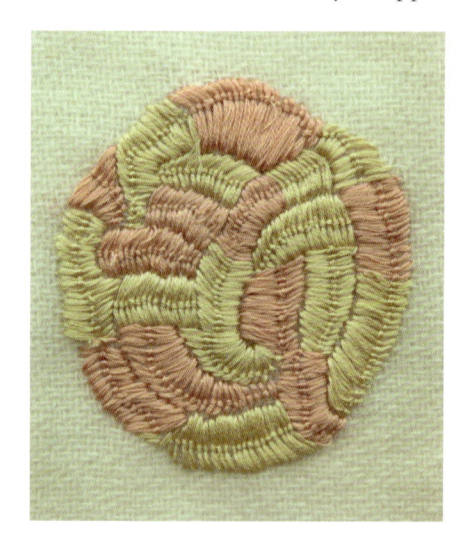

Rebecca Fielding
Romanian stitch, 2011. Stranded silk on wool, 20 x 20 cm (8 x 8 in.). MMU–Coats hand-stitch project. In the sample, entitled *Compact*, the emphasis is on stitch direction, with the lustre of the silk standing out against the matt wool base cloth. Photo: Mary Stark.

Sophie Brown
Sheaf (filling stitch), 2011. String on cardboard, 18 x 24 cm (7 x 9½ in.). MMU–Coats hand-stitch project. The simplicity and raw quality of the materials gives emphasis to the form of the stitch. Photo: Mary Stark.

Bella Leonard
Bullion stitch, 2011. Cotton thread on chiffon layered over printed cotton, cut away to reveal the print. 24 x 21 cm (9½ x 8¼ in.). MMU–Coats hand-stitch project. Photo: Mary Stark.

Fiona Rainford
Wave stitch (open), 2011. Paper and photograph, 8.5 x 11 cm (3⁵⁄₁₆ x 4½ in.). MMU–Coats hand-stitch project. The paper stitches are worked on a distressed photograph as a background, the spacing of the stitches deliberately varied to echo the quality of marks in the paper base. Photo: Mary Stark.

Maker unknown
Long and short stitch, c.1930. Embroidered picture in silks on plain white cotton. 27 x 34 cm (10¾ x 13½in.) Also contains French knots and seeding. RBKS Collection. Acc. no. 11842. Photo: Mary Stark.

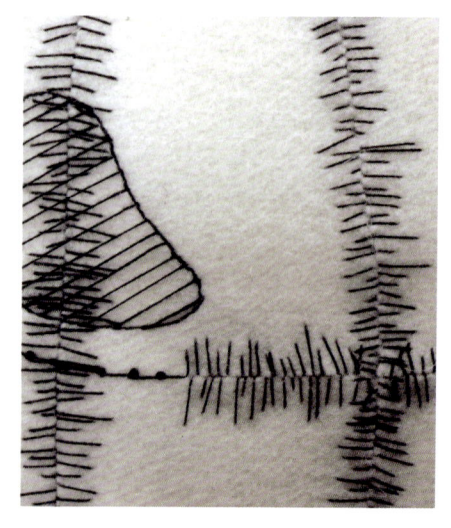

Emma Galbraith
Insertion stitch. *Home Is Where My Heart Is* (detail), 2009. Insertion stitch. Wool fabric with insertion stitch and cross-hatching from the 'Mapping' collection. 500 x 580 cm (197 x 228¼ in.). Photo: Mary Stark.

GLOSSARY OF STITCHES

Chloe Hamill
Picot stitch, 2011. Gold thread on wool, creating a fully 3D form that stands almost independent of the base. 24 x 22 cm (9½ x 9 in.). MMU–Coats hand-stitch project. Photo: Mary Stark.

Emma Louise Minshall
Spanish knotted feather stitch, 2011. Paper string on cotton, 15 x 7 cm (6 x 2¾ in.). MMU–Coats hand-stitch project. The paper string used here holds the shape of the stitch, connecting with basketry. Photo: Mary Stark.

Claire Ford
Brick stitch, 2009. 20 x 15 cm (8 x 6 in.). Stitch with materials that almost obliterate the form; only close inspection shows how the surface is constructed. Photo: Mary Stark.

Natalie Davies
(*right*) French knots, 2011. Mixed hand threads and ribbon, 10 x 13 cm (4 x 5¼ in.). MMU–Coats hand-stitch project. Masses of knots are set side by side; the materials change the surface whilst the stitch remains the same. Photo: Mary Stark.

Jane McKeating
(*far right*) Fly stitch. *No Particular Value*, 2009. Silk floss on linen with digital print, using stitch to create pattern in image-making. 22 x 22 cm (9 x 9 in.). Special Collections at Manchester Metropolitan University. Photo: Steve Yates.

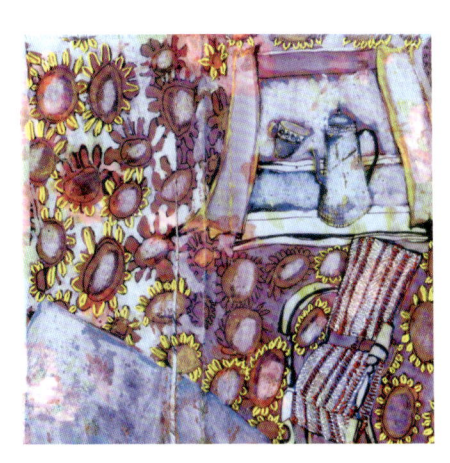

Influence of Stitch

Artists who have an understanding of stitch continue to be influencd by the process as work moves away from making an actual stitch.

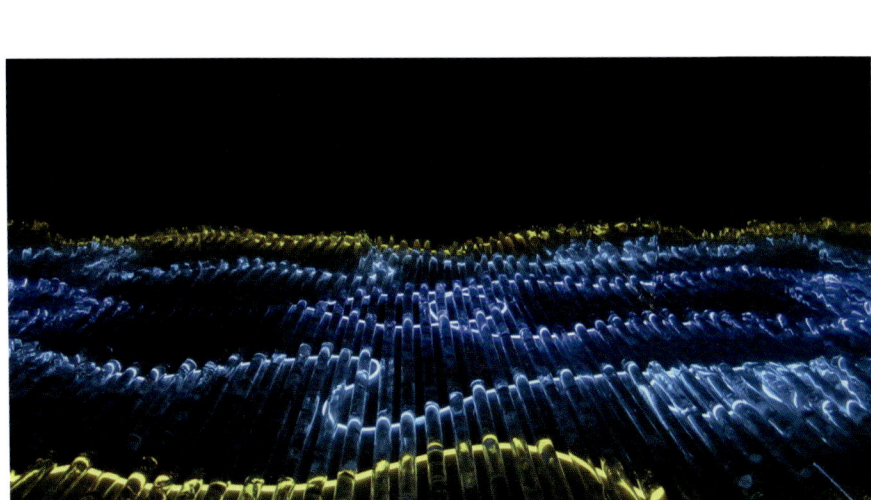

Frances Rocca
Digital Stitch, 2011. Here, a graduate of an embroidery degree course demonstrates how understanding stitch has informed and influenced digital practice. Photo: Frances Rocca.

Artists' Profiles

DAVID OWEN
David Owen is Professor of Social and Political Philosophy at the University of Southampton. He has published nine books including, most recently, *Nietzsche's Genealogy of Morality* (Acumen, 2007) and, with Bert van den Brink, *Recognition and Power* (CUP, 2007). In addition, he has lectured on philosophical aspects of the arts at Winchester School of Art, and given public lectures and gallery talks at venues such as ARTSway and the John Hansard Gallery. His most recent essay in this field is 'Returning Time', in the catalogue for Bashir Makhoul's exhibition 'Return' (2007).

TOM LUNDBERG
Tom Lundberg lives in Fort Collins, Colorado. He is a Professor of Art at Colorado State University, where he coordinates the programme in Fibres. Lundberg has lectured and taught in the United States, England, Italy and New Zealand. He completed a BFA in Painting at the University of Iowa and an MFA in Textiles from Indiana University. His embroideries are exhibited internationally and are in the permanent collections of Arkansas Arts Center, Little Rock, Arkansas; State of New Mexico; Chase Manhattan Bank, New York; Indianapolis Museum of Art; Museum of Arts and Design, New York; and the Renwick Gallery, Smithsonian American Art Museum, Washington, DC.

JANE MCKEATING
Jane McKeating studied at Goldsmiths College, followed by Manchester Polytechnic. She led the BA (Hons) Embroidery programme at Manchester Metropolitan University until 2005 when she moved on to take up a post addressing widening participation at the University. As Director of Studies in Manchester School of Art, Manchester Metropolitan University she is still very much involved in embroidery education. As a practitioner Jane exhibits internationally, recently becoming a member of the 62 Group of textile artists in 2010. Publications include co-authoring the companion book to this volume with Alice Kettle, *Machine Stitch: Perspectives* (A&C Black, 2010).

ALICE KETTLE
Alice Kettle is Senior Research Fellow MIRIAD at Manchester School of Art, Manchester Metropolitan University. She edited the companion to this volume, *Machine Stitch: Perspectives*, with Jane McKeating (A&C Black, 2010). At MMU, she has become increasingly interested in the cross-fertilisation of material practice. Her work is represented in various public collections (see www.alicekettle.com). She is also currently Visiting Professor at the Centre for Real World Learning, University of Winchester.

ARTISTS' PROFILES

KATE EGAN
Kate Egan was born in Manchester and spent her childhood in Vancouver in Canada. She studied embroidery at Manchester Metropolitan University in 1988–91, after which she worked as a practitioner and lecturer simultaneously for 20 years. Her current role is programme leader for the BA (Hons.) Textiles in Practice programme at Manchester School of Art, Manchester Metropolitan University. In 2002, Kate set up the art label FLOAT as a platform for interdisciplinary and collaborative projects.

HEATHER BELCHER
Heather Belcher has developed a special interest in handmade felt processes, and travelled to Kyrgyzstan in Central Asia, funded by a Research and Development Grant from Arts Council England, to study traditional felt techniques. Heather is an exhibiting member of the Contemporary Applied Arts Gallery in London and the 62 Group of textile artists.

ANNE MORRELL
Anne Morrell was born in Chennai, India. She studied at Goldsmiths College in London, where she subsequently taught. She joined Manchester Metropolitan University, leading the embroidery specialism within the Textiles and Fashion course, and was appointed professor in 1992. She works with the Calico Museum in Ahmedabad, India as consultant. She exhibits her own work internationally. Significant publications are: *Techniques in Indian Embroidery* (originally published by Batsford, 1994), *Indian Embroideries II* (Sarabhai Foundation, 2011), and *The Migration of Stitches & the Practice of Stitch as Movement* (Sarabhai Foundation, 2007).

JUNE HILL
June Hill is a freelance curator, writer and textile historian, closely associated with Bankfield Museum, Halifax, where she curated the textile collection (1989–2005). June has been publishing ongoing research into UK textile collections for *Embroidery* since January 2006 is a contributor to the *Encyclopedia of World Dress* (Berg, 2010) and the author of a monograph on Diana Springall (A&C Black, 2011). Recent ventures include *The Sleeping Bag Project* (2011–12) and exhibitions on the work of Beryl Dean (2011), Jilly Edwards (2011) and Michael Brennand-Wood (2012).

MELANIE MILLER

Melanie Miller is a lecturer, maker, writer and curator. She has worked at Manchester School of Art, Manchester Metropolitan University for 20 years, teaching on the BA Embroidery programme and the MA Textiles programme. Melanie's specialism is machine embroidery: she completed her PhD in this subject in 1997 and has co-curated exhibitions around this theme, notably 'Mechanical Drawing – The Schiffli Project' with June Hill in 2007. This was a layered project using the historic multi-needle pantograph schiffli embroidery machine.

JAMES HUNTING

James is an artist, an educator and a professional embroiderer. He trained at Goldsmiths College, London, and then worked in the fashion and commissioning world for nearly 20 years as a freelance hand-embroiderer. He is now the course leader of the only hand embroidery-focused degree delivered by the Royal School of Needlework, in collaborative partnership with the University for the Creative Arts Farnham. His own practice is stitch-based hand work, which explores desire, pattern and the evocative potential of the stitched mark.

IAN WILSON

Ian Wilson was born in Africa and has taught English literature and language at universities in England, Ethiopia, Botswana, Malawi and Qatar. He has worked in Central and Eastern Europe, Central Asia and Siberia. Since 2005 he has concentrated on writing and lecturing on the applied arts and design, with a special interest in textiles and ceramics. In 1997 he won the Crafts Council Silver Jubilee prize for critical writing. His work has been translated into German, Chinese, Japanese, Hungarian, Welsh, Spanish and Portuguese, and he has been invited to speak at conferences in China, Germany and Hungary.

NIGEL HURLSTONE

Nigel Hurlstone studied embroidery at Manchester School of Art, Manchester Metropolitan University followed by a Ph.D. in 2000. He has lectured at Glasgow School of Art, Liverpool John Moores University and the University of the West of England, and was the BA Embroidery programme leader at Manchester School of Art, Manchester Metropolitan University, where he now combines teaching with his work as a freelance embroiderer.

ARTISTS' PROFILES

LESLEY MITCHISON
Lesley Mitchison studied woven textiles at the Surrey Institute (Farnham), and went on to complete her master's degree at the University of Central England. She has taught in many institutions in the UK and abroad, including Canberra School of Art, Australia, and the Kawashima Weaving School in Japan. Lesley is currently a programme leader at Manchester University. Her work is in the collections of the Whitworth Art Gallery, Manchester, Nottingham Castle Contemporary Textile Collection, and Gallery Gallery, Kyoto, Japan.

ANN FRENCH
Ann French trained as a textile conservator at the Victoria and Albert Museum, and is currently employed at the Whitworth Art Gallery, the University of Manchester. She is working towards a PhD in the Department of Museology on the Greek Embroidery Collecting of RM Dawkins and AJB Wace. This research combines her love of, and fascination with, historic embroideries and her own family history, as Alan Wace was her grandfather whom she never knew.

TRACY GILL
Tracy Gill studied embroidery at Manchester Metropolitan University. After graduating in 2003, she worked in community arts, organising and delivering workshops for local groups and schools. She embarked on teaching at Blackburn College of Art and Design. Her experiences led her to pursue a master's degree in textiles. It was during this programme of study that Tracy found her pathway into the Rachel Kay-Shuttleworth Collection, where she is the education liaison officer.

SUE PRESTBURY
Sue Prestbury studied fashion manufacturing at Oldham College of Technology, followed by various posts within the fashion industry as designer, pattern-cutter and maker. She is now Senior Technician at Manchester School of Art, Manchester Metropolitan University. She has a BA History of Art and Design with Practice from Manchester Metropolitan University, and continues to undertake commissions for reproduction costume, including contributing to the recent King Henry VIII's costume for the New York Metropolitan Opera.

MARY STARK
Mary Stark is an artist, photographer and film maker based in Manchester. Her practice focuses on exploring media and materiality in a digital age. She has worked in education and with young offenders, teaching media production and project managing professional short films and documentaries. After completing a degree in embroidery in 2006, Mary is now studying for an MA in Photography at Manchester School of Art, Manchester Metropolitan University.

Further Reading

Adamson, Glenn, *The Craft Reader* (Oxford: Berg, 2010).
Andere, Mary, *Old Needlework Boxes and Tools* (Newton Abbot: David and Charles, 1971).
Belger Krody, Sumru, *Embroidery of the Greek Islands and Epirus Region: Harpies, Mermaids and Tulips* (London and Washington: The Textile Museum and Scala Publishers, 2006).
Bolton, Lissant, *Baskets & Belonging: Indigenous Australian Histories* (London: British Museum, 2011).
Borensztein, Leon, *One is Adam One is Superman: The Outsider Artists of Creative Growth* (Oakland, CA: Creative Growth Art Center and Chronicle Books, 2004).
Breskin Adams, Renie, *Inside Out, Selected Works 1978–1996* (Cambridge, MA: Mobilia Gallery, 1996).
Brett Guy, *Through Our Own Eyes: Popular Art and Modern History* (London: Heretic/GMP, 1986).
Bucherer, Paul, and Cornelia Vogelsanger, *Gestickte Gebete* (Embroidered Prayers) (Liestal, Switzerland: Stiftung Bibliotheca Afghanica, 2000).
Bunn, Stephanie, *Nomadic Felts* (London: British Museum, 2010).
Buszek, Maria Elena, *Extra/ordinary Craft* (Durham and London: Duke University Press, 2011).
Butler, Anne, *The Arco Encyclopedia of Embroidery Stitches* (New York: Arco, 1979).
Butler, Anne, *The Batsford Encyclopaedia of Embroidery Stitches* (London: B. T. Batsford [1979] 1982).
Chadwick, Whitney, *Women, Art and Society* (London: Thames and Hudson, 2007).
Constantine, Mildred and Laurel Reuter, *Whole Cloth* (New York: Monacelli Press, 1997).
Corrin, Lisa, *Loose Threads* (London: Serpentine Gallery, 1998).
Corwin, Nancy, and Barbara Eckhardt, *Barbara Eckhardt: Poetic Space* (New Bedford, MA: University Art Gallery, College of Visual and Performing Arts, University of Massachusetts, Dartmouth, 1998).
Crompton, Rebecca, *Modern Design in Embroidery* (London: B. T. Batsford, 1936).
Curtis, E. A., *Needlework: Schedule 111. Exemplified and Illustrated* (London: Griffith & Farran, 1865).
Day, Lewis F., *Art in Needlework* (London: B. T. Batsford, 1900).
Dean, Beryl, *Ecclesiastical Embroidery* (London: B. T. Batsford, 1958).
Dean, Beryl, *Ideas for Church Embroidery* (London: B. T. Batsford, 1968).
Dean, Beryl, and Pamela Pavitt, *Rebecca Crompton and Elizabeth Grace Thomson: Pioneers in Stitchery in the 1930s* (London: Beryl Dean, 1996).
Edwards, Eiluned, *Textiles and Dress of Gujarat* (London: Victoria and Albert Museum in association with Maplin Publishing, 2011).

FURTHER READING

Frater, Judy, *Threads of Identity: Embroidery and Adornment of the Nomadic Rabaris* (Ahmedabad: Mapin, 1995).

Hambridge, E. R., *Blackboard Diagram Drawing for Teachers of Needlecraft* (London: Pitman, 1909).

Hann, M., C. A. Senturk and G. M. Thomsen, *The Pesel Embroideries*, exhibition catalogue (Leeds: University of Leeds International Textiles Archive, 1995).

Harris, Jennifer, and Pennina Barnett, *The Subversive Stitch* (exhibition catalogue) (Manchester: Cornerhouse and Whitworth Art Gallery, 1988).

Harvey, Virginia I., *The Techniques of Basketry* (London: B. T. Batsford, 1975).

Hogarth, Mary, *Modern Embroidery* (New York: Garden City Publishing, 1938).

Hornstein, A. Gail, *Agnes's Jacket: A Psychologist's Search for the Meaning of Madness* (Emmaus, PA: Rodale Books, 2009).

Illian, Clary, *A Potter's Workbook* (Iowa City: University of Iowa Press, 1999).

Ilse-Neuman, Ursula, *Diane Itter* (New York: American Craft Museum, 1995).

Itter, William and Tom Rhea, *William Itter: A Retrospective Paintings and Drawings 1969–2009* (Bloomington, IA: Indiana University, 2009).

Johnstone, Pauline, *Greek Island Embroidery* (London: Alec Tiranti, 1961).

Johnstone, Pauline, *Guide to Greek Island Embroidery* (London: Her Majesty's Stationery Office, 1972).

Kendrick, A. F., Louisa Pesel and E. W. Newberry, *A Book of Old Embroidery*, ed. Geoffrey Holme (London, Paris, New York: 'The Studio' Ltd., 1921).

Livingstone, Joan, and John Ploof, *The Object of Labor: Art, Cloth and Cultural Production* (Cambridge, MA: MIT Press, 2007).

McFadden, David Revere, *Radical Lace and Subversive Knitting: Process + Materials 1* (New York: Museum of Arts and Design, 2007).

McFadden, David Revere, *Pricked: Extreme Embroidery: Process + Materials 2* (New York: Museum of Arts and Design, 2008).

MacGregor, John, PhD thesis, *Metamorphosis: The Fiber Art of Judith Scott*, Oakland, CA: Creative Growth Art Center, 1999).

Maizels, John, *Raw Creation: Outsider Art and Beyond* (London, New York: Phaidon, 1996).

Marsh, Gail, *Early 20th Century Embroidery Techniques* (Lewes: Guild of Master Craftsman Publications, 2011).

Mayer-Thurman, Christa C., *Raiment for the Lord's Service: A Thousand Years of Western Vestments* (Chicago: Art Institute of Chicago, 1975).

Millar, Lesley, *Cloth and Culture Now* (Norwich: Sainsbury Centre for Visual Arts, 2007).

Monem, Nadine, *Contemporary Textiles: The Fabric of Fine Art* (London: Black Dog Publishing, 2008).

Morrell, Anne, *Techniques of Indian Embroidery* (London: B. T. Batsford, [1994] 1995; Loreland, CO: Interweave, paperback 1995).

Morrell, Anne, *The Guide to Structural Sewing Terms and Techniques* (Ahmedabad, India: Sarabhai Foundation, 1998).

Morrell, Anne, *Indian Embroidery Techniques at the Calico Museum of Textiles. A Working Guide to the Embroidery Gallery* (Ahmedabad, India: Sarabhai Foundation, 1999).

Morrell, Anne, *The Migration of Stitches & the Practice of Stitch as Movement* (Ahmedabad, India: Sarabhai Foundation, 2007).

Morrell, Anne, *Indian Embroideries 11* (Ahmedabad, India: Sarabhai Foundation, 2011).

Morrell, Anne and I. L. Finkel, *The Calico Museum of Textiles: Monograph Folder Series 1–5* (Ahmedabad, India: Sarabhai Foundation, 2002).

Naik, D. B., *The Art and Literature of Banjara Bambanis* (New Delhi, India: Abhinav Publications, 2000).

Nicholson, Virginia, *Singled Out* (Oxford: Oxford University Press, 2008).

Norris, Lucy, *Recycling Indian Clothing: Global Contexts of Reuse and Value* (Bloomington, IA: Indiana University Press, 2010).

Paine, Sheila, *Embroidered Textiles: A World Guide to Traditional Patterns* (London and New York: Thames & Hudson, 2008).

Parker, Roszika, 'The Subversive Stitch: Embroidery and the Making of the Feminine', 1st edition, (London: The Women's Press, 1984; new edition I. B. Tauris, London, 2010).

Pesel, Louisa, *Stitches from Eastern Embroideries Portfolio II* (London: Percy Lund, Humphreys & Co., 1913).

Pritchard, Frances, *Clothing Culture: Dress in Egypt in the First Millennium AD* (Manchester: University of Manchester, 2006).

Rebetz, Pascal, *On m'appelait Judith Scott* (Lausanne: Collection de l'Art Brut, Lausanne, 2006).

Rudenko, Sergei I., *Frozen Tombs of Siberia: The Pazyryk Burials of Iron Age Horsemen* (Berkeley: University of California Press, 1970).

Schuette, Marie, and Sigrid Müller-Christensen, *A Pictorial History of Embroidery* (New York: Praeger Publishers, 1964; copyright 1963).

Scott, Joyce, *EnTWINed: The Silent World of Judith Scott: Of Loss, Love and Transformation* (to be published)

Shrujan Trust, *Under the Embroidered Sky: Embroidery of the Ahirs of Kutch* (Gujarat: Shrujan Trust, 2010).

Smith, Amy K., *Needlework for Student Teachers* (London: City of London Book Depot, 1899, 5th edition).

Smith, Esther K., *How to Make Books* (London: Potter Craft, Random House, 2007).

Smith, Zadie, *Changing My Mind: Occasional Essays* (London: Hamish Hamilton, 2009).

Springall, Diana, *Twelve British Embroiderers* (Japan: Gakken, 1984).

Taylor, John, *The Needles Excellency* (London, 1631).

Taylor, Roderick, *Embroidery of the Greek Islands and Epirus* (New York: Interlink Books, 1998).

Trilling, James, *Aegean Crossroads: Greek Island Embroideries in the Textile Museum* (Baltimore: The Textile Museum Washington and Schneidereith & Sons, 1983).

Wace, A. J. B., *Mediterranean and Near Eastern Embroideries from the Collection of Mrs F. H. Cook*, 2 vols (London: Halton, 1935).

Walter, Agnes, *Needlework and Cutting Out* (Peterborough: Blackie, 1911).

Index

Aids Memorial Quilt 119
Anzeri, Maurizio 203
ari hook 94–5
arthur+martha 121–2
Aviks, Ilze 25–6

Bajević, Maja 13–14
Bayeux Tapestry 58
Beadle, Joan 97–9
Belcher, Heather 56–63, 217
Bispo do Rosário, Arthur 83–5
Bjørne Linnert, Lise 13, 56–7
Blackwood, Jilli 200
Bourgeois, Louise 202–3
Brafield, Stacy 49, 54–5
Breskin Adams, Renie 24
Brimelow, Elizabeth 196, 198

Caldwell, Dorothy 201–2
Casswell, Tasmin 150–1
Chan, Kai 199
Changi quilts, the 160–1
Charles I 186–7
Cheney, Nigel 32
Chicago, Judy 117, 130
Chilean arpilleras 120
Chorley, Primmy 204–5
Cogan, Orly 118–19
community-based textile work 56–63, 119–20
craftivism 120–1
Crompton, Rebecca 91–2, 106, 108–9

Dean, Beryl 104–15
'Desconocida: Unknown' 13, 56–8
Dezsö, Andrea 118–19
Drew, Jane 189

ecclesiastical embroidery 110–12
Echelman, Janet 39, 43–7
Eckhardt, Barbara 22–3

Egan, Kate 48–55, 98–9, 217
Egan, Neela 59
Emin, Tracey 129, 151–3

feminism 116–31
Fine Cell 31
Fisher, Henry Robert 88
Foreman Day, Lewis 169
Fraoli, Maddy 68–9
Frater, Judy 69–72
French, Ann 164–75, 219
Fry, Gavin 32–3

Garfen, Caren 126–8
George, Rachel 182
Gill, Madge 83–4
Gill, Tracy 176–85, 219
Gladwell, James 79–80
Greer, Betsy 121

Haigh, Janet 207
hand stitch
    concept of 17
    history of 93–7, 141–5, 165–6, 186–7
    in literature 149–50, 152
Harbord, Elzbieta 82–3
haute couture 133
Hill, June 104–15, 217
Hmong people 12–13
Hollick, Graham 67–8
Hulme 59–60
Hunting, James 132–7, 218
Hurlstone, Nigel 146–53, 218

Illian, Clary 21
Itter, Diane 24–5
Itter, William 24–5

Jones, Anne 2, 13

Kala Raksha Trust 69–72
Kant, Tanvi 206
Kay-Shuttleworth, Rachel 176–7, 179
'Keeping Glasgow in Stitches' 58–9
Kettle, Alice 38–47, 78–89, 196–207, 216
Kutch 64–77, 100
Kyoko Moses, Tabitha 159–63
Kyrgyz hand-stitched carpets 62–3

Lacey, Jacqueline 193
Leahy, Bernie 205
Lee Knowles, Mark 41
Littler, David 40–3
Lundberg, Tom 18–27, 216

Manchester Metropolitan University 59–62
Materson, Raymond 84, 87
McKeating, Jane 28–37, 64–77, 196–216
McKenzie Nicholson, Anne 23–4
McVetis, Richard 206–7
Millar, Lesley 12–14, 56–7
Miller, Melanie 116–31, 218
Mills, Eleri 202
Mitchison, Lesley 154, 219
Morfill, Sally 40–4
Morrell, Anne 90–103, 217
Morris & Co. 166
museum collections of hand stitch 164–75

Nelson, Deirdre 123
NGO embroidery initiatives 65–75

Olliver, Clyde 200–1
Outsider Art 78–88
Owen, David 16–17, 216

Pepper, Betty 206
Pesel, Louisa 93, 169–74
Pollit, Belinda 100–1
Potter, Valerie 84, 86
Prestbury, Sue 186, 219

Qasab 72–6
Quaker tapestry 58

Raste, Meena 73, 75–6
RBKS Collection 31, 176–85
Reichek, Elaine 117, 148–9
'Respect and protect' project 60–2
Richter, Agnes 80–1
Riviere, Antonia 53–5
Royal School of Needlework 166

sampler-cultureclash 40–3
samplers 30, 40, 178, 193
Scheving, Kristin 49, 53–4
Schwarz, Tilleke 205
Scott, Judith 82
SEWA Trade Facilitation Centre 66–7
Shah, Pankaj 73–4
Shaikh, Asif 28–9
Sharif, Rabia 181–2
Short, Eirian 35
Smyth, Debbie 198–9
South Kensington Museum *see* Victoria and Albert Museum
Staircase House 186, 188, 192–4
Staircase Stitchers 186, 189, 192–4
Stark, Mary 199, 219
Steeper, Lauren 206–7
Stetterington, Lynn 59–62, 124–5

Takadoi, Kazuhito 196–7
Torma, Anna 34

Ullah, Farzana 11

Verran, Jo 60–1
Victoria and Albert Museum 167–72

Waldren, Chaz 84, 86
Walker, Audrey 33
wedding dress embroidery 134–5
Wells, Rosanna 196–7
Willoughby, Alison 206
Wilson, Anne 154–9, 162
Wilson, Ian 138–45, 218
Wintsch, Johanna Natalie 81